ALFRED DE MUSSET
SEVEN PLAYS

Alfred de Musset

SEVEN PLAYS

Translated by Peter Meyer

MARIANNE

FANTASIO

DON'T TRIFLE WITH LOVE

THE CANDLESTICK

A DIVERSION

A DOOR MUST BE OPEN OR SHUT

YOU CAN'T THINK OF EVERYTHING

OBERON BOOKS

LONDON

First published in this edition in 2005 by Oberon Books Ltd

521 Caledonian Road, London N7 9RH

Tel: +44 (0) 20 7607 3637 / Fax: +44 (0) 20 7607 3629

e-mail: info@oberonbooks.com

www.oberonbooks.com

These translations originally published by Hill and Wang, 1962

A catalogue record for this book is available from the British Library.

PB ISBN: 9781840025866

E ISBN: 9781783192830

Converted by Replika Press PVT Ltd., India

Visit www.oberonbooks.com to read more about all our books and to buy them. You will also find features, author interviews and news of any author events, and you can sign up for e-newsletters so that you're always first to hear about our new releases.

Contents

INTRODUCTION

ALTHOUGH THE PLAYS of Alfred de Musset are virtually unknown in England and America, the French generally acknowledge him as their leading dramatist of the first half of the nineteenth century, and his influence in Europe has been widespread. He was one of the very few playwrights admired by Ibsen, and Turgenev's plays are derived directly from his work.

Since Musset's plays were first performed, they have held the stage in France, whereas those of his contemporaries are now rarely seen. The reason is a strange one. After his first play, *La Nuit vénitienne,* failed so disastrously in 1830, Musset decided never to write for the theatre again. However, he had a natural gift for dialogue and situation, and doubtless for this reason he cast much of his work in dramatic form. But it was written for publication, not the stage, and so was free of the theatrical conventions of the time, which produced the plays of the elder Dumas and Scribe.

After Musset achieved success in the theatre in 1847, Scribe asked him how he managed it, adding, 'I write to amuse people, but I can never make them laugh as you do.' 'Ah,' replied Musset, 'but I write to amuse myself.'

Louis Charles Alfred de Musset was born in Paris on December 11, 1810, in a house that was eventually destroyed by the construction of the Boulevard Saint Germain. His family prided themselves on being able to trace their descent back to the twelfth century, but his father, Victor Donatien de Musset-Pathay, had been forced by the Revolution into unusual paths. He served in the armies of the Republic until after the Battle of Marengo, and then entered the civil service, where he remained for the rest of his life. But he also had literary inclinations and published a biography of Jean-Jacques Rousseau, followed by an edition of his work.

With this background of Rousseau and military service under Napoleon, it is not surprising that the atmosphere of the Musset home was staunchly liberal and Bonapartist. Alfred was the second of three children, and the family life, both in Paris and with numerous relatives in the country, was a happy one. When he left school at the age of seventeen, he had no clear idea what he wanted to do. The two most popular careers for young men of his position were the law and medicine, but the first he considered too dull, and although he reluctantly agreed to become a doctor, he was immediately revolted by the dissection lessons.

However, he had shown some talent for drawing and decided that his only possible future was as an artist. He began to take lessons and to study at the Louvre and might well have had a successful career in this field: the drawings that have survived have a certain charm and some of his work was praised by Delacroix.

While he was still at school, Musset had been introduced by his friend, Paul Foucher, to Victor Hugo, who, although only eight years his senior, had been since 1825 a Chevalier of the Légion d'Honneur and in possession of a government pension. Hugo's house was the centre of the new Romantic Movement in literature and his circle, known as the Cénacle, included Sainte-Beuve, Prosper Mérimée and Alfred de Vigny, none of whom was then over thirty.

The accent of the Cénacle was on youth and its members were only too willing to welcome any new talent that appeared. Inspired by this example and by the work of André Chénier, Musset began to write poetry, and, with the help of Paul Foucher, one of his poems appeared on 31 August 1828 in a small Dijon newspaper, *Le Provincial*. He then started writing seriously: one morning a few months later a surprised Sainte-Beuve was abruptly awakened and forced to listen to an elegy about a priestess of Diana, followed by a number of ballads. It says much for Saint-Beuve's good humour and the spirit of the times that Musset was sufficiently encouraged to read his poems aloud to the Cénacle, which received them with enthusiasm.

It was presumably the success of his poems that gave Musset the confidence he had previously lacked. He had entered society the year before, a shy youth, ignored by men and women, but he suddenly lost his childish appearance and manner and was welcomed everywhere. Paris society at that time does not seem to have been so very different from the one which the young Proust knew fifty years later and although Musset did not set out to describe it in the same detail, the plays in this volume reflect the life he found there.

At the age of eighteen, Alfred de Musset was remarkably handsome. He was tall and fair-haired, with an aquiline nose and a full, rather sensual mouth; but what most attracted people, both men and women, was his wit and gaiety and general high spirits. It is not surprising that the salons of Paris were opened to him and he rapidly acquired a passion for wine and gambling and, scarcely less rapidly, for women. He soon found himself among a circle of young men considerably richer than himself and began patronising the best tailors, hiring horses, playing for high stakes, and generally leading a life he could ill afford. He was thus unable to offer any resistance when his father found him a job in the office of a friend who had recently obtained a contract for the supply of fuel to the army.

Musset had just translated anonymously for a Paris publisher Thomas de Quincey's *The Confessions of an English Opium Eater* (having added to the hero's dreams some recollections of his own anatomy lessons) and this literary exercise, coupled with the success of his poems at the Cénacle, seemed to offer an escape from the drudgery of office life. He therefore presented his manuscripts to the publisher of the Romantic faction, Urbain Canel, who, after requesting and quickly obtaining a further five hundred lines to complete the necessary octavo format, agreed to publish them.

The final proofs reached the author in December 1828 and his father gave a party on Christmas Eve, when some of the poems were read. Mérimée and Vigny were among the guests and there was unanimous agreement that the volume was bound to be successful.

A few days later *Tales of Spain and Italy* was published. The Mediterranean has always exercised a great attraction for young writers and artists, then perhaps more than at any other time: Shelley had been drowned off La Spezia in 1822 and Byron died at Missolonghi two years later; Mérimée had already begun to write about Spain; and in 1832 Delacroix was to make the visit to Morocco that revolutionised his art. Musset's book was in the broad stream of the Romantic tradition, but it was marked by a highly personal wit and cynicism, together with a mastery that is astonishing in a young man of barely eighteen.

The Romantics were distinguished not only for their choice of subject, but for their opposition to what they considered sterile rules of prosody and subject. In *Tales of Spain and Italy,* the poem that created the greatest sensation was the 'Ballad to the Moon', not merely because the scenes the moon witnessed were indelicate, but because they were bourgeois and not therefore a fit subject for poetry. Worst of all, however, the poet had dared to describe the moon appearing above a church spire, 'like the dot on an 'i' and such a prosaic description of an essentially poetic subject caused a scandal which can hardly be realised today.

Although *Tales of Spain and Italy* was more successful than the author had dared to hope, only five hundred copies were printed and it was clear that poetry would not be sufficiently remunerative to enable him to leave his office. So at the beginning of 1830, he wrote *La Quittance du diable,* a short play in three scenes, each containing an episode in verse, designed to be set to music. This was the usual form for the *vaudeville* of the time and as such it was accepted by the Théâtre des Nouveautés. The management went so far as to cast the leading parts, but for some reason, probably the July Revolution, it was never performed. It is a trivial work, based on an episode in *Redgauntlet,* and the only remarkable thing about it is the name of one of the characters, 'The Sir of Redgnauntley'.

With the accession of Louis-Philippe, the theatre found itself for a few brief years in possession of a freedom it had never known and quickly took advantage of it. The manager of the Odéon immediately mounted a play about Napoleon – who until then had been a forbidden subject – and, finding a further gap in his repertory, he asked the author of *Tales of Spain and Italy* for something new and bold. Musset was only too eager to accept and on 1 December 1830, the curtain rose on the first performance of *La Nuit vénitienne.*

To understand the reasons for the tumultuous failure of *La Nuit vénitienne,* it is necessary to examine the position of the drama in France at that time. In literature, the Romantic Movement had already made itself felt, but it was very slow to invade the theatre. This is in marked contrast to England and Germany. Shelley's *The Cenci* was written in 1819, although it was not performed because its subject was incest, and all of Byron's plays were written between 1817 and 1824. Of the latter, only *Marino Faliero* was staged in the author's lifetime, but both Byron and Shelley were admired in France and their work was known. In Germany, Goethe and Schiller had been played for many years and Madame de Staël had written about them as early as 1810 in *De l'Allemagne*. Although the book was confiscated by the police, it was reprinted abroad in 1813 and circulated widely.

In France, however, the stage was still held by the Classicists, who proclaimed a slavish devotion to the Rules, formulated by Boileau in the seventeenth century. The Rules were based on Greek tragedy: Boileau had in effect codified the existing practice. Indeed, Corneille's successful defiance of the three unities of time, place, and action had been one of the reasons which led Cardinal Richelieu to found the Académie.

The Rules governed style, subject, and poetry. The unities were supreme; but, in addition, there must be no comic element in a tragedy (the converse was true of comedy) and subjects always had to he taken from the Bible or antiquity. Everyday language was to be avoided and there must be strict adherence to the alexandrine, with alternate pairs of feminine rhymes and the end of a sentence only at the end of a line or at the prescribed caesura.

When used by a master like Racine, the Rules produced plays of exceptional austerity, precision and beauty, but by the nineteenth century only their letter was being observed and the underlying spirit was completely dead.

The time was ripe for change and the first assault came in 1828 when Charles Kemble and his company visited Paris with *Lear*, *Othello*, *Macbeth* and *Hamlet*. For the first time, French audiences saw the plays of Shakespeare performed as they had been written and were able to note for themselves the mingling of tragedy and comedy, the use of scenes from everyday life and poetry handled with absolute freedom.

It so happened, also in 1828, that Victor Hugo met Talma, then the leading actor in France, and mentioned that he was writing a romantic play, *Cromwell*. Talma agreed to act in it, but died within a few months. Not only was his acknowledged successor, Frédéric Lemaître, only twenty-six years old and clearly too young for the part, but there were serious doubts as to whether the play itself was actable (it would take six hours to perform).

Cromwell was not staged therefore, but was published the following year and, under the influence of Charles Kemble, Hugo wrote a lengthy preface that was to become the manifesto of the Romantic Movement. He investigated the nature of poetry and drama and considered exactly what modem drama should be. This led him to a devastating attack on the Rules and a plea that the dramatist should revert to nature. He did not go so far as might have been expected and insisted on the retention of verse and rhyme, but this was no doubt due to an awareness of his own virtues.

The first Romantic play to be seen in Paris was *Henri III et sa cour* by Alexandre Dumas in 1829 and this was followed by Alfred de Vigny's version of *Othello*. However, the play which finally sealed the success of the Romantic Movement was Hugo's *Hernani,* which was first performed at the Comédie Française on 25 February 1830. On this occasion Hugo disdained the services of the usual claque and gave their seats to his friends. The Romantics were therefore present in strength, headed by Théophile Gautier, resplendent in a cherry-coloured doublet and pale green trousers, with his hair in long ringlets.

The first line of *Hernani* was enough to shock the Classicists because the sentence was carried on into the second. The booing that started was promptly countered by the cheers of Gautier and his friends, and the uproar continued throughout the performance. Surprisingly, the critics were not unkind and although similar scenes continued to take place until the play was withdrawn after forty-five performances, because of the illness of Mademoiselle Mars (who played Dona Sol), it was generally agreed that the Romantics had won their battle.

La Nuit vénitienne is a slight play about which it is difficult nowadays to feel any emotion, but from the moment the curtain rose, it was clear that there were groups in the theatre determined that it should not succeed. The Classicists were still resentful of the success of *Hernani* and, even if Musset had not been known to be a member of the Cénacle, the Romantic spirit of *Tales of Spain and Italy* would have been enough to arouse their hostility.

The first scene was played in comparative quiet, but booing started in the second and continued to drown a great part of the play. The author was astonished, but continued to hope that all would be well with the scene between the Prince and Laurette. Mademoiselle Béranger, a beautiful young actress, exquisitely dressed in white satin, leaned against the balcony trellis and looked out over the moonlit canal. Unfortunately, the scenery had just been painted and when she turned back to face the audience, her skirts were heavily barred with the green diamonds of the trellis. Pandemonium broke out and the management were forced to lower the curtain. On the following night the reception was much the same and Musset turned his back on the theatre, to devote himself to a life of pleasure.

In April 1832, Musset's father died of cholera and when the family examined their resources, it was clear that Alfred would have to look to literature for an income. Although he had renounced the theatre, he hastily wrote for publication, not performance, two plays in verse, *La coupe et les lèvres* and *À quoi rêvent les jeunes filles*. In later years he was to publish them among his collected poems, not with his plays (he was clearly more interested in the poetry than the stagecraft). With the addition of another poem, they were published as the first volume of *Spectacle d'un fauteuil,* or *Armchair Theatre,* the title that he was to continue to use until 1840 for the publication of his plays in book form.

Spectacle d'un fauteuil was an almost complete failure. Only Mérimée of his friends and Sainte-Beuve among the critics were favourably impressed, but in spite of this the author's object was attained. Shortly after the publication of Sainte-Beuve's article, Buloz, the editor of *La Revue des deux mondes,* a fortnightly literary magazine, persuaded the poet to become one of his contributors.

On 1 April 1833, Musset made his first appearance in the magazine with *André del Sarto,* which it is difficult to believe was written for the occasion, as has always been assumed. The abundance of plot and absence of characterisation are defects typical of a first play. Even *La Nuit vénitienne,* slight as it is, is more mature and it seems improbable that within six weeks he could have written *Les Caprices de Marianne.*

Les Caprices de Marianne is the first of Musset's plays to reveal his particular dramatic genius and although ostensibly set in mediaeval Italy, the characters are clearly taken from the Paris which the author knew. Hermia is his mother and Octavio and Celio are, as George Sand pointed out and he admitted, the two sides of his own character. As for the original of Marianne, Musset himself said, 'She's not a woman, she is woman'.

Les Caprices de Marianne was published on 15 May 1833. On 20 June, Buloz gave a dinner party for the contributors to his magazine, at which all the guests, with one exception, were men. The exception was George Sand, and Musset was placed next to her. On 29 July, she became his mistress.

George Sand, a great-granddaughter of Marshal de Saxe, was born six years before Musset. In January 1831, she had left her husband and come to Paris to live with a young writer, Jules Sandeau. They collaborated on a novel, using half of Sandeau's name (Jules Sand) to avoid recognition, and when they parted shortly afterwards, she retained Sand as a *nom de plume,* adding a first name, George, that was widely used in her home country near Bourges.

By 1833, George Sand was celebrated as the authoress of *Indiana* and *Lélia,* and her intelligence and sincerity made an immediate impression on Musset, in spite of his dislike of blue-stockings. They became friends immediately and within a few weeks, almost against his will and certainly to his astonishment, he found he was in love with her. For her part, she was afraid to fall in love with him, afraid of his reputation, afraid perhaps of herself, and she yielded almost reluctantly. Soon afterwards at Fontainebleau, her worst fears were realised. Musset first upset her by talking of his previous mistresses and was then terror-stricken by hallucinations. Later, he became jealous of her past life and made her miserable with his cross-questioning. Within a matter of hours it was over, and he was once again the charming, attentive lover he had been before.

These two sides of his character, this alternating between the ardent romantic and the libertine, the Celio and Octavio of *Les*

Caprices de Marianne, persisted throughout his life. George Sand described him later as suffering from a sort of moral epilepsy and possessed by an angel and a demon. But in the summer and autumn of 1833 the angel predominated and they were happy enough to decide to pay a long visit to Italy. They set out in December, financed by an advance of four thousand francs from Buloz against her next novel. Later in the month they arrived in Genoa from Marseilles, having travelled part of the way with Stendhal (who disgusted them with his obscenity and heavy drinking), and George Sand, conscious of her obligations to Buloz, began to write regularly every day. As Musset was accustomed to write only when possessed by his Muse or for financial reasons, he sought what amusement he could find in the theatres and streets of Genoa. He was bored and bad-tempered and they quarrelled frequently. They therefore moved on to Florence, and then, in January 1834, to Venice.

No sooner had they reached Venice than George Sand became ill and once again Musset found himself alone. He began drinking heavily, was unfaithful, as he had already been in Genoa, and, thinking he had caught venereal disease, had to confess to her. Their quarrels became more frequent and more bitter, until he finally announced that he did not love her and she replied that they were neither of them in love any more and never had been. The door between their rooms was closed and they would have parted, if they had had enough money to do so.

The next day Musset caught malaria, followed by brain fever and George Sand nursed him devotedly for three weeks, including thirteen days of delirium. In her state of exhaustion and misery it is not surprising that she needed someone's sympathy, and Musset's doctor, Paolo Pagello, was a young Italian of Austrian origin; George Sand, always quick to champion the causes of the poor or downtrodden and no doubt regarding him as the representative of the oppressed Austrians, fell in love with him, told him so, and became his mistress.

When Musset was well enough to travel, it was decided that he should return to France, and realising that George and Pagello were in love, but with no suspicion that they were already lovers, he joined their hands together and left Venice.

While Musset was in Venice, *Fantasio* was published in *La Revue des deux mondes*. It was probably inspired by the marriage in 1832 of Leopold I of Belgium to Princess Louise, daughter of Louis-Philippe, and writing in the full flush of his happiness with George Sand, Musset portrayed himself, with the utmost sincerity and introspection, as the chief character. The play was not performed until 1866, when Musset had been dead for nine years, the title role being played by Delaunay, who bore a remarkable resemblance to the young Musset of thirty years before, so it is easy to imagine the emotions aroused among the author's friends who filled the theatre. For this production, Paul de Musset, Alfred's brother, extended the play to three acts, which the author had contemplated but refrained from doing as he considered it unperformable. His opinion was shared by Delaunay and by the public of 1866, and the play did not succeed until it was played in its original form.

On 10 April 1834, Musset returned to Paris a changed man. He was subject to attacks of nerves, was incapable of writing, and shut himself in his room, emerging only at night to play chess with his mother. He continued to correspond with George Sand, the tone of their letters being one of profound friendship and devotion. It was clear to them both that their love was dead, but that something different and equally strong had taken its place.

Both his family and Buloz pressed him to start writing again and he reluctantly took up the first scene of a verse play which he had begun some time before under the name of *Camille et Perdican*. This was to become *On ne badine pas avec l'amour*, which appeared in the *Revue* on 1 July, the poetic origin being plainly visible in the first scene between the Chorus and Blazius. The title, *Don't Trifle with Love*, reflects the author's state of mind when he finished the play. So do the characters of Camille and Perdican; in fact, the last few lines of the second act are taken directly from a letter which George Sand wrote to him on 2 May and Camille's description of life in her convent derives from George Sand's experiences.

Also in 1834, Musset published the first two prose volumes of *Spectacle d'un fauteuil*, including all the prose plays he had then written, together with *Lorenzaccio,* whose extraordinary deficiencies of construction, which overshadow a passionate plea for liberty, do not prevent it from being widely regarded as Musset's most important dramatic work. Its chief character, Lorenzo de Medici, shared a life of debauchery with his cousin, Alessandro, Duke of Florence, in order to have the opportunity of murdering him and so free Florence of tyranny, only to find that he had been so contaminated that redemption was impossible. It was no doubt the parallel with the author's own life that enabled Musset to draw this character with such insight and the part has attracted players as different as Sarah Bernhardt and Gérard Philipe. The problems of translating the rolling periods of French prose into English – an over-faithful translation would be only too reminiscent of Max Beerbohm's *Savanarola* – mean that *Lorenzaccio* has had only rare outings on the British stage. There was, however, a notable production starring Greg Hicks at the National Theatre in 1983, in a version by John Fowles.

In August 1834, George Sand returned to Paris for a few days. When she met Musset, they talked quietly as old friends and then they both left, he to Baden and she to her home at Nohant. Once again they corresponded. The tone of his letters changed to a pleading, passionate note, full of phrases such as 'Forget me, I can suffer without complaining'. She replied resignedly, pointing out that she was no longer in love with him.

At the end of October they both returned to Paris and within a few days she was once again his mistress. Almost immediately his old jealousy returned. He discovered that she had slept with Pagello while he was ill in Venice, and, when he taxed her with it, she replied with dignity that he had forfeited all rights to question her on such a subject. There followed a succession of partings and reconciliations, the latter now entirely at her instigation, as for the first time she was passionately in love with him, until she left Paris on 6 March 1835 and broke with him forever.

Since November 1834, Musset had been cured of his passion for George Sand. He now had to work for financial reasons, but the break with George Sand had temporarily cured him of the desire to be continually seeking entertainment and the next four years were marked by a considerable literary output (which reflected the personal assessment he had been undertaking since the previous May) and the only other important love affairs he was to have.

In these years he wrote a number of novels and poems, and also four plays. *La Quenouille de Barberine* (*Barberine's Distaff*), first published in two acts in August 1835, and later rewritten in three acts as *Barberine,* now seems excessively verbose, distinguished only by a characteristic climax. But *Il ne faut jurer de rien* (*You Can't Think of Everything*), published the following year, is a *proverbe* of considerable charm in spite of a rather abrupt ending.

Proverbe in this context is not a proverb but a well-known saying and in its dramatic form was originally a sort of charade designed to illustrate the saying which formed the last line. The *proverbe* was expanded into a short play in the eighteenth century – notably by Carmontelle – and Musset developed it still further; he had already used it to a certain extent in *On ne badine pas avec l'amour* and reverted to it again in later years.

The other two plays of this period are both translated in this volume. *Le Chandelier* was first published in November 1835, and is based on Musset's own experiences. At the age of eighteen he had found himself in the position of Fortunio in the play – except that the lady remained unmoved by his reproaches – and again in 1835 he believed he recognised the same situation. This time he was mistaken, but after the explanations that ensued, they did fall in love and the lady in question, Madame Jaubert, became his mistress.

Musset's affair with Madame Jaubert lasted for two brief periods of three and two weeks, on the first occasion ended by the jealousy which had caused similar breaks with George Sand, and on the second at Madame Jaubert's request because of the jealousy and unhappiness of someone else. They remained in love, obtaining a certain pleasure from their self-sacrifice, and a close friendship developed, which lasted until his death. She became his 'godmother', one of the few people who exercised any influence on him and to whom he could always turn for sympathy and understanding.

The year 1836 was distinguished by an uncharacteristic love affair with a young milliner, Louise Durand, who lived opposite his house. They spent an idyllic two months together in the country and for once the relationship ended, not in quarrels, but in the discovery that they had too little in common to be interested in each other any longer. His peace of mind at this time was reflected in his poetry and a novel, but not in any play, possibly because he realised the difficulties of portraying simple happiness in dramatic form.

In April 1837, Musset began a love affair with a cousin of Madame Jaubert's, Aimée d'Alton, who was to remain his mistress for nearly two years and eventually married his brother. She was a gentle girl who was devoted to him and she succeeded in persuading him to write. She lent him money and would have liked to marry him, but he refused on the grounds of having no fortune, doubtless remembering also that at one time he would have married George Sand, if she had been free.

In March 1837, Aimée d'Alton was shocked by Musset's gambling and, in an attempt to cure him, sent him a purse anonymously, with a note advising him to be more economical. He guessed who had sent it and the episode formed the basis of *Un Caprice,* which was published in the *Revue* on June 15, the characters being portraits of Aimée d'Alton, Madame Jaubert, and the author. *Caprice* has a wider meaning in French than in English, and *A Diversion,* the title of this translation, is one of the ways the word has been used in the text.

Musset's love affair with Aimée d'Alton, like the previous one with Louise, was unusual in ending without an open quarrel and by the end of 1838 he was once again leading the life of Octavio. Since the days of the Cénacle he had always worshipped youth and his feverish search for entertainment was no doubt due to the approach of his thirtieth year and a fear of growing old. His reply to his friends' remonstrations was that he was too old to write and his life's work was finished (it is a fact that most of his best work had already been created).

Musset's reluctance to write was only partly caused by his break with Aimée d'Alton and his gradual reversion to his former habits. Since 18 October 1838, his financial worries had largely disappeared with his appointment as librarian at the Ministry of the Interior, a post he was to retain until the Revolution of 1848, by which time he was beginning to be assured of an income from the performances of his plays. The appointment had been offered to Buloz, who refused it, but recommended Musset, only to find that the Minister knew of him by hearsay as the author of the scandalous 'Ballad to the Moon'. Musset was forced to obtain the support of Louis-Philippe's son, the Duke of Orléans, a former schoolfellow.

From 1839 Musset's drinking began to affect his health and his disposition, and his charm and gaiety became less and less apparent. In 1840 and on two later occasions he was seriously ill with pneumonia and was weakened by his doctors constantly bleeding him, when they mistook his lung congestion for brain fever. His government salary had relieved him of the necessity of writing the novels which he detested and it was only occasionally that his emotions were aroused sufficiently to inspire a poem. Rachel, who had made a brilliant debut at the Comédie Française in 1838, asked him to write a tragedy for her, but he only achieved a few fragments (observing the Rules, which, in a tragedy he considered it would have been monstrous to disobey), and it was to the surprise of his friends that in 1845 he wrote *Il faut qu'une porte soit ouverte ou fermée*. Paul de Musset thought that, with the exception of the ending, this *proverbe* represented one of the author's own experiences. But although Musset himself is recognisable, it is unlikely that he was thinking of marriage and presumably rather more than the last few speeches has been altered.

In 1845 also, Musset was made a Chevalier of the Légion d'Honneur and soon afterwards, perhaps because this brought him back into the public eye, it was proposed to stage *Un Caprice* at the Odéon. But nothing came of this and Musset must have become resigned to never having his plays performed, when on 17 November 1847, *Un Caprice* was mounted at the Comédie Française. According to Paul de Musset, Madame Allan-Despréaux was living in St Petersburg when she saw a short play which enchanted her, but when she asked for it to be translated into French so that she could take it back to Paris, she was told that it was a French play. This story is probably apocryphal and the true version appears to be that Buloz, who was then manager of the Comédie Française, had already decided to stage it when Madame Allan returned to Paris and insisted on playing Madame de Léry as she had done in Russia. Whatever the reason for its production, the play had an immediate success and the author's other plays began to be in demand. Those which had originally been written in one act, such as *Un Caprice* and *Une Porte,* were performed almost as they had been written, but new versions had to be made of the longer ones, including *Les Caprices de Marianne* and *Le Chandelier.* Of the other plays in this volume, *Fantasio* and *On ne badine pas* were not considered suitable for performance during the author's lifetime, and he never revised them.

The plays were also staged abroad. Shortly afterwards *Un Caprice* was produced in London at the Royal Lyceum Theatre with the surprising title of A *Charming Widow,* but this title may have been considered too provocative for publication, as another version was printed as *A Good Little Wife.*

Another consequence of Musset's success in the theatre was that actresses began to ask him for new plays. The tragedy that had been promised to Rachel remained unwritten, but in 1849 he created *Louison,* a delightful little comedy in verse in an eighteenth-century manner, for Augustine Brohan, who eventually did not play it; and two years later for Rose Chérie, *Bettine,* a comedy in one long act, which failed completely and is clearly too verbose and lacking in wit to sustain the slender plot.

Musset wrote two other plays that were published in his lifetime: *On ne saurait penser à tout,* in 1849, for a charity matinée, in which Madame Allan, who shortly afterwards became his mistress, took part; and *Carmosine,* the following year, at the insistent request of a magazine editor, who paid him a very high fee.

On ne saurait penser à tout (*You Can't Think of Everything*) was adapted from a typical *proverbe* by Carmontelle. Although a success at the charity matinée (as most works usually are), it was received coldly at the Comédie Française a few weeks later, the author even being accused of plagiarism, although his debt to Carmontelle was acknowledged in the programme. He eventually made a number of additions, particularly in the opening scene, and these may indicate a reason for its failure. It is played nowadays as a farce with a number of cuts in the opening scene, but if it was originally directed without the business and speed which farce demands (and the additions, which would slow down the action, tend to show this), it could easily have been dismissed as a diffuse adaptation of a play that was already well known in a more concise form.

Carmosine is based on a story by Boccaccio and this tale of a young girl dying of love for her sovereign touched a responsive chord in Musset, always sensitive to the emotions of youth. But although the characters are firmly drawn and individual scenes are delicately written, the romantic plot seems strangely artificial without the poetry or fantasy it evidently needs.

It was popularly believed that Musset owed his post of librarian to a poem on the birth of the Comte de Paris, which he published in September 1838: this identification with the Orléanist regime led to his dismissal after the Revolution of 1848 – ironically enough in view of his ingrained Bonapartist sympathies which had not been destroyed by his friendship with the Duke of Orléans.

To provide some financial compensation, the Académie awarded him a prize, but as it was one designed to help and encourage young writers and poor artists, Musset felt humiliated and gave it to charity. Two years later he had swallowed his indignation sufficiently to seek election to the Académie for the second time and failed only slightly less ignominiously than on the first occasion just before the 1848 revolution. However, at the instigation of Mérimée, he tried once more and duly became an Academician in 1852, on the same day as Balzac.

In 1853, Musset wrote a short play in verse, *The Dream of Augustus,* at the suggestion of the Minister of Education, who himself selected the subject and although for various reasons the play was not published, he was rewarded with the post of librarian at the Ministry. In 1855, the Minister requested another play and Musset wrote a one-act comedy in prose, *The Ass and the Brook,* which, not surprisingly, was a complete failure when read by the author at a reception given by the Minister at the Tuileries.

Musset was now living alone under the care of a housekeeper, as his mother had joined his sister at Angers. Since at least 1842 he had been suffering from heart trouble, which had manifested itself in a twitch of the head, and in the winter of 1856 his condition deteriorated rapidly, culminating the following April in a series of fainting fits. On 2 May 1857, he died. The next day a young man appeared at his door and asked to be allowed to render solitary homage, but the housekeeper refused to admit him. It was Villiers de l'Isle-Adam, aged nineteen, come to pay the tribute that Musset with his love of youth would have most appreciated.

Peter Meyer

Note by the Translator

The text used is that of the *Collected Edition* of 1853, reprinted in 1856, the last to be published in the author's lifetime. However, in accordance with the current practice of the Comédie Française, Madame de Léry's lines about her furs have been reinstated from the original version of *Un Caprice*, and some of the additions to the opening scene of *On ne saurait penser à tout* have been omitted. Other amendments (and they are extensive), now made by the Comédie Française, have not been adopted, except for certain of the cuts mentioned below.

Some of the plays have been given new titles for reasons set out in the Introduction. First names and titles of characters have been anglicised, or, in the case of Octavio, Italianised, and some have been altered where this appeared desirable: in *Un Caprice*, for example, Ernestine and Matilda have been rechristened Flora and Charlotte.

In *On ne badine pas avec l'amour*, which the author never revised for the stage, the scenes have been reduced in number, by changing the locations of some and amalgamating others, but this has not involved any alteration of the text. In all the translations, characters do not go down on their knees (as Musset so often directed) except where necessary to the plot; references which an audience today would be unlikely to understand have been changed; and a few lines have been cut, chiefly in soliloquies, where the Romantic conceit or elaboration of metaphor would now seem exaggerated to English ears.

I am grateful to the Archivist of the Comédie Française for allowing me to examine the original prompt copies of the plays and for answering a number of written queries.

MARIANNE
(Les Caprices de Marianne)

Characters

CELIO, a young man

PIPPO, his servant

CLAUDIO, Chief Magistrate

TIBIA, his servant

OCTAVIO, a young man

MARIANNE, Claudio's wife

HERMIA, Celio's mother

MALVOLIO, her steward

SERVING MAN

SERVANTS

ASSASSINS

Scene: A square in Naples: on the one side Claudio's house, with a balcony, and on the other a tavern, with tables in an arbour in front of it.

The action takes place on a single day in the early sixteenth century; there is a short lapse of time between Acts One and Two.

ACT ONE

CELIO and PIPPO enter.

CELIO. Well, Pippo, you've just seen Marianne?

PIPPO: Yes, my lord.

CELIO: What did she say?

PIPPO: More pious and proud than ever. She'll tell her husband, she says, if you don't stop pursuing her.

CELIO: Can any woman be so cruel? There's nothing left for me but death. What plan can I think of now? What do you advise, Pippo?

PIPPO: I'd first of all advise you not to stay here. Her husband's coming.

(*They move upstage.*
CLAUDIO and TIBIA enter.)

CLAUDIO: You're my faithful servant, my devoted retainer? Well, know that I must be revenged for an outrage.

TIBIA: You, sir?

CLAUDIO: Me. These impudent guitars never stop murmuring beneath my wife's windows. But be patient! All is not yet lost. (*He notices CELIO and PIPPO.*) Come over here. There's someone who might hear us. This evening you'll find me an assassin, as I told you.

TIBIA: Whatever for?

CLAUDIO: I think Marianne has lovers.

TIBIA: You think that, sir?

CLAUDIO: Yes. There's an odour of lovers around my house. No one passes naturally before my door. It rains guitars and secret messages.

TIBIA: Can you prevent people serenading your wife?

CLAUDIO: No. But I can post a man behind the gate and get rid of the first one who enters.

TIBIA: For shame! Your wife has no lovers. You might as well say I have mistresses.

CLAUDIO: Why shouldn't you, Tibia? You're very ugly, but you've a lot of intelligence.

TIBIA: I agree, I agree.

CLAUDIO: There, Tibia, you agree yourself. You mustn't doubt it any more. My dishonour is public.

TIBIA: Why public?

CLAUDIO: I tell you it is public.

TIBIA: But, sir, the whole town knows your wife is a dragon of virtue. She sees no one, she never goes out except to Mass.

CLAUDIO: Leave this to me. I don't feel angry. After all the presents I've given her! Yes, Tibia, at this moment I'm weaving a terrible plot and I feel I'm almost dying of grief.

TIBIA: Oh no, no!

CLAUDIO: When I tell you something, you'll be so good as to believe me.

(*CLAUDIO and TIBIA go out.*)

CELIO: How unhappy is the man who in the flower of his youth yields to a hopeless love! How unhappy is the man who surrenders to a charming dream, without knowing where it will lead him or if his love will be returned! Joyfully he ventures slowly from the shore; he can see in the distance enchanted plains, green meadows, the mirage of his Eldorado. The waves bear him forward in silence, but when reality awakens him, he's as far from the goal he craves as from the shore he's left. He can't continue his voyage or retrace his steps. (*Music can be heard.*) What is this masquerade? Isn't that Octavio I can see?

(*OCTAVIO enters, wearing a long, open domino, with a mask on his face and a harlequin's cane in his hand.*)

OCTAVIO: (*To the other masquers offstage.*) That's enough, all of you, go back home. We've had enough for today. (*To CELIO, taking off his mask.*) Well, my worthy gentleman, how fares this gracious melancholy?

CELIO: Octavio! Oh, why are you so mad? You've a pound of rouge on your cheeks. Where did you get this costume? Aren't you ashamed in the middle of the day?

OCTAVIO: Oh, Celio! Why are you so mad? You've a pound of chalk on your cheeks! Where did you get this great black cloak? Aren't you ashamed in the middle of the carnival?

CELIO: I was going to your house.

OCTAVIO: I was going to my house too. How is my house? I haven't seen it for a week.

CELIO: I've a favour to ask you.

OCTAVIO: Speak, dear boy. Do you want money? I've none left. Do you want my sword? Here's a harlequin's cane. Go on, go on, I'm at your service.

CELIO: How long will this last? A week without going home! You'll kill yourself.

OCTAVIO: Never with my own hand, my dear fellow, never. I'd rather die than try to kill myself.

CELIO: Isn't this life you're leading suicide?

OCTAVIO: Imagine a tightrope walker, in silver slippers, his balancing pole in his hand, suspended between heaven and earth. On either side, shrivelled little old faces, thin, pale phantoms, sharp-witted creditors, relations and toadies, a whole legion of monsters, cling to his cloak and tug at him in all directions to make him lose his balance. Frivolous remarks, elaborate witticisms, cavalcade around him; a cloud of sinister predictions blinds him with black wings. He continues lightly on his way from East to West. If he looks down, his head turns; if he looks up, his foot stumbles. He goes faster than the wind and all the hands stretched out towards him won't make him spill one drop of the cup of happiness his own hand carries. That's my life, my dear fellow; it's my own faithful portrait.

CELIO: How happy you are to be mad!

OCTAVIO: How mad you are not to be happy! Tell me what it is you want.

CELIO: I want peace of mind, the sweet content that makes life a mirror where all objects are painted for a moment and across which everything lightly skims. A debt, for me, is a reproach. Love, which you all treat as a pastime, disturbs my whole life. Oh, my dear fellow, you still don't know what it is to love as I do! My study is deserted; for a month I've wandered around this house day and night. What pleasure I feel at moonrise to bring my modest choir of musicians under the trees at the back of this square and hear them hymn the beauty of Marianne! But she has never appeared at the window, never leaned her charming face against the blind.

OCTAVIO: Who is this Marianne? She's not my cousin, is she?

CELIO: That's who it is. Old Claudio's wife.

OCTAVIO: I've never seen her; but it's certain she's my cousin. Claudio's done it on purpose. Tell me your troubles, Celio.

CELIO: Every method I've tried, to make her aware of my love, has been useless. She has just left the convent, she loves her husband, she respects her duties. Her door is closed to every young man in town; no one can approach her.

OCTAVIO: Hm! Is she pretty? How silly of me! You love her, that scarcely matters. What can we think of?

CELIO: Can I speak freely? You won't laugh at me?

OCTAVIO: Speak freely and let me laugh at you.

CELIO: You're a relation, you must be welcome in her house?

OCTAVIO: Am I welcome? I've no idea. Let's assume I'm welcome. To tell the truth, we're not a very close circle in my illustrious family. We hardly keep in touch except by letter. However, Marianne does know my name. Should I speak to her on your behalf?

CELIO: A dozen times I've tried to talk to her. A dozen times I've felt my knees give way as I've approached her. When I see her, my throat tightens. I suffocate, as if my heart were rising to my lips.

OCTAVIO: I've felt that. In the depths of the forest, when a deer advances with tiny steps over the dry leaves and the hunter hears the bracken slide across its quivering flanks like the rustle of a silken dress, then the beating of his heart overcomes him in spite of himself. He raises his gun in silence, without moving a step, without breathing.

CELIO: Why do I feel like this? Why can't I love this woman as you would, Octavio, as I'd love any other woman? Why am I saddened, paralysed, when you would be happy and ardent, you would be attracted, as iron is attracted by a magnet? Who can say: 'This is happy or sad'? Reality is only a shadow. What makes it divine, call imagination or madness. Then madness is beauty itself. Every man is enveloped in a transparent net that covers him from head to foot. He thinks he can see woods and rivers, heavenly places, and beneath his gaze universal nature changes colour with the infinite shades of a magic cloak. Octavio! Octavio! Help me! Help me!

OCTAVIO: I like your love, Celio. It diffuses in your brain like Syracusan wine. Give me your hand, I'll help you. Wait, wait! The air on my face is making me think again. I know this Marianne; she hates me without ever having seen me. She's a thin girl, who always has her own way, a spoiled child.

CELIO: Do what you like, but don't deceive me, I implore you. It's easy to deceive me; I can't fight against something I'd never do myself.

OCTAVIO: Why don't you climb over the wall?

CELIO: What's the use, if she doesn't love me?

OCTAVIO: Why don't you write to her?

CELIO: She tears up my letters or sends them back to me.

OCTAVIO: Why don't you fall in love with someone else?

CELIO: My life's breath belongs to Marianne. With a single word from her lips she can set it aflame or snuff it out. To live for someone else would be as difficult for me as dying for her. Sh! Here she comes.

OCTAVIO: Go away, I'll speak to her.

CELIO: How can you? In the dress you're wearing! Wipe your face; you look like a madman.

OCTAVIO: (*Taking off his domino.*) There! Madness and I, my dear Celio, are too fond of each other ever to quarrel. We each obey the other's wishes. Have no fears about that. When a student on holiday waltzes at his first ball, you expect him to lose his reason. My imagination is my reason. I think by letting my tongue wag and at this moment I'd speak to the King as I will to your lady.

CELIO: I don't know what I feel. No, don't speak to her.

OCTAVIO: Why?

CELIO: I can't say why. I feel you're going to deceive me.

OCTAVIO: Give me your hand. I've never deceived any one since the day I was born. I shan't start with my best friend.

(*CELIO goes out. MARIANNE enters from her house.*)

Don't turn away, princess of beauty. Let your gaze fall for a moment on the most humble of your servants.

MARIANNE: Who are you?

OCTAVIO: My name is Octavio. I'm your husband's cousin.

MARIANNE: Have you come to see him? Go into the house; he'll be back soon.

OCTAVIO: I haven't come to see him and I certainly won't go into the house for fear you'll turn me out again when you've heard what brings me here.

MARIANNE: Then don't trouble to tell me or keep me here any longer.

OCTAVIO: I'm afraid I must. I beg you to stay and listen to me. Cruel Marianne! Your eyes have caused a great affliction and your words are not designed to cure it. What has Celio done to you?

MARIANNE: Who are you talking about? What affliction have I caused?

OCTAVIO: The cruellest of all afflictions, because it's hopeless; the most terrible, as it feeds on itself and rejects the healing draught even from the hand of friendship; an affliction that strikes colour from one's lips at the touch of poisons sweeter than ambrosia and, like Cleopatra's pearl, melts the hardest of hearts in a torrent of tears; an affliction no perfume, no human science, can relieve. It's nourished by the passing wind, the scent of a faded rose, the chorus of a song. It draws food for its suffering from all that surrounds it, as a bee draws its honey from all the flowers in the garden.

MARIANNE: Will you tell me the name of this affliction?

OCTAVIO: Let him who is worthy to pronounce it tell you. Let your dreams at night teach it you, your orange trees in springtime. Seek it some lovely evening and you'll find it on your lips. Without itself, its name does not exist.

MARIANNE: Is it so dangerous to say, so fearfully infectious, that it terrifies a tongue that pleads in its favour?

OCTAVIO: Is it so sweet to hear, that it makes you ask? You have learned it from Celio.

MARIANNE: Then it's without wishing to. I don't know him or it.

OCTAVIO: It's the wish of my heart that you should know them together and never separate them.

MARIANNE: Is it?

OCTAVIO: Celio is my best friend. If I wanted to make you feel envious, I'd tell you he is handsome as the day, young, noble, and I should not be lying. But I only want to make you feel sorry, so I'll tell you he's been sad as death, since the day he saw you.

MARIANNE: Is it my fault he's sad?

OCTAVIO: Is it his fault you're beautiful? He only thinks of you. Night and day he prowls around this house. Have you never heard singing beneath your windows? Have you never raised your blind at midnight?

MARIANNE: Everyone can sing at night and this square belongs to everyone.

OCTAVIO: Everyone can love you, but no one can tell you so. How old are you, Marianne?

MARIANNE: What a charming question! If I were only eighteen, what would you want me to think?

OCTAVIO: Then you've still five or six years to be loved, eight or ten to be in love yourself, and the rest to pray to God.

MARIANNE: Really? Well, to make good use of the time I have, I love Claudio, your cousin and my husband.

OCTAVIO: My cousin and your husband put together will never make more than a priggish boor. You're not in love with Claudio.

MARIANNE: Or with Celio. You can tell him so.

OCTAVIO: Why?

MARIANNE: Will you tell me why I'm listening to you? Goodbye, sir. This little joke has lasted long enough. (*Goes out.*)

OCTAVIO: Heavens! Heavens! She has lovely eyes. Ah! Here comes Claudio. That's not quite the same thing. I don't exactly care to continue the conversation with him.

(*CLAUDIO and TIBIA enter.*)

CLAUDIO: (*To TIBIA.*) You're right…

OCTAVIO: (*To CLAUDIO.*) Good evening, cousin.

CLAUDIO: Good evening. (*To TIBIA.*) You're right.

OCTAVIO: Cousin, good evening.

CLAUDIO: Good evening, good evening.

(*OCTAVIO goes out.*)

You're right, my wife's a treasure of purity. What more can I say? Her virtue is undoubted.

TIBIA: You think so, sir?

CLAUDIO: Can she prevent people singing beneath her windows? The signs of impatience she shows stem from her character. Did you notice, as soon as I mentioned the subject, her mother was immediately of the same opinion as myself?

TIBIA: Concerning what?

CLAUDIO: Concerning people singing beneath her windows.

TIBIA: There's no harm in singing. I very often hum myself.

CLAUDIO: It's difficult to sing well.

TIBIA: Difficult for you and me. Nature didn't endow us with a voice and we've never cultivated it. But look how cleverly actors do it.

CLAUDIO: They spend their lives on the stage.

TIBIA: How much a year do you think one earns?

CLAUDIO: Who? A judge?

TIBIA: No, a singer.

CLAUDIO: I've no idea. A judge gets a third of what my post is worth. Judges of appeal have double.

TIBIA: If I were chief magistrate of this town, and if I were married and my wife had lovers, I'd sentence them myself.

CLAUDIO: To how many years in the galleys?

TIBIA: To death. A death sentence is a superb thing to read aloud.

CLAUDIO: The magistrate doesn't read it; the clerk of the court does.

TIBIA: The clerk of your court has a pretty wife.

CLAUDIO: No, it's the other magistrate who has a pretty wife. I had supper with them last night.

TIBIA: The clerk has too. The assassin who's coming tonight is the clerk's wife's lover.

CLAUDIO: What assassin?

TIBIA: The one you asked for.

CLAUDIO: There's no point in his coming, after what I've just told you.

TIBIA: What did you tell me?

CLAUDIO: About my wife.

TIBIA: Why, here she comes.

(*MARIANNE enters.*)

MARIANNE: Do you know what's happened to me, while you've been strolling round the town? I've received a visit from your cousin.

CLAUDIO: Who can that be? Name him by his name.

MARIANNE: Octavio. He made love to me on behalf of his friend Celio. Who is Celio? Do you know the man? Take care he doesn't set foot in our house, or Octavio.

CLAUDIO: I do know him. He's Hermia's son. She lives next door. How did you answer him?

MARIANNE: It doesn't matter how I answered. Do you understand what I'm saying? Order your servants to bar the door to this man and his friend. I'm expecting some further action on their part and I want to avoid it. (*Goes out.*)

CLAUDIO: What do you think of this, Tibia? There's some plot behind it.

TIBIA: You think so, sir?

CLAUDIO: Why didn't she want to tell me her answer? The man was impertinent, it's true, but the answer deserved to be known. I've a suspicion it's Hermia's son who arranged all these guitars.

TIBIA: Preventing these men entering your house is an excellent method of keeping them away.

CLAUDIO: Listen to me. I must report this discovery to my mother-in-law.

TIBIA: Why, sir, here she is.

CLAUDIO: Who? My mother-in-law?

TIBIA: No, Hermia, our neighbour. Weren't you talking about her just now?

CLAUDIO: Yes, as the mother of this man Celio, and that's the truth, Tibia.

TIBIA: Well, sir, she's coming this way with one, two, three servants. She's a worthy woman.

CLAUDIO: Yes, her wealth is considerable.

TIBIA: I've also heard she's high-principled. Suppose you spoke to her, sir?

CLAUDIO: What! The mother of a man I may be forced to have stabbed to death this very evening! His own mother, Tibia! For shame! I don't recognise your usual sense of the proprieties. Come, Tibia, let's go indoors.
(*CLAUDIO and TIBIA go out.*
HERMIA enters with MALVOLIO and two SERVANTS.)

HERMIA: Has everything been done as I ordered? Have the musicians been told to come?

MALVOLIO: Yes, madam, this evening they'll be at your orders, or I should say...

HERMIA: What else? Is everything prepared for supper, as I said? You'll tell my son I'm sorry I haven't seen him. What time did he go out?

MALVOLIO: To go out, you first of all have to come in. He hasn't been home all night.

HERMIA: You don't know what you're saying. He had supper with me yesterday and brought me home. Has the picture I bought this morning been taken to his study?

MALVOLIO: In his father's lifetime it wouldn't have been like this.

HERMIA: In his mother's lifetime, Malvolio, it is. Who asked you to watch over his conduct? Remember this. Don't let Celio ever came across a face of ill omen as he goes by. Don't let him hear you muttering like this between your teeth, or, by heaven, not one of you will pass the night under his roof.

MALVOLIO: I'm not muttering. There are no forebodings on

my face. You ask me what time my master went out and I
tell you he didn't come home. Since he's been in love, you
don't see him twice a week.

HERMIA: Why are Celio's books covered with dust? Why
is his room untidy? Why do I have to put my hand to
everything in my son's house, if I want to get something
done? You take it upon yourself to cast your eyes on
matters that don't concern you, when your work's only half
finished and the tasks you've been given fall on others. Be
off with you and keep a guard on your tongue.

(*MALVOLIO and the SERVANTS go out.*
CELIO enters.)

HERMIA: Well, my dear boy, what are your pleasures today?

CELIO: Whatever yours are, Mother.

HERMIA: (*Taking his arm.*) What! Common pleasures, but
no common cares? That's an unfair division, Celio. Have
secrets from me, my child, but not those which prey on
your mind and make you unconscious of everything
around you.

CELIO: I have no secrets and if I did have any, please God
they wouldn't be the kind I'd be ashamed of.

HERMIA: When you were ten or twelve years old, all
your cares, all your little worries, attached themselves to
me. Upon a harsh or gentle look of these eyes of mine
depended the sorrow or joy of yours: your little fair head
was tied by such a slender thread to your mother's heart.
Now, my child, I'm only your sister, incapable perhaps of
relieving your anxieties, but not of sharing them.

CELIO: Mother! You too, you once were beautiful! Under
this long veil you now wear, the eye can still recognise
the bearing of a queen. Oh, Mother! You have inspired
love! The sound of guitars has murmured beneath your
half-open windows; in these burning streets, in the whirl of
these festivities, you once walked, young, carefree, superb.
You never fell in love; a kinsman of my father's died for
love of you.

HERMIA: What memories would you recall to me?

CELIO: If your heart can bear the sorrow, if it won't make

you weep, tell me this story, please; I want to know the details.

HERMIA: (*Sadly.*) My child, what's the use? What sad fantasy possesses you?

CELIO: I beseech you. I'm listening.

HERMIA: You want me to? At that time your father had never seen me. As a connection of my family, he undertook to obtain their approval of the young Orsini, who wanted to marry me. He was received by your grandfather as his rank deserved and admitted into the intimacy of our home. Orsini was an excellent match, yet I refused him. Your father, in pleading for him, had killed the little love he had inspired in my heart after two months of constant attentions. I had never suspected the strength of his passion for me. When he received my answer, he fell unconscious into your father's arms. However, a long absence, a journey which he then undertook, was to dispel his grief. Your father changed his role and asked for himself what he had been unable to obtain for Orsini. I loved him sincerely and the respect he had inspired in my parents did not allow me to hesitate. The marriage was decided the same day and the church opened its door to us a few weeks later. At this moment Orsini returned. He came to see your father, reproached him bitterly, accused him of betraying his confidence and causing the refusal he had received. 'What's more,' he added, 'if you wanted to destroy me, you'll be satisfied.' Terrified by these words, your father ran to mine and asked him to testify so that Orsini might be disabused. Alas, it was too late. The poor man was found in his room, struck down by his own sword.

CELIO: He died?

HERMIA: Yes; it was terrible.

CELIO: No, Mother, death is never terrible, when it comes to the aid of a hopeless love. The only reason I feel sorry for him is that he thought he was deceived by his friend.

HERMIA: What is the matter, Celio? You turn away your head.

CELIO: You, too, Mother, you are moved. Oh, I see this story was too painful for you. I was wrong to ask you to tell it.

HERMIA: Don't think about my sorrows, they are only memories. Your own touch me more deeply. If you refuse to fight against them, they will live a long time in your young heart. I don't ask you to tell them to me, but I can see them. As you are sharing mine, come, let us fight together. There are friends at home, let us go and try to enjoy ourselves. Let us attempt to live, my child, and to look cheerfully, me at the past, you at the future. Come, Celio, give me your hand.

ACT TWO

OCTAVIO and PIPPO enter.

OCTAVIO: He's giving up, you say?

PIPPO: Poor man! He's more in love than ever! I almost believe he doesn't trust you, or me, or anyone he knows.

OCTAVIO: No, by heaven, I won't give up. I feel like Marianne, I want to be obstinate. If Celio's not successful, I'll cut my tongue out.

PIPPO: Will you go against his wishes?

OCTAVIO: Yes, if they happen not to be mine, which are elder sister to his, and if it's to send Claudio to hell. I loathe, despise and detest him from head to foot.

PIPPO: Well, you can give him your answer in person, here he comes. But I won't have any more to do with it. (*Goes out.*)

(*CELIO enters.*)

OCTAVIO: Why, Celio, you're giving up the struggle?

CELIO: (*A book in his hand.*) What do you want me to do?

OCTAVIO: Don't you trust me? You look so pale. Where have you been?

CELIO: At my mother's.

OCTAVIO: Why are you so sad?

CELIO: I don't know. I'm sorry, I'm sorry, do whatever you like. Go and find Marianne; tell her: if she deceives me, she'll kill me and my life lies in her eyes.

OCTAVIO: What the devil have you to do with death? What makes you think about that?

CELIO: My dear fellow, it's here before my eyes.

OCTAVIO: Death?

CELIO: Yes, Love and Death.

OCTAVIO: What does that mean?

CELIO: Love and Death, Octavio, are linked together. One is the source of the greatest happiness man can find on earth. The other puts an end to all sorrows, all afflictions.

OCTAVIO: Is that a book you have there?

CELIO: Yes. You probably haven't read it.

OCTAVIO: Very probably. When you've read one, there's no reason to read all the others.

CELIO: (*Reading.*) 'When the heart experiences sincere and profound feelings of love, it also experiences, as it were, a weariness, a languor, that gives rise to a desire for death. Why? I do not know.'

OCTAVIO: Nor do I.

CELIO: (*Reading.*) 'Perhaps it's the effect of falling in love for the first time; perhaps this vast desert we live in, suddenly becomes so terrifying that it seems uninhabitable without this new, unique, infinite happiness, that is revealed by one's heart.'

OCTAVIO: Well, really, what's the matter with you?

CELIO: (*Reading.*) 'A peasant, a coarse, ignorant workman, a shy, young girl, who would ordinarily shudder at the mere thought of death, grows bold enough to gaze upon the tomb, when she's in love.' Octavio, Death leads us to God, and I tremble, when I think of it. Good night, my dear friend.

OCTAVIO: Where are you going?

CELIO: I have business in town. Goodbye, do whatever you wish.

OCTAVIO: You look as though you're going to drown yourself. You're not by any chance frightened of death?

CELIO: Oh, if I'd been able to make a name for myself in battles or tournaments! If I'd been allowed to wear Marianne's colours and stain them with my blood! If I'd been given a rival to fight, a whole army to defy! If sacrificing my life could have been useful to her! I can act, but I can't speak. My tongue can't help my heart and I shall die without making myself understood, like a mute in prison.

OCTAVIO: Look, Celio, what are you thinking about? There are other Mariannes on earth. Let's dine together and laugh at this one.

CELIO: Goodbye, goodbye, I can't stay any longer. I'll see you tomorrow. (*Goes out.*)

OCTAVIO: Celio, do listen! We'll find you a charming

Marianne, sweet as a lamb. Really, this is strange! No
matter, I won't give up. I'm like a man playing faro and
holding the bank for someone else, with the luck against
him. He'd rather drown his best friend than give up and
he's a hundred times more furious at losing someone
else's money than if he were ruining himself. Ah, here
is Marianne. Going to vespers, no doubt. She's walking
slowly.

(*MARIANNE enters.*)

OCTAVIO: Lovely Marianne, you'll sleep in peace tonight.
Celio's heart belongs to another; he won't serenade
beneath your windows.

MARIANNE: What a pity! How unfortunate I couldn't share
a great love like that! See how I'm thwarted by fate! I was
about to fall in love with him.

OCTAVIO: Is that true?

MARIANNE: Yes, tonight or tomorrow, Sunday at the
latest, I swear it on my soul. Who could not succeed with
an ambassador like you? I think his passion for me was
something like Chinese or Arabic, to need an interpreter
and be unintelligible on its own.

OCTAVIO: Go on joking, go on. We're not afraid of you any
more.

MARIANNE: Or perhaps his love was still only a poor little
baby. Like a nurse, you took it out on leading strings and
let it fall on its head, as you strolled through the town.

OCTAVIO: But the nurse made it drink a certain milk, which
yours must have given you; and given generously. You still
have a drop on your lips that mingles with everything you
say.

MARIANNE: What is the name of this wonderful milk?

OCTAVIO: Indifference. You're unable to love or hate. You're
like roses from India, without thorns and without scent.

MARIANNE: Well said! Did you prepare this in advance? If
you don't burn the draft of your speeches, give it to me,
please, so I can teach it to my parrot.

OCTAVIO: What was there in that to hurt you? If a flower
has no scent, it's none the less beautiful; quite the contrary,

they're the most beautiful God has made. I think you've no right to complain on that score.

MARIANNE: My dear cousin, don't you feel sorry for women? Look what happens to me. It is decreed by fate that Celio should fall in love with me, or think he does, that the said Celio should tell his friends, and the said friends should in their turn decree that on pain of death I should fall in love with him. The youth of Naples deigns to send me, in your person, a worthy representative, charged with telling me I have to fall in love with my lord Celio within one week. Consider that, will you. Is it not a most contemptible woman who can obey such a proposition at a given hour and date? Won't she be slandered, pointed at, sung about in taverns? If she refuses, on the other hand, is there a monster to compare her with? Is there a statue colder than she? And the man who speaks to her, who dares to stop her, prayerbook in hand on the public highway, has the right to tell her, 'You're a rose from India, without thorn or scent'.

OCTAVIO: Cousin, cousin, don't get angry.

MARIANNE: Decency and marriage vows are ridiculous, aren't they? So is a girl's upbringing, the pride of a heart that imagined it was worth something and to deserve the respect of others should start by respecting itself? That is all a dream, a bubble, to evaporate at the first sigh of a fashionable gallant?

OCTAVIO: You're mistaken about me and about Celio.

MARIANNE: After all, what is a woman? The occupation of a moment, a vain shadow you pretend to love for the pleasure of saying so. A woman! She's a distraction! When you meet one, couldn't you say, 'There's a lovely fantasy going by!' And wouldn't it be a great scholar in such matters, who would lower his eyes before her and whisper, 'There goes perhaps the happiness of an entire life' and would let her go? (*Goes out.*)

OCTAVIO: Tra tra, pom pom, tra la, tra la. What a strange little woman! (*Calling toward the inn.*) Hi, there! (*SERVING MAN enters.*)

47

Bring me a bottle of something. Out here.

SERVING MAN: Whatever you like, Excellency. Some lacrima christi?

OCTAVIO: All right, all right. (*He writes a few words with a pencil.*) Go and look for my lord Celio in the streets around here. He's wearing a dark cloak and a doublet that's even darker. Tell him one of his friends is here drinking lacrima christi on his own. Then you'll go to the main square and give this (*Giving him what he has written.*) to a certain Rosalinda, who has red hair and is always at her window. (*SERVING MAN goes out.*) I don't know what's the matter with my throat; I feel as wretched as the day after a party. I might as well dine here. Do I want to sleep? I feel absolutely paralysed.

(*CLAUDIO and TIBIA enter.*)

Ah, cousin Claudio, you're a good judge; where are you going at this speed?

CLAUDIO: What do you mean by that?

OCTAVIO: I mean that as a magistrate, you've a good style.

CLAUDIO: My language or my clothes?

OCTAVIO: Language, language. Your gown is full of eloquence and your arms form two charming parentheses.

CLAUDIO: Let me say in passing that my door knocker seems to have burnt your fingers.

OCTAVIO: In what way, most learned cousin?

CLAUDIO: By trying to use it, most crafty cousin.

OCTAVIO: Be bold and add most respectful, Claudio, for the knocker that is. But you can have it painted, without my being afraid of soiling my hands on it.

CLAUDIO: In what way, most facetious cousin?

OCTAVIO: By never using it, most caustic cousin.

CLAUDIO: It so happens that you have, as my wife has given strict orders for it to be slammed in your face.

OCTAVIO: Your spectacles are inadequate, most charming cousin. Your compliment is addressed to the wrong person.

CLAUDIO: My spectacles are excellent, most witty cousin. Didn't you make love to my wife?

OCTAVIO: What reason should I have, subtle magistrate?

CLAUDIO: Whatever reason your friend Celio has, obliging messenger. Unfortunately I heard everything.

OCTAVIO: With whose ears, incorruptible senator?

CLAUDIO: My wife's; she's told me everything, beloved bumpkin.

OCTAVIO: Absolutely everything, passionate husband? Did nothing remain in her charming ear?

CLAUDIO: Only her answer, charming tavern loafer, and I am charged to give it to you.

OCTAVIO: But I'm not charged to hear it, darling affidavit.

CLAUDIO: Then my door will give it you in person, if you ever decide to consult it, delightful croupier.

OCTAVIO: That's something I don't exactly care for, dearest death sentence. I'll live happily without it.

CLAUDIO: May you do so in peace, diminutive dice thrower. I wish you a thousand successes.

(*CLAUDIO goes out, followed by TIBIA.*)

OCTAVIO: Don't worry about that, dear bolts and bars. Sleep in peace, as you do in court.

(*SERVING MAN enters.*)

SERVING MAN: Sir, the red-haired lady isn't at her window; she can't accept your invitation.

OCTAVIO: Damnation take her, and you too!

SERVING MAN: The gentleman in the dark cloak isn't in the streets around here. But I met his servant and told him to go and look for him.

(*SERVING MAN goes into the inn.*)

OCTAVIO: Damnation take the whole universe! Is it decreed I'll dine alone today? What the devil am I going to do?

(*SERVING MAN enters, with a flask of wine and a glass. He puts them on the table and goes back into the inn.*)

All right, this will do. (*He sits down and pours out same wine.*) I can bury my misery in the wine, or at least the wine in my misery. Ah-ha! Vespers are finished. Here's Marianne returning home.

(*MARIANNE enters.*)

MARIANNE: Still here, cousin Octavio, and at table already? It's rather sad to get drunk all alone.

OCTAVIO: Everyone's abandoned me. I'm trying to see double, to provide a companion for myself.

MARIANNE: What! Not one of your friends, no one to relieve you of this terrible burden of solitude?

OCTAVIO: Shall I tell you my thoughts? I invited a certain Rosalinda, a girl I know. But she's dining in town like a lady of quality.

MARIANNE: That's annoying for you, of course; your heart must be feeling a terrible void.

OCTAVIO: A void which I can't express and I'm communicating in vain to this glass. The vespers bell's left my skull split open for the whole evening.

MARIANNE: Tell me, cousin, is that cheap wine you're drinking?

OCTAVIO: Don't make fun of it. It's lacrima christi, if you want to know, and it's delicious.

MARIANNE: I'm surprised you don't drink cheap wine. Have some, do.

OCTAVIO: Why should I?

MARIANNE: Try it. I'm sure there's no difference between the two.

OCTAVIO: All the difference between the sun and a lantern.

MARIANNE: No, I tell you they're the same thing.

OCTAVIO: Heaven forbid! Are you making fun of me?

MARIANNE: You think there's a great difference?

OCTAVIO: Definitely.

MARIANNE: I thought it was the same with wine as it is with women. What a wretched heart you must have then, for your lips to have to teach you the lesson. You won't drink the wine the people drink, but you love the women they love. The generous, poetic spirit of this golden flask, this marvellous essence, distilled by the lava of Vesuvius under its burning sun, will give you some banal semblance of pleasure. You'd blush to drink a common wine, your throat would rise. Oh, your lips are delicate, but your heart gets drunk cheaply. Good night, cousin. I hope Rosalinda will console your troubles.

OCTAVIO: Lovely Marianne, two words, I beg you. My

answer will be short. How long do you think I have to pay court to this bottle here to obtain a favourable response? As you say, it's filled with a celestial spirit and it's as different from the wine of the people as a lord is from his peasants. See how obliging it is. One word was enough to bring it out of the cellar. Still covered with dust, it's emerged to give me ten minutes of oblivion and then die. Its crown, purple with sweet-smelling wax, immediately fell into fragments and itself, I can't conceal it, almost passed my lips in a single draught in the warmth of its initial kiss.

MARIANNE: Are you sure it's worth any more? If you were really one of its lovers and the recipe were lost, wouldn't you go into the volcano's mouth in search of the last drop?

OCTAVIO: That is what it's worth, precisely. God didn't hide its source at the top of an inaccessible peak or the bottom of an unplumbed cavern. He spread it in golden bunches on our shining hillsides. It's true it is rare and precious, but it doesn't forbid one to approach it. No, it lets itself be seen in the sunshine and a whole court of bees and butterflies murmurs about it day and night. The thirsty traveller can rest under its green branches; it has never let him hope in vain, never refused him the sweet tears that fill its heart. Oh, Marianne, what a fatal gift beauty is! The wisdom it vaunts so proudly is the sister of avarice and its weaknesses sometimes earn more mercy than its cruelty. Good night, cousin, I hope Celio forgets you.

(*OCTAVIO goes into the inn. CLAUDIO enters.*)

CLAUDIO: Do you think I'm a puppet and I walk about this earth to scare away the birds?

MARIANNE: Where have you got this charming idea?

CLAUDIO: Do you think a man of my standing doesn't know the value of words and you can make a game of his credulity, as if he were a tightrope walker?

MARIANNE: Who has upset you this evening?

CLAUDIO: Do you think I didn't hear your own words? 'If this man or his friend appears at our door, slam it in his face.' Do you believe I consider it proper to see you talking to him openly in an arbour?

MARIANNE: You saw me in an arbour?

CLAUDIO: Yes, yes, with these eyes of mine, at this inn here. The arbour of an inn's no place for conversation for a magistrate's wife and there's no point in slamming the door on him when you chatter here with so little modesty.

MARIANNE: Since when have I been forbidden to talk to one of your relations?

CLAUDIO: When one of my relations is one of your lovers, it's advisable to refrain.

MARIANNE: Octavio, one of my lovers! Are you out of your mind? He's never paid court to anyone in his life.

CLAUDIO: He's a depraved man; he spends his time in brothels.

MARIANNE: The more reason for him not to be, as you so charmingly put it, one of my lovers. I like talking to Octavio in the arbour of a tavern.

CLAUDIO: Don't drive me to do something distressing with your extravagant behaviour. Consider what you're doing.

MARIANNE: What do you expect me to drive you to? I'm curious to know what you'll do.

CLAUDIO: I forbid you to see him and exchange a single word with him in my house, or anyone else's house or in the open air.

MARIANNE: Ha-ha, really this is something new! Octavio's my relation just as much as yours and I intend to speak to him whenever I think fit, in the open air, or anywhere else; and in our house, if he cares to come there.

CLAUDIO: Remember these last words of yours. I'm preparing an exemplary punishment for you, in case you don't do as I wish.

MARIANNE: Let me tell you I'll do as I wish and you can prepare whatever you like. I don't give that much for it.

CLAUDIO: Let us cease this conversation. Either you see the impropriety of conversing in an arbour or you'll drive me to violence that is beneath my position. (*Goes out.*)

MARIANNE: Hey! Come here, somebody!

(*SERVANT enters.*)

Do you see a young man in that tavern sitting at a table?

Go and tell him I must speak to him and will he be so good as to come here. (*SERVANT goes out.*) This is something new! Who does he take me for? What harm is there? How do I look today? What a dreadful dress! What did he mean? 'You'll drive me to violence'! What violence? I wish my mother were here. Pah! She agrees with him as soon as he opens his mouth. I feel I want to hit someone. I'm very good-natured, that's a fact. Oh, so this is the beginning, is it? I was told so, I knew, I expected it! Patience, patience! He's preparing a punishment! Well what, I wander? I'd like to know what he means.

(*OCTAVIO enters.*)

Come here, Octavio, I want to talk to you. I've thought about what you said on behalf of your friend, Celio. Tell me, why doesn't he speak for himself?

OCTAVIO: For a very simple reason. He's written to you and you've torn up his letters. He's sent a messenger and you've forbidden him to speak. He's serenaded you, you've left him in the street. Heavens, if he gave himself to the devil, he'd achieve something.

MARIANNE: In other words he thought of you.

OCTAVIO: Yes.

MARIANNE: Well, talk to me about him!

OCTAVIO: Seriously?

MARIANNE: Yes, yes, seriously. Here I am, I'm listening.

OCTAVIO: You're joking.

MARIANNE: Why, what sort of pitiful advocate are you? Speak, whether I'm joking or not.

OCTAVIO: Why are you looking all about you? It's a fact, you are angry.

MARIANNE: I want to be in the fashion, Octavio. I want to have a squire. Is that the right expression? If I understood you correctly just now, about your bottle, you were blaming me, weren't you, for appearing too severe and repulsing the men who are in love with me? All right, I agree to listen to them. I'm threatened, I'm insulted, and I ask you, do I deserve it?

OCTAVIO: Certainly not, far from it.

MARIANNE: I can't lie or deceive anyone, and it's just for that reason I don't want to have to. What woman in Italy does not tolerate the presence of men who want to make love to her, without people seeing anything wrong? You tell me men serenade me and I leave them in the street? Well, I shall go on doing so, but my shutter will be half open, and I'll be there, I'll be listening.

OCTAVIO: Can I tell Celio?

MARIANNE: Celio or anyone else, I don't mind! What do you advise, Octavio? You see, I rely on you. Well, you don't speak? I tell you, it's what I want. Yes, this very evening I've a desire to be serenaded, and I'll enjoy listening to it. I'm curious to see if I'll be forbidden to. (*Giving him a knot of ribbons from her dress.*) Look, here are my colours. Anyone you like can wear them.

OCTAVIO: Marianne, whatever reason has inspired you to be kind for one minute, as you sent for me, as you agree to listen, for heaven's sake, remain like this for one minute more. Let me speak to you.

MARIANNE: What do you want to say?

OCTAVIO: If ever a man on earth were worthy of understanding you, worthy of living and dying for you, that man is Celio. I've always been pretty worthless, but I will do myself this justice, that the passion I'm pleading for has found a wretched spokesman. You're so lovely, so young! If you only knew what a treasury of happiness you possess, and he possesses! In this fresh dawn of youth, this divine dew of life, this initial harmony of twin souls! I won't talk about his suffering, this sweet, tender melancholy that has never tired of your hardness and would die of it without complaining. Yes, Marianne, he will die of it. What can I say? What can I think of, to give my words the force they lack? I don't know the language of love. Look into your soul; it might speak to you of his. Is there any power capable of touching you? You know how to pray to God. Does any prayer exist to convey all that fills my heart? (*He kneels.*)

MARIANNE: Get up, Octavio. Really, to hear you talk, any passer-by would believe you were pleading for yourself.

OCTAVIO: Marianne, Marianne! For heaven's sake, don't smile! Don't close your heart to the first spark that may ever have touched it.

MARIANNE: Are you sure I'm not allowed to smile?

OCTAVIO: *(Rising.)* Yes, you're right, I know what harm my friendship can do. I know who I am; I feel it; from my mouth such language sounds like a joke. You doubt the sincerity of my words. Never perhaps have I felt more bitterly than I do now how little confidence I can inspire.

MARIANNE: Why is that? You see I'm listening. I don't like Celio; I don't want anything to do with him. Talk to me about someone else, whoever you wish.

OCTAVIO: Oh woman, three times woman! You don't like Celio! But perhaps you will like the first man you happen to see. There's a man who loves you, who dogs your footsteps, who'd gladly die at one word from your lips, but you don't like him! He's young, handsome, rich and in every way worthy of you. But you don't like him! Yet you'll like the next man you happen to see!

MARIANNE: Do what I tell you or never see me again.
(MARIANNE goes into the house.)

OCTAVIO: You're very pretty, Marianne, and this little whim of getting angry is a charming peace treaty. I wouldn't need much pride to understand it; a little treachery's enough. However, it's Celio who'll reap the benefit.
(CELIO enters.)

CELIO: You sent for me, my dear fellow. Well, what news?

OCTAVIO: Pin this ribbon in your hat, Celio. Take your guitar and your sword. Our cause is half won.

CELIO: For heaven's sake, don't laugh at me.

OCTAVIO: It will be a lovely night. The moon will soon appear over the horizon. This evening Marianne will be alone behind her shutter. She's agreed to listen to you.

CELIO: Is that true? Is that true? You've saved my life, Octavio, or else you're pitiless.

OCTAVIO: I tell you it's all settled. A song beneath the

window, a good, long cloak, a dagger in your pocket, a mask on your face. Have you a mask?

CELIO: No.

OCTAVIO: No mask? In love, and it's carnival time! The boy never thinks of anything. Go and get ready as quick as you can.

CELIO: Oh, my heart fails me.

OCTAVIO: Courage, my dear fellow! On your way! You can embrace me when you come back. On your way! On your way! Night's drawing on. (*CELIO goes out.*) His heart fails him, he says. So does mine, I've only half dined. As a reward for my troubles, I'm going to enjoy my supper. (*Calling.*) Hey! Holla! Giovanni! Beppo!
(*OCTAVIO goes into the inn.*
CLAUDIO and TIBIA enter with two ASSASSINS.
MARIANNE appears on the balcony.)

CLAUDIO: (*To the ASSASSINS.*) Let him come in and attack him as soon as he reaches those trees.
(*One of the ASSASSINS goes out.*)

MARIANNE: (*Aside.*) Who's that I see? My husband and Tibia!

TIBIA: (*To CLAUDIO.*) And if he comes from the other side?

CLAUDIO: What, Tibia, the other side? Will my whole plan be wrecked?

MARIANNE: (*Aside.*) What are they saying?

TIBIA: This square is a crossroads, he can come from either side.

CLAUDIO: You're right. I didn't think of that.

TIBIA: What shall we do, sir, if he comes from the left?

CLAUDIO: Wait for him at the corner of the wall.

MARIANNE: (*Aside.*) Heavens, what did I hear?

TIBIA: And if he appears on the right?

CLAUDIO: Let me think. You'll do the same.
(*The other ASSASSIN goes out.*)

MARIANNE: (*Aside.*) How can I warn Octavio?

TIBIA: Here he comes. Look, sir, see how big his shadow is! He's a very tall man.

CLAUDIO: Let's move away. When the time comes, strike.

(*CLAUDIO goes out.*
TIBIA hides.
CELIO enters, masked.)

CELIO: (*Approaching the balcony.*) Marianne! Marianne! Are you there?

MARIANNE: Run away, run away, Octavio!

CELIO: God, what name was that?

MARIANNE: The house is surrounded by assassins. My husband heard us talking and your death is certain, if you stay another minute.

CELIO: Is this a dream? Am I Celio?

MARIANNE: Octavio, Octavio, for heaven's sake, don't wait! There may still be time to escape. Be outside the garden at noon tomorrow, I'll be there. (*Goes indoors.*)

CELIO: (*Unmasking and drawing his sword.*) Death, you're there, so come to my aid. Octavio, Octavio, traitor! I can't guess your aim, your interest, in sending me into this terrible trap, but as I'm here I'll find out. Though it costs me my life, I'll learn the answer to this dreadful mystery.
(*CELIO goes out, followed by TIBIA.*
OCTAVIO enters from the inn.)

OCTAVIO: Ah! Where shall I go now? I've done something to make someone else happy, what can I think of for my own pleasure? Heavens, it's a lovely night and it really should be put down to my account. It's a fact, the girl is beautiful and her little fit of temper suited her. What was the reason? I don't know. What does it matter why the ivory ball falls on the number you've backed? Cheating a friend out of a mistress is too ordinary a trick for me. It's more important to have supper! Celio's obviously doing without. Oh, Marianne, how you'd have hated me, if I'd been in love with you! How you'd have slammed the door in my face! You'd have thought your fool of a husband an Adonis, compared with me. What's the reason for all this? The reason for everything is luck! It's the way things are in this world. This morning Celio was in despair, wasn't he? And now…
(*A muffled noise and a clash of swords are heard.*)

What did I hear? What's that noise?

CELIO: (*Offstage, in a choking voice.*) Help!

OCTAVIO: Celio! It's Celio's voice. (*Running to CLAUDIO's house.*) Open the gate, or I'll break it down.
(*CLAUDIO enters.*)

CLAUDIO: What do you want?

OCTAVIO: Where is Celio?

CLAUDIO: I don't think he's accustomed to sleep in this house.

OCTAVIO: If you've killed him, Claudio, take care. I'll twist your neck with these hands of mine.

CLAUDIO: Are you mad or walking in your sleep? Look in the garden, if you think fit to do so. I've seen no one enter. And if anyone had wanted to, I think I have the right not to open the door to him.
(*OCTAVIO goes into the inn. TIBIA enters.*)
Is it all over? Are my orders carried out?

TIBIA: Yes, sir, don't worry. They can search as much as they wish.

CLAUDIO: Now let's think about my wife and go and warn her mother.
(*CLAUDIO and TIBIA go out.*
MARIANNE enters.)

MARIANNE: It's certain. I'm not mistaken. I saw it all, I heard it all. Through the trees behind the house I saw scattered shadows suddenly merge and pounce. I heard the sound of swords, then a stifled cry, the most sinister, the last appeal. Poor Octavio! Brave as he is, and he is brave, they surprised him, trapped him. Is it possible, is it believable that such an error should be paid for so dearly? Is it possible far so little sense to cause so much cruelty? I acted so frivolously, so madly, out of pure fun, pure caprice! I must see him, I must find out...
(*OCTAVIO enters, sword in hand, looking about him.*)

MARIANNE: Octavio, is that you?

OCTAVIO: Yes, Marianne, it is. Celio is dead.

MARIANNE: Celio, you said? How could...

OCTAVIO: He is dead.

MARIANNE: Oh God!

OCTAVIO: He is dead. Don't go that way.

MARIANNE: Where do you want me to go? I'm ruined! This is no place to stay, Octavio! Surely Claudio isn't in the house?

OCTAVIO: No. They took the necessary precautions and wisely left me on my own.

MARIANNE: I know them, I'm ruined; perhaps you are too. Let's go, they'll come back, immediately.

OCTAVIO: Go, if you want to. I'm staying. If they have to come back, they'll find me, and whatever happens, I'll be waiting for them. I want to watch over him in his last sleep.

MARIANNE: Will you abandon me? Do you know what danger you're running and how far their vengeance might go?

OCTAVIO: Look over there, behind those trees, that little dark place at the corner of the wall. There lies my only friend. I don't care about anything else.

MARIANNE: Not even for your life? Or mine?

OCTAVIO: Not even for that. Look over there! I'm the only man in the world who knew him. Place on his tomb an alabaster urn, covered with a mourning veil; that will be his perfect image. That's how a gentle melancholy veiled the perfections of this tender, delicate soul. The woman who loved him would have been very happy.

MARIANNE: Would he have defended her, if she'd been in danger?

OCTAVIO: Yes, no doubt he would. He alone was capable of unlimited devotion. He alone would have pledged his whole life to the woman he loved, as easily as he braved death for her.

MARIANNE: Wouldn't you do that, Octavio?

OCTAVIO: Me? I'm only a heartless rake. I don't respect women. The love I inspire is like the love I feel, the fleeting drunkenness of a dream. My gaiety's a mask. My heart is older. Oh, I'm just a coward. I've not avenged his death. (*He throws down his sword.*)

MARIANNE: How could you have? Claudio's too old

to accept a duel and too powerful in this town to fear anything from you.

OCTAVIO: Celio would have avenged my death, if I'd died for him as he died for me. His tomb is mine. I'm the man they felled in that dark alley; I'm the man they sharpened their swords for, I'm the man they killed! Farewell the gaiety of my youth, the carefree folly, the free, happy life at the foot of Vesuvius! Farewell the joyous suppers, the evening gossip, the serenades under golden balconies! Farewell Naples and its women, torchlight masquerades, suppers in shady forests! Farewell love and friendship! My place on earth is empty.

MARIANNE: Are you so sure of that, Octavio? Why do you say farewell to love?

OCTAVIO: I don't love you, Marianne. It was Celio who loved you.

FANTASIO

Characters

THE KING OF BAVARIA

RUTTEN, his secretary

HARTMAN, young man of Munich

FACIO, young man of Munich

SPARK, young man of Munich

FANTASIO, young man of Munich

OFFICER

TAILOR

PRINCE OF MANTUA

MARINONI, his aide-de-camp

ELSBETH, the King of Bavaria's daughter

GOVERNESS

FIRST PAGE

SECOND PAGE

COURTIERS

TOWNSPEOPLE

Scene: The action takes place in and near Munich.

ACT ONE

Scene I

THE KING OF BAVARIA's palace.
THE KING, attended by RUTTEN, is surrounded by his COURTIERS.

THE KING: My friends, a long time ago I announced the
betrothal of my beloved Elsbeth to the Prince of Mantua.
Today I have to announce that the Prince will visit us. This
evening perhaps, tomorrow at the latest, he will be in this
palace. Let there be a public holiday: open the prisons
and let the people pass the night in merrymaking. Rutten,
where is my daughter?
(COURTIERS go out.)

RUTTEN: Sire, she is in the garden with her governess.

THE KING: Why haven't I seen her yet today? Is she sad or
happy to think that she will soon be married?

RUTTEN: I thought the Princess' face was veiled with a
certain melancholy. What young girl does not daydream
just before her wedding? Saint-Jean's death has upset her.

THE KING: Do you think so? The death of my jester! A court
fool, hunchbacked and almost blind!

RUTTEN: The Princess loved him.

THE KING: Tell me, Rutten, you've seen the Prince; what
kind of man is he? *(He sighs.)* I'm giving him my most
precious possession and I don't know him at all.

RUTTEN: I stayed a very short time in Mantua.

THE KING: Speak freely. Through whose eyes can I see the
truth, if not through yours?

RUTTEN: It's a fact, Sire, I can't say anything about the mind
or character of the noble Prince.

THE KING: Is that really so? You hesitate, you, a courtier!
Tomorrow the Prince will be my son-in-law. If you had
thought him worthy of the title, how the air of this room
would be filled with hyperboles and eulogies and flattering
metaphors. Was I wrong, my friend? Have I made a bad
choice?

RUTTEN: Sire, the Prince is considered the best of kings.

THE KING: Politics are a fine spider's web, where so many poor, mutilated flies lie struggling. I won't sacrifice my daughter's happiness for anything.

(*They go out.*)

Scene II

A street. The same evening.
SPARK, HARTMAN, and FACIO are sitting around a table, drinking.

HARTMAN. As it's the Princess' wedding day, let's drink and smoke and make a noise.

FACIO: Why don't we join the crowds in the streets and smash a few lanterns on the heads of our worthy citizens?

SPARK: Come now, let's sit here quietly and smoke our pipes.

HARTMAN: I won't do anything quietly. I want to ring in the holiday, even if I have to get strung up as a clapper in a belfry. Where the devil is Fantasio?

SPARK: Let's wait for him. We won't do anything till he comes.

FACIO: Bah, he'll always find us. He's getting drunk somewhere. Hey there! A final glass! (*He raises his glass.*)

(*An OFFICER enters.*)

OFFICER: Gentlemen, I've come to ask you to be good enough to go further away, if you don't want your celebrations to be disturbed.

HARTMAN: Why is that?

OFFICER: The Princess is on the terrace over there and you'll understand of course that it's not proper for your shouting to reach her ears. (*Goes out.*)

FACIO: This is intolerable.

SPARK: What does it matter whether we enjoy ourselves here or somewhere else?

HARTMAN: How do we know we shall be allowed to enjoy ourselves somewhere else? You'll see, some strange man in uniform will spring out from every cobblestone in town to tell us to go and enjoy ourselves in the moon.

(*MARINONI enters, wrapped in a cloak.*)

SPARK: The Princess has never done anything autocratic. May God preserve her! If she doesn't want to hear us laughing, she must be sad or else she's singing. Let's leave her in peace.

FACIO: Hm! Look at that cloak over there, ferreting for news! The fellow wants to talk to us.

MARINONI: (*Approaching.*) I'm a stranger here, gentlemen. What is the occasion of these festivities?

SPARK: Princess Elsbeth is getting married.

MARINONI: Ah, ah! She's a fine woman, or so I presume?

HARTMAN: Inasmuch as you're a fine man, correct.

MARINONI: Beloved by her people, I venture to say, as I think the whole town's illuminated.

HARTMAN: You're not mistaken, worthy stranger. All these lighted lanterns that you see, are, as you've so wisely remarked, none other than illuminations.

MARINONI: What I meant was, is the Princess the cause of these signs of happiness?

HARTMAN: The one and only cause, oh powerful orator. We could all of us get married without any sign of joy in this ungrateful town.

MARINONI: Happy the Princess who earns her people's love!

HARTMAN: Lighted lanterns don't make a people happy, my beloved, primitive man. They don't prevent the aforesaid Princess being as capricious as a wagtail.

MARINONI: Is that a fact? Did you say capricious?

HARTMAN: I said so, beloved stranger, that is the word I used.

(*MARINONI bows and goes out.*)

FACIO: What the devil does that Italian babbler want? There he goes accosting someone else. You can smell he's a spy a mile off.

HARTMAN: You can't smell anything at all. He's just a fool.

SPARK: Here comes Fantasio.

HARTMAN: What's the matter with him? He's sauntering along like an alderman. Unless I'm very much mistaken, there's some plot hatching in that brain of his.

FACIO: Well, my dear fellow, what shall we make of this lovely evening?

(*FANTASIO enters.*)

FANTASIO: Anything you like, except a new novel.

FACIO: I was saying we ought to plunge into this rabble and enjoy ourselves.

FANTASIO: The essential thing is to get false noses and fireworks.

HARTMAN: And kiss the girls and trip up the citizens; and break lanterns. Come on, let's go, that's it.

FANTASIO: Once upon a time there was a King of Persia.

HARTMAN: Come on, Fantasio.

FANTASIO: I won't join you, I won't join you.

HARTMAN: Why?

FANTASIO: Give me a glass of that stuff. (*He drinks.*)

HARTMAN: You've the month of May on your cheeks.

FANTASIO: I know; and the month of January in my heart. My head's like an old, empty fireplace, full of wind and ashes. Brrr! (*He sits down.*) I'm so bored by everybody celebrating. I wish this great, heavy sky were an enormous nightcap to envelop the whole of this stupid town and its stupid inhabitants. Come on, tell me an old joke, please, something really hackneyed.

HARTMAN: Why?

FANTASIO: To make me laugh. I don't laugh at new jokes any more; perhaps I'll laugh at ones I know.

HARTMAN: You seem rather misanthropic and inclined to melancholy.

FANTASIO: Not at all; you see, I've just left my mistress.

FACIO: Will you join us, yes or no?

FANTASIO: I'll join you, if you'll join me. Let's stay here a while. We'll talk about this and that, and look at our new clothes.

FACIO: No, we certainly won't. You may be tired of standing up, but I'm tired of sitting down. I want to do everything that can be done in the open air.

FANTASIO: I couldn't. I'm going to smoke here under the chestnut trees with my old friend Spark, who's going to keep me company. Aren't you, Spark?

SPARK: If you like.

HARTMAN: In that case, goodbye. We're going to enjoy ourselves.

(*HARTMAN and FACIO go out. FANTASIO sits down next to SPARK.*)

FANTASIO: What a failure this sunset is! Nature is pitiful this evening. Just look at that valley over there, those four or five wretched clouds climbing up the mountain. When I was twelve, I used to make landscapes like that on the covers of my exercise books.

SPARK: Good tobacco! Good beer too!

FANTASIO: How I must bore you, Spark, don't I?

SPARK: No. Why do you say that?

FANTASIO: You bore me terribly. Don't you mind seeing the same, faces every day? What on earth are Hartman and Facio going to do in all this revelry?

SPARK: They're energetic young fellows, they can't stay still.

FANTASIO: *The Arabian Nights*, what a wonderful book! Oh Spark, my dear Spark, if you could transport me to China! If I could only get out of this skin of mine for an hour or two! If I could be that man over there!

SPARK: I'd say that was rather difficult.

FANTASIO: How charming he is, that man over there. Look. What lovely silk breeches! What lovely red flowers on his waistcoat! The seals on his watch bounce on his stomach, to balance the tails of his coat flapping on his legs. I'm sure that in that man's head are hundreds of thoughts that are completely foreign to me. His essence is peculiar to him. (*Sighing.*) But everything men say to each other is so similar. The thoughts they exchange are almost always the same in every conversation. But inside those isolated machines, what recesses, what secret compartments! It's a complete world that each one carries within himself! An unknown world that's born and dies in silence! How solitary are all those human bodies!

SPARK: Have a drink, you idle man, instead of ploughing up your brains.

FANTASIO: There's only one thing that's amused me in the last three days; my creditors have obtained a judgement against me, and if I set foot in my house, four great bailiffs will come and seize me by the neck.

SPARK: That's good news, I must say. Where will you sleep tonight?

FANTASIO: With the first girl I find. Do you realise my furniture's being sold tomorrow? Let's buy some of it, shall we?

SPARK: Do you need money, Henry? Can I give you my purse?

FANTASIO: Idiot! If I'd no money, I'd have no debts. I want a ballet dancer for a mistress.

SPARK: It would bore you to extinction.

FANTASIO: Not at all. My imagination would be filled with pirouettes and white satin slippers. One of my gloves would reserve a seat in the circle from the first of January to New Year's Eve and I'd hum clarinet solos in my dreams, while waiting to die of a surfeit of strawberries in the arms of my beloved. Consider this, Spark. We have absolutely nothing to do. We don't practise any profession.

SPARK: Is that what's making you unhappy?

FANTASIO: A fencing master's never melancholy.

SPARK: You don't seem to care for anything any more.

FANTASIO: My dear fellow, to be able not to care for anything any more, you must once have cared a great deal.

SPARK: Well then?

FANTASIO: Well then! What do you want me to care about? Look at this smoky old town. There's not a square or street or lane where I haven't wandered thirty times. There's not a cobblestone where I haven't dragged these shabby heels, not a house where I don't know the girl or woman whose stupid head is eternally outlined at the window. I can't take a step without walking in my footprints of the day before. Well, my dear fellow, this town's nothing, compared with my brain. Every cranny's a hundred times more familiar.

Every street, every place in my imagination is a hundred times more tired. I've walked in a hundred times more directions through this ramshackle brain, with me its sole inhabitant! I've got drunk in every tavern; I've driven like an absolute monarch in a golden coach; I've ridden like a worthy citizen on a peaceful mule; and the only thing I daren't do now is enter like a thief with a dark lantern in my hand.

SPARK: I can't understand this perpetual self-examination. When I smoke, for instance, my thoughts become tobacco smoke; when I drink, they become Spanish wine or Flanders beer; when I kiss my mistress' hand, they enter the tips of her slender fingers and spread through her whole being on electric currents. I need the scent of a flower to make me happy, and the humblest object in universal nature is enough to change me into a bee and make me flit here and there with a pleasure that's always new.

FANTASIO: Let's speak plainly, you're capable of sitting all day fishing.

SPARK: If it amuses me, I'm capable of anything.

FANTASIO: Even making bricks without straw?

SPARK: No, that wouldn't amuse me.

FANTASIO: Ah-ha, how do you know? Making bricks without straw is not to be despised. Let's go and play cards.

SPARK: No, I really won't.

FANTASIO: Why?

SPARK: Because we'll lose our money.

FANTASIO: Heavens, what are you imagining? You rack your brains, you don't know what to think up. Do you see the worst side of everything, you wretched man? Lose our money! Does your heart contain no hope or faith in God? Are you some frightful atheist who'll wither my heart and destroy my illusions? Me, full of youth and energy! (*He begins to dance.*)

SPARK: It's a fact, there are moments when I wouldn't swear you aren't mad.

FANTASIO: (*Still dancing.*) Give me a bell, a glass bell.

SPARK: What do you want a bell for?

FANTASIO: Didn't some philosopher say that a man absorbed in great thoughts is like a diver in a bell in the middle of the ocean? I've no bell, Spark, no bell at all, and I'm dancing like Jesus Christ upon the waters of the ocean.

SPARK: Become a journalist, Henry, or a man of letters. That's the best way to relieve misanthropy and suppress the imagination.

FANTASIO: Oh, I'd like to have a passion for grilled lobster, or a barmaid, or a group of minerals! Spark! Let's try to build a house on our own.

SPARK: Why don't you write down all your dreams? They'd make a charming volume.

FANTASIO: A sonnet's better than a long poem and a glass of wine's better than a sonnet. (*He drinks.*)

SPARK: Why don't you travel? Go to Italy.

FANTASIO: I've been.

SPARK: Well, don't you think it's a beautiful country?

FANTASIO: It's full of flies as big as cockchafers and they bite you all night long.

SPARK: Go to France.

FANTASIO: There's no good Rhine wine in Paris.

SPARK: Go to England.

FANTASIO: That's where I am. Have the English a country? I'd just as soon see them here as in their own home.

SPARK: Well, go to the devil, then!

FANTASIO: Oh, if there were a devil in the sky! If there were a hell, how I'd blow my brains out to go and see it all. What a wretched thing man is! Can't even jump out of a window without breaking his legs! Forced to play the violin for ten years to become a tolerable musician! To have to learn how to be a painter or a potboy! To have to learn how to make an omelette. You know, Spark, sometimes I want to sit down on a parapet and watch the river flow past; and begin to count one, two, three, four, five, six, seven and so on till the day I die.

SPARK: What you're saying would make a lot of people laugh. It makes me shudder. It's the history of the whole century. Eternity's a great nest and every century flies away from it one after the other like young eagles, to cross the sky and vanish. Our own has reached its turn at the edge of the nest. But its wings have been cut off and it's waiting for death, as it looks into space and can't take off.

FANTASIO: (*Singing.*)

You call me your life, but call me

your soul,

For the soul is immortal and life's

but a day...

Do you know a more exquisite song than that, Spark? It's Portuguese. It never comes into my mind without making me want to fall in love with someone.

SPARK: Who, for instance?

FANTASIO: Who? I've no idea. Some lovely girl, round and plump, like the ones Mieris painted. Something soft as the west wind, pale as moonbeams. Something thoughtful, like those little serving maids in Flemish pictures who give a stirrup cup to a top-booted traveller, straight as a post on a great white horse. What a lovely thing a stirrup cup is! A young woman in her doorway, the fire burning, you can see it at the back of the room, supper cooked, children asleep! All the peace of a quiet, contemplative life in one corner of the picture! And there's the man, still breathless, but firm in the saddle, having done twenty leagues and with thirty still to do. A mouthful of brandy and goodbye. The night is deep there, the weather threatening, the forest dangerous. The good woman follows him with her eyes for a minute, then as she turns back to her fire, she lets fall the sublime alms of the poor, 'May God protect him'.

SPARK: If you were in love, Henry, you'd be the happiest man on earth.

FANTASIO: Love doesn't exist any more, my dear fellow. It was suckled by religion, but religion now has pendulous breasts, like an old purse with a single penny lying in the bottom. Love's a host you must break in two at the foot of the altar and swallow together in a kiss. There's no altar any more, there's no love any more. Long live nature! We still have wine. (*He drinks.*)

SPARK: You'll get drunk.

FANTASIO: I'll get drunk, you're right.

SPARK: It's a little late for that.

FANTASIO: What do you call late? Noon, is that late? Midnight, is that early? When does your day begin? Let's leave it at that, Spark, please. Let's drink, gossip, analyse, talk nonsense, play politics. Let's think up government coalitions. Let's catch all the moths flying round this candle and put them in our pockets. Do you know that steam cannons are wonderful material for philanthropy?

SPARK: How do you mean?

FANTASIO: Once upon a time there was a king who was very wise, very wise, very happy, very happy…

SPARK: Well?

FANTASIO: The one thing he needed, to make his happiness complete, was children. He had prayers said in public in all the mosques.

SPARK: What are you trying to say?

FANTASIO: I'm thinking of my beloved *Arabian Nights*. That's the way they all begin. Why, Spark, I'm drunk. I must do something. Tra-la, tra-la! Come along, let's go.

(*A funeral goes by.*)

(*To the men carrying the coffin.*) Hey! Who are you burying? This is no time to bury anyone.

MAN: We're burying Saint-Jean.

FANTASIO: Saint-Jean is dead? The King's jester dead? Who's taken his place? The Minister of Justice?

MAN: His place is empty, you can take it if you like.

(*They go out.*)

SPARK: You deserved that insolence. What are you thinking about, stopping those people?

FANTASIO: There's nothing insolent in that. It was good advice that man gave me; I'm going to follow it immediately.

SPARK: You're going to become the court jester?

FANTASIO: Yes. Tonight if they'll have me. As I can't sleep

in my own house, I want to enjoy this puppet show they're performing tomorrow and from the royal box itself.

SPARK: That's very clever of you. You'll be recognised and they'll turn you out. You are the godson of the late Queen, aren't you?

FANTASIO: That's very stupid of you. I'll wear a hump and a red wig like Saint-Jean, then no one will recognise me, though I'd three dozen godmothers at my heels. (*He knocks at a door.*) Hey, fellow, open the door, if you haven't gone out and your whole family with you.

(*A TAILOR opens the shop door.*)

TAILOR: What does your lordship want?

FANTASIO: You're the court tailor, aren't you?

TAILOR: At your service.

FANTASIO: Are you the man who used to make Saint-Jean's clothes?

TAILOR: Yes, sir.

FANTASIO: You knew him? You know which side his hump was, how he curled his moustache, what kind of wig he wore?

TAILOR: Ha-ha! You will have your little joke, sir.

FANTASIO: I'm not having any little joke, fellow. Go into your shop. If you don't want to be poisoned in your breakfast coffee tomorrow, remember to be as silent as the grave about everything you hear.

(*FANTASIO goes into the shop with the TAILOR. SPARK follows.*)

Scene III

An inn on the road to Munich. Later that evening.
The PRINCE OF MANTUA and MARINONI enter.

PRINCE: Well, Colonel?

MARINONI: Highness?

PRINCE: Well, Marinoni?

MARINONI: Melancholy, capricious, deliriously happy, a dutiful daughter, very fond of green peas.

PRINCE: Write it down. I only understand copperplate handwriting.

MARINONI: (*Writing.*) Melancho…

PRINCE: Write in a whisper. I have been considering an important plan since dinner.

MARINONI: There, Highness, that's what you asked for.

PRINCE: Good. I name you my intimate friend. In my whole kingdom I don't know any handwriting more beautiful than yours. Sit down at a certain distance. Well, my friend, you think you have secretly discovered the character of the Princess, my future bride?

MARINONI: Yes, Highness. I frequented the neighbourhood of the palace and these notes contain the principal features of the different conversations in which I was engaged.

PRINCE: (*Looking in a mirror.*) I think I am powdered like an innkeeper.

MARINONI: The clothes are magnificent.

PRINCE: Marinoni, what would you say if you saw your master wearing a plain green coat?

MARINONI: Your Highness is making fun of my credulity.

PRINCE: I am not, Colonel. Know that your master is the most romantic of men.

MARINONI: Romantic, Highness?

PRINCE: Yes, my friend – I have granted you that title. The important plan I have been meditating upon is unheard of in my family. I intend to arrive at the court of the King, my father-in-law, in the clothes of an ordinary aide-de-camp. It is not sufficient to have sent a man of my household to gather public rumours about the future Princess of Mantua – that man, Marinoni, being yourself – but I want to observe further with my own eyes.

MARINONI: Is that true, Highness?

PRINCE: Don't stand there petrified. The intimate friend of a man such as myself must have a mind that is vast and daring.

MARINONI: Only one thing appears to me to thwart your Highness' scheme.

PRINCE: What is that?

MARINONI: The idea of such a disguise could only come from the glorious Prince who rules over us. But if my gracious sovereign is concealed among the staff, who will the King of Bavaria honour with the splendid banquet he is giving in the palace?

PRINCE: You're right; if I'm disguised, someone else must take my place. That is impossible, Marinoni. I didn't think of that.

MARINONI: Why impossible, Highness?

PRINCE: I can of course lower the princely dignity to the rank of colonel. But how can you believe I'd agree to raise an ordinary man to my station? Besides, do you think my future father-in-law would forgive me?

MARINONI: The King is considered to be sensible and intelligent, with a pleasant disposition.

PRINCE: Ah, I shan't willingly give up my plan. To enter this new court without display or fuss, observe everything, approach the Princess under a false name and perhaps make her fall in love with me... Oh, I'm wandering. It's impossible. Marinoni, my friend, try on my dress coat. I can't resist it.

MARINONI: (*Bowing.*) Highness!

PRINCE: Do you think that future centuries will ever forget such an unparalleled incident?

MARINONI: Never, gracious Prince.

PRINCE: Come and try on my coat.

(*They go out.*)

ACT TWO

Scene I

THE KING OF BAVARIA's garden. The next morning.
ELSBETH and her GOVERNESS enter.

GOVERNESS. It has made my poor eyes weep, weep in
floods.

ELSBETH: You're so good. I loved Saint-Jean too. He had
such wit. He was no ordinary clown.

GOVERNESS: To think that the poor man departed this life
the day before your betrothal! You were all he ever talked
about at dinner and supper, as long as daylight lasted. Such
a happy fellow, so amusing, he made you love ugliness
and your eyes followed him all the time in spite of yourself.

ELSBETH: Don't talk about my marriage. That's another
great misfortune.

GOVERNESS: Don't you know the Prince of Mantua's
arriving today? They say he's a Don Juan.

ELSBETH: What's that you're saying, my dear? He's stupid
and horrible, everybody knows it here.

GOVERNESS: Is that so? I was told he was a Don Juan

ELSBETH: I wasn't asking for a Don Juan, my dear. But it's
sometimes cruel to be only a king's daughter. My father is
the best of men. This marriage he's arranged will ensure
the peace of his kingdom and he'll receive in reward
the blessing of his people; but I (*Sighing.*) shall have his
blessing and nothing more.

GOVERNESS: How sadly you're talking!

ELSBETH: If I refused the Prince, war would soon start
again. What a tragedy that peace treaties are always signed
with tears! I wanted to be sensible and resign myself to
marrying anyone that politics required me to. Being the
mother of one's people may console strong minds, but not
weak wills. I'm only a poor dreamer. Perhaps it's the fault
of your novels; you always have one in your pocket.

GOVERNESS: Heavens! Don't tell anyone.

ELSBETH: I've known so little of life and dreamed so much.

GOVERNESS: If the Prince of Mantua is the man you say he is, God won't let the matter come about, I'm certain.

ELSBETH: You think so! My poor friend, God lets men act and doesn't value our complaints much more than the bleating of a sheep.

GOVERNESS: I'm sure if you refused the Prince, your father would not compel you.

ELSBETH: No, he certainly would not compel me; and that's why I'm sacrificing myself. Do you want me to go and tell my father to break his word and with one stroke of the pen strike his name off a contract that makes thousands happy? What does it matter, if it makes one girl unhappy? I am letting my good father be a good king. (*The GOVERNESS weeps.*) Don't weep for me, my dear. You might perhaps make me weep myself, and a royal bride must not have red eyes. Don't worry about it. After all I shall be a queen; perhaps that's amusing. Who knows, perhaps I'll take pleasure in my clothes, my carriages, my new court? Fortunately there's more for a princess in marriage than just a husband. Perhaps I'll find happiness in the heart of my wedding bouquet.

GOVERNESS: You are an absolute paschal lamb.

ELSBETH: Look, my dear, let's anyway start by laughing at it, ready to weep when we have to. The Prince of Mantua's said to be the most ridiculous thing on earth.

GOVERNESS: If Saint-Jean were here!

ELSBETH: Oh, Saint-Jean! Saint-Jean!

GOVERNESS: You loved him very much, my child.

ELSBETH: It's strange. His wit attached me to him with invisible threads that seemed to come from my heart. His perpetual mockery of my romantic ideas pleased me enormously, though I find it difficult to tolerate a great many people who entirely agree with me. I don't know what there was about him, in his eyes, his gestures, the way he took snuff. He was an extraordinary man. When he spoke to me, enchanting pictures appeared before my eyes. His words gave life to the oddest things, as if by magic.

GOVERNESS: He was an absolute Rigoletto.

ELSBETH: I've no idea about that. But he was the prince of fools.

GOVERNESS: Look at those pages coming and going. I don't think it can be long before the Prince appears. You must go back to the palace and get dressed.

ELSBETH: Please leave me another ten minutes. Go and set out whatever I need. (*Sighing.*) I haven't much time left for dreaming.

GOVERNESS: Heavens, can this marriage possibly take place, if you don't like it? A father sacrificing his daughter! The King would be an absolute Jephthah, if he did it.

ELSBETH: Don't malign my father. My dear, go and set out whatever I need. (*The GOVERNESS goes out.*) I believe there's someone behind those bushes. Is that the ghost of my poor fool that I see sitting on the grass among the cornflowers? Answer me. Who are you? What are you doing, picking those flowers?

(*She goes toward a bank of flowers.*
FANTASIO can be seen, sitting on the ground, dressed as a jester with a hump and wig.)

FANTASIO: I'm a respectable flower picker who bids good day to your pretty face.

ELSBETH: What is the meaning of this dress? Who are you to come and mock a man I loved with this red wig? Are you learning to be a jester?

FANTASIO: May it please your Serene Highness, I am the King's new jester. The steward welcomed me cordially; I was introduced to your father's valet; the kitchen boys have been looking after me since yesterday evening; and I'm quietly picking flowers while waiting to acquire some wit.

ELSBETH: That's a flower I doubt if you'll ever pick.

FANTASIO: Why? An old man can acquire wit, as well as a young girl. It's sometimes so difficult to distinguish between a flash of wit and crass stupidity. What matters is to keep on talking. The worst shot can hit a target with a pistol, if he fires seven hundred and eighty times a minute, as easily as a better one who only fires once or twice with a good aim. All I ask is to be fed sufficiently for the size of my stomach and I'll look at my shadow in the sun to see if my wig grows.

ELSBETH: So that's why you're here, wearing Saint-Jean's clothes? You're right to talk of your shadow; as long as you wear that costume, I think it will always be more like him than you.

FANTASIO: At the moment I'm composing an elegy to decide my fate.

ELSBETH: In what way?

FANTASIO: It will prove clearly that I'm the most important man on earth or else it will be completely valueless. I'm busy demolishing the universe to put it into an acrostic; the sun, the moon, and the stars are fighting to get into my rhymes like schoolboys at the entrance to a circus.

ELSBETH: Poor man! What a task you're undertaking! Creating wit at so much an hour! Haven't you arms or legs? Wouldn't you do better to plough up the earth than your own brains?

FANTASIO: Poor girl! What a task you're undertaking! Marrying an idiot you've never seen! Haven't you a heart or mind? Wouldn't you do better to sell your clothes than your own body?

ELSBETH: That's very bold of you, sir.

FANTASIO: What would you call that flower, please?

ELSBETH: A tulip. What are you trying to prove?

FANTASIO: A red tulip or a blue tulip?

ELSBETH: Blue, so it seems to me.

FANTASIO: Not at all, it's a red tulip.

ELSBETH: Are you trying to clothe an old expression in a new dress? There's no need to, in order to say that colour, like beauty, is in the eye of the beholder.

FANTASIO: I'm not saying anything of the sort. I'm telling you this tulip's a red one, although I agree it's blue.

ELSBETH: How do you manage that?

FANTASIO: In the same way as your marriage contract. Who on earth can know if it was born red or blue? Tulips themselves have no idea. Gardeners and notaries do the most extraordinary grafting, so that apples become pumpkins and thistles emerge from the jaws of an ass, to lie soaking in cream on a bishop's silver platter. This tulip here was expecting to be red, but it's been married. It's quite astonished to be blue. That's how the whole world's transformed by the hand of man. Poor Dame Nature must sometimes roar with laughter, when in her lakes and rivers she surveys her eternal masquerade. Do you think you could smell roses in the Garden of Eden? All you could smell was green grass. The rose is the daughter of civilisation. It's a marquise like you and me.

ELSBETH: The pale flower of the hawthorn can become a rose and a thistle can become an artichoke. But one flower can't become another. So what does Nature care? It can't be changed, it's either beautified or killed. The poorest violet would rather die than yield, if by artificial means you tried to alter its form by a stamen.

FANTASIO: That's why I value a violet higher than a king's daughter.

ELSBETH: There are some things even jesters have no right to joke about. Remember that. If you heard me talking to my governess, watch out for your ears.

FANTASIO: No, my tongue, not my ears. You've lost your way. You must weigh your words.

ELSBETH: Don't make puns to me, if you want to earn your money. And don't compare me to tulips if you don't want to earn something else.

FANTASIO: Who knows? A joke comforts a great many sorrows and playing with words is as good as any other way of playing with thoughts, actions, and people. Everything on earth is a joke and the expression of a four-year-old child is as difficult to understand as all the nonsense of three modern plays.

ELSBETH: You seem to look at the world through a rather changing prism.

FANTASIO: We all have our own spectacles; but no one really knows what colour the glass is. Who can really tell me whether I'm happy or unhappy, good or bad, stupid or witty?

ELSBETH: You're ugly, anyway. That's certain.

FANTASIO: No more certain than your beauty. Here comes your father with your future husband. Who can know if you'll marry him? *Goes out.*

ELSBETH: I can't avoid meeting the Prince of Mantua, so I might as well go towards him.

(*THE KING enters with MARINONI, in the PRINCE's costume, and the PRINCE, dressed as an aide-de-camp.*)

THE KING: Prince, here is my daughter. Forgive her informal dress. This is the home of a bourgeois who rules over other bourgeois, and our etiquette is as indulgent to us as it is to them.

MARINONI: Allow me to kiss this charming hand, if that is not too great a favour for my lips.

ELSBETH: Your Highness will excuse me if I go back to the palace. I will see you, I think, more suitably at this evening's reception.

PRINCE: The Princess is right. What divine modesty!

THE KING: (*To MARINONI.*) Who on earth is this aide-de-camp who follows you about like your shadow? I cannot stand hearing him add some inept remark to everything we say. Send him away, please.

(*MARINONI speaks to the PRINCE.*)

PRINCE: (*Aside to MARINONI.*) It's extremely clever of you to persuade him to dismiss me. I'll try to join the Princess and drop a delicate hint or two, quite without emphasis.

(*The PRINCE goes out.*)

THE KING: That aide-de-camp's an imbecile, my dear fellow. How can you put up with the man?

MARINONI: Ahem! Let us continue our walk, if your Majesty will allow. I think I see a most charming pavilion beyond that shrubbery.

(*They go out.*)

Scene II

Another part of the garden. Immediately afterwards.
The PRINCE enters.

PRINCE. My disguise is a complete success; I observe; and I
    charm them all. Till now everything is going as I desired.
    The father seems a great king, though somewhat offhand,
    and I'd be surprised if he didn't like me immediately. I see
    the Princess returning to the palace; fortune favours me
    particularly.
    (*ELSBETH enters.*
    The PRINCE stops her.)
    Highness, allow a faithful servant of your future husband
    to offer the sincere congratulations that at the sight of you,
    his humble and devoted heart cannot repress. Happy are
    the great ones of this earth! They can marry you; I cannot.
    That for me is quite impossible. I am of humble birth. All
    I possess is a name, fearful to my enemies. A pure and
    stainless heart beats beneath this modest uniform; I am
    a poor soldier, riddled with bullets from head to foot. I
    haven't a ducat; I'm all alone, an exile from my native land
    and also from my realm divine, that is, the heaven of my
    dreams; I have no woman's heart to press unto my own; I
    am accursed and silent.

ELSBETH: (*Gently.*) What is it you want, sir? Are you mad or
    are you asking for charity?

PRINCE: How could I ever find words to express my feelings!
    I saw you pass alone along this path. I thought it my duty
    to throw myself at your feet and offer you my company as
    far as the postern door.

ELSBETH: I'm very grateful. Be so good as to leave me in
    peace. (*Goes out.*)

PRINCE: Was I wrong to speak to her? But I had to, as I plan
    to conquer her in my assumed disguise. Yes, I did well to
    speak to her. But she answered in an unpleasant manner.
    Perhaps I should not have spoken so warmly. But of
    course I had to, as her marriage is almost assured and I'm
    supposed to supplant Marinoni who is taking my place.

But her answer is unpleasant. Would her heart be cold or
false? I'd be wise to investigate with care.

(*The PRINCE goes out.*)

Scene III

A room in the palace. Later the same day.
FANTASIO is alone.

FANTASIO. How delightful it is being a jester! I must have
been drunk last night when I put on this costume and
appeared at the palace. But it's a fact, cold reason would
never have inspired me to anything so worthwhile as
this insane behaviour. I arrive and here I am, received,
cosseted, recorded, and, better still, forgotten. I come and
go in this palace as if I'd lived here all my life. I met the
King just now. He hadn't even the curiosity to look at me.
His jester's dead and he's been told, 'Sire, here's another
one'. It's admirable! My brain's on holiday, thank heavens,
and I can talk all the nonsense imaginable without
anyone trying to stop me. I'm one of the King of Bavaria's
household pets and, if I like, provided I keep my hump
and wig, I'll be allowed to live the rest of my life between
a spaniel and a guinea fowl. In the meantime my creditors
can stub their toes on my door in complete comfort. In this
wig I'm as safe here as in the West Indies. (*Looking through
a window.*) Isn't that the Princess I can see in the next
room? She's adjusting her wedding veil; two long tears
run down her cheeks; now one breaks away like a pearl
and falls upon her chest. Poor child! I heard her talking
to her governess this morning; in fact it was by chance; I
was sitting on the grass and all I wanted to do was to go to
sleep. Now she sits there weeping, with no suspicion that I
can see her again. Oh, if I were a student of rhetoric, what
profound reflections I'd make on this coroneted misery,
this poor sheep, with a pink ribbon placed round her neck
to lead her to the slaughter! This little girl is no doubt
romantic; she thinks it cruel to marry a man she doesn't
know. Yet she sacrifices herself in silence. How capricious

fortune is! I have to get drunk, see Saint-Jean's funeral, take his costume and his place, in fact commit the greatest folly possible, so that I can look through this window and see the only two tears that this child will probably weep on her unhappy wedding veil. (*Goes out.*)

Scene IV

The garden. Later the same day.
The PRINCE is talking to MARINONI.

PRINCE. You're just a fool, Colonel.

MARINONI: Your Highness is most painfully mistaken about me.

PRINCE: You're a master numbskull. Couldn't you have prevented it? I entrust you with the greatest plan that's been begotten for an incalculable period of years and you, my best friend, my most faithful servant, you pile one inanity upon another. No, no! There's no use talking, it's quite unforgivable.

MARINONI: How could I prevent your Highness suffering these annoyances? They're the necessary consequences of the part you're playing. You order me to take your name and behave as the real Prince of Mantua. Can I prevent the King of Bavaria reproving my aide-de-camp? You were wrong not to stop interrupting our conversation.

PRINCE: I'd be glad if a fool like you would stop giving me orders.

MARINONI: But, Highness, do remember I must be either the Prince or the aide-de-camp. I'm only acting on your orders.

PRINCE: Telling me I'm impertinent in front of the whole court, because I wanted to kiss the Princess' hand! I'm ready to declare war on him and go back to Mantua to put myself at the head of my armies.

MARINONI: But Highness, do consider that this insult was addressed to the aide-de-camp, not the Prince. Do you hope to be respected in this disguise?

PRINCE: That's enough. Give me back my coat.

MARINONI: (*Taking off the coat.*) If you command it,
Highness, I'm ready to die for you.

PRINCE: Really, I don't know what to decide. On the one
hand I'm furious at what's happening; on the other, I'd be
heartbroken to give up my plan. I'm continually pursuing
the Princess with remarks that have a double meaning, and
her answers do not appear to be indifferent. Two or three
times already I've succeeded in whispering unbelievable
things. Come, let us think the matter over.

MARINONI: (*Holding the coat.*) What shall I do, Highness?

PRINCE: Put it on, put it on. Let's go back to the palace.
(*They go out.*)

Scene V

A room in the palace. Later the same day.
THE KING is talking to the PRINCESS.

THE KING. You must answer frankly what I'm asking you.
Do you dislike this marriage?

ELSBETH: Sire, it's for you yourself to answer. I like it, if you
like it; I dislike it, if you dislike it.

THE KING: I thought the Prince an ordinary man, it's
difficult to say anything about him. To my mind the idiocy
of his aide-de-camp is the only thing against him. He
may be a Prince, but he's not an educated man. There is
nothing about him that repels me or attracts me. What can
I say to you? Women's hearts have secrets I cannot know.
Sometimes they create such strange heroes; they seize so
oddly on one or two aspects of a man they meet that it's
impossible to decide for them; there's nothing tangible to
guide one. So tell me plainly what you think of the Prince.

ELSBETH: I think that he's the Prince of Mantua and war will
start again tomorrow if I don't marry him.

THE KING: That is certain, my child.

ELSBETH: So I think I will marry him and there will be no
war.

THE KING: May the blessings of my people thank you for
your father's sake! Oh, my dearest daughter! This union

will make me happy, but I'd rather not see in your lovely blue eyes this sadness that belies their resignation. Think about it for a few days more.

(*THE KING goes out.*

FANTASIO enters.)

ELSBETH: There you are, poor man. How do you like it here?

FANTASIO: Like a bird at liberty.

ELSBETH: You'd have answered better if you'd said like a bird in a cage. This palace is a beautiful cage, but a cage it is.

FANTASIO: The size of a palace or a room does not make man more or less free. The body moves where it can. The imagination sometimes opens wings as big as the sky, in a cell as big as a hand.

ELSBETH: So you're a happy fool then?

FANTASIO: Very happy. I make conversation with the dogs and the kitchen boys. There's a puppy in the kitchen no bigger than that and it tells me charming things.

ELSBETH: In what language?

FANTASIO: In the purest style. It doesn't make a single grammatical error in the space of a whole year.

ELSBETH: Could I hear a few words in this style?

FANTASIO: I would really prefer not. It's a special tongue. Only puppies can talk it. Trees and grains of corn know it too; but kings' daughters don't. When is your wedding?

ELSBETH: In a few days it will all be over.

FANTASIO: That's to say it will all begin. I'm thinking of giving you a present myself.

ELSBETH: What present? I'm curious to know.

FANTASIO: I'm thinking of giving you a pretty little stuffed canary that sings like a nightingale.

ELSBETH: How can it sing, if it's stuffed?

FANTASIO: It sings perfectly.

ELSBETH: Really, you're making fun of me with unusual spirit.

FANTASIO: Not at all. My canary has a little whistle in its stomach. You press very gently a little spring under its left claw and it sings all the new operas, just like Madame Grisi.

ELSBETH: This is an invention of your wit, I suppose?

FANTASIO: Certainly not. It's a court canary. There are a great many very well-brought-up little girls whose behaviour is identical. They have a little spring under their left arm, a little diamond spring, like a dandy's watch. The tutor or governess touches the spring and you immediately see the lips open in the most gracious smile, a charming cascade of honeyed words emerges in a gentle murmur, and all the social graces immediately begin to dance like airy nymphs on tiptoe round the magic spring. The fiancé opens his eyes in amazement, the onlookers whisper indulgently, and the father, secretly filled with content, gazes with pride at the golden buckles on his shoes.

ELSBETH: You seem to take pleasure in returning to certain subjects. Tell me, jester, what have those poor girls done to you, to make you laugh at them so gaily? Doesn't respect for one's duty find favour in your eyes?

FANTASIO: I've a great respect for ugliness. That's why I respect myself so profoundly.

ELSBETH: You sometimes seem to know more than you say. Well, where do you come from? And who are you, after only one day here to be able to penetrate secrets that even princes themselves will never suspect? Are your sallies addressed to me or are you speaking to your shadow?

FANTASIO: To my shadow. I often speak to it. It's my closest confidant.

ELSBETH: It does in fact seem to have taught you things you should not know. I could easily believe you were spying on everything I say and do.

FANTASIO: Heaven knows. What does it matter to you?

ELSBETH: More than you could think. In this room just now, when I was putting on my veil, I suddenly heard someone walking behind the tapestry. I'd be very much mistaken if it weren't you.

FANTASIO: Rest assured that it remains a secret between your handkerchief and me. I'm no more indiscreet than curious. What pleasure could your sorrows give me? What sorrow could your pleasures give me? You're one thing and I'm another. You're young and I'm old; beautiful and I'm ugly; rich and I'm poor. It's obvious there's no connection between us. We're two wheels on the highway of destiny, rolling in different ruts, incapable of leaving traces in the same dust; what does it matter to you that these two wheels should chance to cross? Is it my fault if one of your tears fell on my cheek as I was sleeping?

ELSBETH: You speak to me in the shape of a man I loved, that's why I listen to you in spite of myself. My eyes think they see Saint-Jean. But perhaps you're only a spy.

FANTASIO: What use would that be to me? If it were true that your marriage cost you a few tears and if by chance I found out, what should I gain by telling people? I shouldn't be given a pistole for it and you wouldn't be put in a dark cell. Of course I understand it must be rather tiresome to marry the Prince of Mantua. But after all it's no business of mine. Tomorrow or the day after you'll have left for Mantua with your wedding dress and I'll still be here on this stool with these old clothes. Why do you expect me to hate you? I've no reason to want your death. You've never lent me money.

ELSBETH: But if chance has let you see something I want no one to know about, should I not turn you out for fear of another accident?

FANTASIO: Are you intending to compare me to a confidant in a dramatic tragedy, afraid I'll follow your every footstep with declamations? Don't dismiss me, please. I'm enjoying myself here. Look, there's your governess arriving with her pockets full of mysteries. To prove I shan't listen to her, I'll go to the pantry and eat a plover's wing the steward's put aside for his wife. (*Goes out.*)

(*The GOVERNESS enters.*)

GOVERNESS: Elsbeth, my dear, do you know something terrible?

ELSBETH: What do you mean? You're trembling all over.

GOVERNESS: The Prince isn't the Prince and the aide-de-camp isn't either. It's an absolute fairy story.

ELSBETH: What farrago of nonsense is this?

GOVERNESS: Sh! Sh! One of the Prince's officers, the Prince's, has just told me. The Prince of Mantua's an absolute Almaviva. He's disguised as one of the aides-de-camp. He must have wanted to see you and get to know you, like in a fairy tale. He's disguised, the dear man, disguised like Lindor. The man you've been introduced to as your future husband is only an aide-de-camp called Marinoni.

ELSBETH: It can't be true.

GOVERNESS: It's certain, definitely certain. The dear man's disguised; it's impossible to recognise him. It's an extraordinary affair.

ELSBETH: You say you've heard this from an officer?

GOVERNESS: One of the Prince's officers. You can ask him in person.

ELSBETH: And he didn't show you which of the aides-de-camp was the real Prince of Mantua?

GOVERNESS: Just imagine, it made him tremble himself, poor man, to tell me. He only confided in me because he wants to be nice to you and he knew I'd warn you. As for Marinoni, that's a fact. But who the real Prince is, he didn't say.

ELSBETH: If that were true, it would give me something to think about. Go and fetch that officer.

(*A PAGE enters.*)

GOVERNESS: What's the matter, Flamel? You seem to be out of breath.

FIRST PAGE: Oh, madam, it will make you die of laughter. I daren't speak in front of Her Royal Highness.

ELSBETH: Go on. What has happened now?

FIRST PAGE: The moment the Prince of Mantua entered the courtyard on horseback at the head of his staff, his wig suddenly rose in the air and disappeared.

ELSBETH: Why was that? How ridiculous!

FIRST PAGE: Madam, may I die if it's not the truth. The wig

rose in the air on the end of a hook. We found it in the pantry next to a broken bottle. No one knows who played the joke. But that doesn't make the Duke less furious, and he swore that if the author isn't sentenced to death, he'll declare war against the King your father and put everything to fire and sword.

ELSBETH: Let's go and listen to this story, my dear. I'm beginning to feel more lighthearted.

(*Another PAGE enters.*)

Well, what news?

SECOND PAGE: Madam, the King's jester's in prison. He's the man who took the Prince's wig.

ELSBETH: The jester's in prison? And on the Prince's orders?

SECOND PAGE: Yes, Highness.

ELSBETH: (*To her GOVERNESS.*) Let us go. I must speak to him.

(*ELSBETH goes out with her GOVERNESS.*)

Scene VI

Another room in the palace. Immediately afterwards.
The PRINCE is talking to MARINONI.

PRINCE. No, no, let me unmask myself. It's time I burst forth! I shan't let it rest there. Fire and sword! A royal wig on the end of a hook! Are we among barbarians, in the deserts of Siberia? Is there anything civilised and respectable left on earth? I'm foaming with rage and my eyes are popping out of my head.

MARINONI: You'll ruin everything by being so violent.

PRINCE: And this father, this King of Bavaria, this monarch eulogised in every one of last year's almanacs! This man, with such a proper appearance, who expresses himself in such measured terms, this man starts laughing at the sight of his son-in-law's wig flying through the air! Yes, I know, Marinoni, I agree it was your wig that was removed. But it's none the less the Prince of Mantua's as it's he they thought they saw in you. When I think that if it had been me, in flesh and blood, my wig might have... Ah,

Providence does exist. When God suddenly gave me
the idea of disguising myself, when the thought 'I must
disguise myself' flashed across my mind, this fatal event
was foreseen by destiny. Yes, destiny saved the head
that governs my people from the most intolerable insult.
But, by heaven, it shall all be known! My dignity's been
demeaned for too long. As divine and human majesties are
pitilessly defaced and desecrated, as men have lost all ideas
of good and evil, as the king of several thousand people
bursts out laughing like a potboy at the sight of a wig,
Marinoni, give me back my coat.

MARINONI: (*Taking off the coat.*) If my sovereign demands it,
I'm ready to suffer a thousand tortures for his sake.

PRINCE: I know your devotion. Come with me, I'll tell the
King exactly what I think of him.

MARINONI: You're refusing the Princess' hand? But she was
making eyes at you unmistakably all through dinner.

PRINCE: You think so? I'm getting lost in an abyss of
perplexities. Still, come with me, let's go to the King.

MARINONI: (*Holding the coat.*) What shall I do, Highness?

PRINCE: Put it on for a moment. You can give it back later.
They'll be much more petrified to hear me adopt the tone I
contemplate in this plain dark coat.

(*They go out.*)

Scene VII

A prison. The same evening.
FANTASIO is alone.

FANTASIO. I don't know if Providence exists, but it's
amusing to believe so. Why, here's a poor little Princess
going to marry a revolting brute against her will; a
provincial boor who had a crown dropped on his head by
destiny, as the eagle dropped the tortoise onto Aeschylus.
Everything was ready; the candles lit, the bridegroom
powdered, the poor girl confessed. She'd wiped away the
two charming tears I saw her shed this morning. Only a
sermon or two was wanted for the tragedy of her life to be

set in motion. In all this lay the fortunes of two kingdoms, the peace of two nations. And I have to get the idea of disguising myself with a hump and come and get drunk once more in our good King's pantry; and then go fishing for his beloved ally's wig on the end of a piece of string. It's a fact, when I'm drunk, I think I've something superhuman in me. Now the marriage is cancelled, and everything called in question. The Prince of Mantua asked for my head in exchange for his wig. The King of Bavaria thought the punishment rather excessive and only agreed to prison. The Prince of Mantua, thank heaven, is such a fool he'd be torn to pieces rather than let go of something. So the Princess remains unmarried, at least on this occasion. If that's not a subject for an epic poem in twelve cantos, I'm an ignoramus. Pope and Boileau have made admirable verses on much less important subjects. Oh, if I were a poet, how I'd paint the scene of that wig flying through the air. But the man who's capable of doing such things scorns to write about them. So posterity will have to do without it. (*He goes to sleep.*)

(*ELSBETH enters with her GOVERNESS, a lamp in her hand.*)

ELSBETH: He's asleep. Shut the door quietly.

GOVERNESS: Look. There's no doubt about it. He's taken off his false wig and his deformity's vanished at the same time. There he is, as he really is, as his people see him in his triumphal chariot. It's the noble Prince of Mantua.

ELSBETH: Yes, it is. Now my curiosity is satisfied. I wanted to see his face, that was all. Let me go closer. (*She takes the lamp.*) Psyche, be careful not to spill the oil.

GOVERNESS: He's as handsome as a real Messiah.

ELSBETH: Why have you given me so many novels and fairy stories? Why have you sown so many strange, mysterious flowers in my poor thoughts?

GOVERNESS: How excited you are, standing there on tiptoe!

ELSBETH: He's waking up. Let's go.

FANTASIO: (*Waking up.*) Am I dreaming? I'm holding the
hem of a white dress.

ELSBETH: Let go. I must leave here.

FANTASIO: It's you, Princess! If it's a pardon for the King's
jester that you're bringing so charmingly, let me put on my
hump and wig. It won't take a moment.

GOVERNESS: Oh, Prince, it ill becomes you to deceive
us like this. Don't put on this costume again. We know
everything.

FANTASIO: Prince! Where do you see a prince?

GOVERNESS: What's the use of pretending?

FANTASIO: I'm not pretending in the slightest. What makes
you call me prince?

GOVERNESS: I know my duty to your Highness.

FANTASIO: (*To ELSBETH.*) Madam, I beg you to explain
what this good woman means. Is there really some absurd
mistake or is it a joke at my expense?

ELSBETH: Why ask, when you're joking yourself?

FANTASIO: Am I by chance a prince, then? Has someone
cast doubts on my mother's honour?

ELSBETH: Who are you, if you're not the Prince of Mantua?

FANTASIO: My name is Fantasio. I'm a citizen of Munich.
(*He shows her a letter.*)

ELSBETH: A citizen of Munich! Well, why are you disguised?
What are you doing here?

FANTASIO: Madam, I beg you to forgive me. (*He kneels.*)

ELSBETH: What does this mean? Get up, fellow, leave here
at once. I forgive you any punishment you may deserve.
Who persuaded you to do this?

FANTASIO: I can't tell the motive that led me here.

ELSBETH: You can't tell? But I want to know.

FANTASIO: I'm sorry, I daren't confess.

GOVERNESS: Let us go, Elsbeth. Don't expose yourself to
speeches that are not worthy of you. This man's a thief or
an insolent fellow who's going to make love to you.

ELSBETH: I want to know the reason that made you wear
this costume.

FANTASIO: I beg you to spare me.

ELSBETH: No, no. If you don't speak, I'll close this door on you for ten years.

FANTASIO: Madam, I'm riddled with debts. My creditors obtained a judgement against me. At this moment, my furniture's sold, and if I weren't in this prison, I'd be in another. I should have been arrested yesterday evening. I didn't know where to spend the night or how to escape the bailiffs, so I had the idea of putting on this costume and seeking refuge in the palace. If you set me free, I'll be seized at once. My uncle's an old miser who lives on cabbage and potatoes and lets me die of hunger in all the taverns in the kingdom. If you must know, I owe twenty thousand crowns.

ELSBETH: Is all this true?

FANTASIO: If I'm lying, I agree to pay them.
(*The noise of horses can be heard.*)

GOVERNESS: There are horses going by. It's the King himself. If only I could signal to a page! (*Calling out of the window.*) Hey, Flamel, where are you going?

FIRST PAGE: (*Off.*) The Prince of Mantua's leaving.

GOVERNESS: The Prince of Mantua!

FIRST PAGE: Yes, war's been declared. There's been a terrible scene between him and the King in front of the whole court and the Princess' marriage has been broken off.

ELSBETH: Do you hear that, sir? You're responsible for destroying my marriage.

GOVERNESS: Good lord in heaven! The Prince of Mantua's going and I haven't seen him!

ELSBETH: How terrible, if war's declared!

FANTASIO: You call that terrible, Highness? Would you rather have a husband who goes to war about a wig? Well, if fighting does break out, we know what to do with these strong arms of ours. All the idle men in town will put on their uniforms; and I'll take my shotgun, if it hasn't yet been sold. We'll take a trip to Italy, and if you ever enter Mantua, it will be as a real queen with no need of any other candles but our swords.

ELSBETH: Fantasio, would you like to remain my father's jester? I'll pay your twenty thousand crowns for you.

FANTASIO: I'd be delighted. But really, if you made me, I'd jump out of the window one of these days to escape.

ELSBETH: Why? You know Saint-Jean is dead. We must have a jester.

FANTASIO: I like this job more than any other; but I can't do any job. If you think getting rid of the Prince of Mantua is worth twenty thousand crowns, give them to me, don't pay my debts. A gentleman without debts wouldn't know what to do. The thought of finding myself without debts has never entered my mind.

ELSBETH: All right, I'll give them to you. But take the key to my garden. The day you're bored with being pursued by your creditors, come and hide among the corn-flowers where I found you this morning. Be careful to put on your wig and your striped coat. Don't appear before me without this twisted body and these silver bells. Because that's the way I came to like you. You'll become my jester again for as long as it pleases you, and then you'll go about your business. Now you are free, the door is open.

GOVERNESS: Is it possible for the Prince of Mantua to have gone without my seeing him!

DON'T TRIFLE WITH LOVE
(On ne badine pas avec l'amour)

Characters

THE BARON

PERDICAN, his son, aged 21

FATHER BLAZIUS, Perdican's tutor

FATHER BRIDAINE, the village priest

CAMILLE, the Baron's niece, aged 18

DAME PLUCHE, her governess

ROSETTE, a village girl, Camille's foster sister

CHORUS OF VILLAGE PEOPLE

PEASANT

SERVANTS

Scene: The action takes place in and near a small French village.

ACT ONE

Scene I

The village square in front of the castle.
CHORUS enters.

CHORUS. Gently rocking on his sharp-eyed mule, Father
Blazius approaches through the sunlit vineyards, his clothes
all new, his inkhorn at his side. Like a baby on a cushion,
he rolls upon his rounded stomach and with eyes half
closed he mumbles a paternoster in his triple chin.
(*FATHER BLAZIUS enters.*)
Good morning, Father Blazius, you come in time for the
grape harvest, like an antique amphora.

FATHER BLAZIUS: If you wish to hear news of great
importance, first bring me here a glass of good cool wine.

CHORUS: Here is our largest pitcher. Drink up, Father
Blazius. The wine is good. You can speak later.

FATHER BLAZIUS: You should know, my children, that
young Perdican, the Baron's son, has just reached his
majority and taken his doctor's degree in Paris. He comes
home here today, his mouth so full of fine and flowery
phrases that half the time you don't know how to answer
him. All his gracious person is a book of gold. If he but
sees a blade of grass, he'll tell you what it's called in Latin.
And if it blows, or pours with rain, he will explain quite
clearly why. You will open your eyes as wide as these castle
gates, when you see him unroll one of the parchments he
has painted with inks of every colour, with his own fair
hands and without a word to anyone. He is, in short, from
top to toe a sparkling jewel. And that is what I've come to
tell the Baron. You realise this does me some honour, I've
been his tutor from the age of four. Now bring me a chair,
so I may get off this mule without breaking my neck. The
brute is rather stubborn and I should not be sorry to drink
another mouthful before I go in.

CHORUS: Drink up, Father Blazius. It will do you good. We

all knew Perdican as a child; there was no need to speak of him at such length. Let us hope we find that child again in the heart of the man.

FATHER BLAZIUS: Good lord, the pitcher's empty. I didn't think I'd drunk it all. Goodbye, my friends. I prepared upon the road a few brief words, quite unpretentious, that will not, I think, displease the Baron. I shall go into see him. (*Goes out.*)

CHORUS: Roughly jolted on a breathless ass, Dame Pluche climbs up the hill. Her groom, with all his might, cudgels the poor beast, which shakes its head, a thistle in its mouth. Her long, thin legs tremble with rage, as with her bony hands she scratches at a rosary.
(*DAME PLUCHE enters.*)
Good day to you, Dame Pluche. You come like influenza with the autumn wind which turns the leaves to yellow.

DAME PLUCHE: A glass of water, scoundrels that you are. A glass of water, with a little vinegar.

CHORUS: Where do you come from, Pluche my sweet? Your false hair is covered with dust. Your wig's awry and your chaste robe pulled up to your venerable garters.

DAME PLUCHE: Know then, you scum, that the lovely Camille, the Baron's niece, comes here today. She has left her convent at her uncle's strict command, to come, in proper time and place, to take, as well she should, the large estate bequeathed her by her mother. Her education, God be thanked, is finished. And all who see her have the joy of savouring a glorious flower of wisdom and devotion. Never has been seen a girl so pure and so angelic, so like a lamb, so like a dove, as this young novice. May the Lord God of Heaven watch over her. So be it. Out of the way, you rabble. I think my legs are swollen.

CHORUS: Calm yourself, good Pluche. And when you pray to God, ask Him for rain; our fields are as dry as your old shins.

DAME PLUCHE: You have brought me water in a pitcher that smells of garlic. Give me your hand to get down. You are ignorant, ill-mannered louts. (*Goes out.*)

CHORUS: Let us put on our best clothes and wait for the Baron to summon us. Unless I'm much mistaken, there's a happy celebration in the air today.

Scene II

A room in the castle, immediately afterwards.
The BARON, FATHER BRIDAINE and FATHER BLAZIUS enter.

BARON. Father Bridaine, you are my friend; let me present to you Father Blazius, tutor to my son. Yesterday at eight minutes past twelve noon my son was twenty-one years old. He has taken his doctor's degree in four separate subjects. Father Blazius, let me present to you Father Bridaine, our village priest. He is my friend.

FATHER BLAZIUS: (*Bowing.*) In four separate subjects, my lord. Literature, botany, Roman law, and canon law.

BARON: Go to your room, my dear Blazius, my son will soon be here. Get ready for dinner and come back when you hear the bell.

(*FATHER BLAZIUS goes out.*)

FATHER BRIDAINE: Shall I tell you what I think, my lord? Every breath of your son's tutor smells of wine.

BARON: Impossible.

FATHER BRIDAINE: I'm as certain as I'm standing here. He spoke to me from very close just now. The smell of wine was frightening.

BARON: That's enough. I tell you it's impossible.

(*DAME PLUCHE enters.*)

There you are, good Dame Pluche. My niece of course is with you?

DAME PLUCHE: She follows me, my lord. I came on a few yards ahead.

BARON: Father Bridaine, you are my friend, let me introduce you to Dame Pluche, governess to my niece. Yesterday evening at seven o'clock, my niece attained the age of eighteen. She has just left the best convent in France.

Dame Pluche, let me present to you Father Bridaine, our village priest. He is my friend.

DAME PLUCHE: (*Bowing.*) The best convent in France, my lord. And, I might add, the best young Christian in the convent.

BARON: Dame Pluche, go and repair the ravages of your journey. My niece, I hope, will soon be here. Be ready in time for dinner.

(*DAME PLUCHE goes out.*)

FATHER BRIDAINE: The old lady seems a model of piety.

BARON: Of piety and propriety, Father Bridaine. Her virtue is unassailable.

FATHER BRIDAINE: But the tutor smells of wine, I'm sure of it.

BARON: Father Bridaine, there are times when I begin to doubt your friendship. Do you take it upon yourself to contradict me? Not another word about it. I have made a plan to marry my son to my niece. They are a well-matched couple. Their education cost me six thousand crowns.

FATHER BRIDAINE: You will have to obtain a papal dispensation.

BARON: I have it, Bridaine. It's on my table in my study. Oh, my dear fellow, now you realise how delighted I am. You know I have always had the most profound horror of solitude. However, the position I occupy forces me to spend three months here in winter and three in summer. It's impossible to please people in general, and one's tenants in particular, without sometimes giving the servants strict orders that no one is to enter. How austere and complicated is the life of a statesman! So what pleasure I should find in tempering, by the presence of my two united children, the heavy melancholy I must needs be a prey to, since I became the King's representative.

FATHER BRIDAINE: Will the wedding take place here or in Paris?

BARON: That's what I was waiting for, Bridaine, I was sure you would ask that question. Well, my dear friend, what

would you say if these hands, yes, Bridaine, your own
hands – don't look at them so piteously – were destined to
give the solemn blessing to the happy confirmation of my
dearest dreams? Eh?

FATHER BRIDAINE: I am silent. Gratitude seals my lips.

BARON: Come here to the window. Look, do you see
my people crowding round the gate? My two children
have arrived at the same time. What a happy chance! I
have arranged for every contingency. My niece will be
introduced by this door on the left and my son by the one
on the right. What do you say to that? I'm so eager to see
how they'll greet each other, what they'll say. Six thousand
crowns is no trifle, there must be no mistakes. Besides,
these children used to love each other very dearly when
they were babies. Bridaine, I have an idea.

FATHER BRIDAINE: What is that?

BARON: During dinner, without appearing to stress it…you
understand, my dear fellow…as you're drinking a happy
toast or two…you know Latin, Bridaine?

FATHER BRIDAINE: Heavens above, yes, I do!

BARON: I should be very pleased to see you dispute with
the boy, discreetly of course, in front of his cousin. That
can only produce a good effect. Make him speak a little
Latin…not exactly during dinner, that would be too
tedious and I of course don't understand a word…but
during dessert…do you see?

FATHER BRIDAINE: If you don't understand a word, my
lord, it's probable your niece doesn't either.

BARON: All the more reason. Surely you don't expect a
woman to admire what she can understand. What are you
thinking of, Bridaine? That's a ridiculous statement.

FATHER BRIDAINE: I know little about women. But
it seems to me difficult to admire what you cannot
understand.

BARON: I know them, Bridaine; I know those charming,
undefinable creatures. Take it from me, they love to have
dust thrown in their eyes. And the more you throw, the
wider they open them so they can take in even more.

(*PERDICAN enters on one side, CAMILLE on the other.*)

BARON: Good morning, children. My dear Perdican, my dear Camille! Come and kiss me; and kiss each other.

PERDICAN: Good morning, Father; and my dearest sister. How wonderful! I'm so happy!

CAMILLE: Father, cousin, I'm glad to see you.

PERDICAN: How tall you are, Camille! And lovely as the dawn!

BARON: When did you leave Paris, Perdican?

PERDICAN: Wednesday, I think, or Tuesday. So here you are, transformed into a woman! And I'm a man! It seems yesterday I saw you no taller than that.

BARON: You must both be tired. It's a long journey and the weather's hot.

PERDICAN: Good lord, no! Do look, Father, how pretty Camille is!

BARON: Now, Camille, kiss your cousin.

CAMILLE: Excuse me.

BARON: A compliment deserves a kiss. Take her in your arms, Perdican.

PERDICAN: If my cousin turns away when I stretch out my hand, it's my turn to say 'Excuse me'. Love can steal a kiss, but not friendship.

CAMILLE: Neither love nor friendship should receive what they cannot return.

BARON: (*To FATHER BRIDAINE.*) That's an ill-omened beginning, eh?

FATHER BRIDAINE: (*To the BARON.*) Too much modesty is no doubt a defect, but marriage removes many scruples.

BARON: (*To FATHER BRIDAINE.*) I'm shocked, offended. That answer's upset me. 'Excuse me!' Did you see she seemed to cross herself? Come here, I want to speak to you. This is extremely painful. This moment should have been so sweet to me, but now it's completely spoiled. I'm vexed, hurt. Damnation, this is very bad.

FATHER BRIDAINE: Say something to them. Look, they're turning their backs on each other.

BARON: Well, children, what are you thinking about? Camille, why are you looking at that picture?

CAMILLE: What a beautiful portrait, uncle! Isn't it our great-aunt?

BARON: Yes, my child, it's your great-grandmother, or rather your great-grandfather's sister, for the dear woman never contributed, other than in prayer, I think, on her part, to the enlargement of the family. She was, indeed she was, a saintly woman.

CAMILLE: Oh yes, a saint. It's my great-aunt Isabel. How well that nun's veil suits her.

BARON: Perdican, why are you looking at that vase of flowers?

PERDICAN: This is a charming flower, Father. It's a heliotrope.

BARON: What a long name for a flower that's no bigger than a fly.

PERDICAN: This little flower may be no bigger than a fly, but it certainly has its price.

FATHER BRIDAINE: Of course! The doctor's right. Ask him its sex, its type, what elements it's made of, where it gets its sap and colour. He'll whirl you into ecstasy by explaining all the phenomena of this tiny blade of grass, from its root up to its petals.

PERDICAN: I don't know as much as that, reverend Father. I know it smells sweet, that's all.

Scene III

The village square, later the same day.
CHORUS enters.

CHORUS: A number of things amuse me and excite my curiosity. Come, my friends, let us sit down under this tree. Two formidable eaters are at this moment face to face in the castle, Father Bridaine and Father Blazius. Have you ever noticed something? When two men, almost identical, equally fat, equally foolish, with the same vices and the same passions, happen by chance to meet, then it follows inevitably that they either love or hate each other. For the same reason that opposites are attracted, that a tall, dried-up man will like one who is small and fat, or fair people make friends with dark, and conversely, I foresee a secret struggle between the tutor and our priest. Both of them are armed with equal impudence; both have a barrel of a stomach; not only are they gluttons, but gourmets too; both will argue at dinner, not only about the quantity but about the quality. If the fish is small, what will they do? And in any case they can't share the tongue of a carp and a carp can only have one tongue. Both of them love to talk; but if necessary they can talk at the same time without listening to each other. Father Bridaine has already tried to put several pedantic questions to Perdican and the tutor raised his eyebrows. He doesn't like anyone to seem to put his pupil to the test. Furthermore each is as ignorant as the other. Again, they are both of them priests: one will boast about his parish, the other will glory in his post as tutor. Blazius is confessor to the son, Bridaine to the father. I can see them already with their elbows on the table, cheeks aflame and eyes agoggle, shaking their triple chins with hatred. They look each other up and down, they open with a light skirmish; soon war will be declared: all kinds of pedantries will be crossed and parried; and, to crown it all, between these two drunkards flutters Dame Pluche, thrusting them off with her sharp elbows. Now dinner is finished and they are opening the castle gates. Here come the company. Let us draw aside.

(*CHORUS go out.*

The BARON and DAME PLUCHE enter.)

BARON: Dame Pluche, I am pained.

DAME PLUCHE: Is that possible, my lord?

BARON: Yes, Pluche, it is possible. I have reckoned for a long time, I had even written down, noted on my tablets, that today was to be the happiest day of my life – yes, good woman, of my life. You are not unaware that I had planned to marry my son to my niece; it was decided, settled; I had mentioned it to Bridaine. And now I see, I think I see, these children speaking coldly to each other. At least they haven't said a word.

DAME PLUCHE: Here they come, my lord. Have they been told of your plans?

BARON: I did say one or two words privately. I think it would be wise, as they are here together, to sit down in that conveniently shady place and leave them alone for a moment.

(*The BARON and DAME PLUCHE go out.*
CAMILLE and PERDICAN enter.)

PERDICAN: Camille, do you realise it was not at all kind to refuse to kiss me?

CAMILLE: I am like that, it's my manner.

PERDICAN: Will you take my arm and walk round the village?

CAMILLE: No, I'm tired.

PERDICAN: Wouldn't you like to see the meadow again? Do you remember our parties in the boat? Let's go down to the mill. I'll take the oars and you can steer.

CAMILLE: I have no desire to.

PERDICAN: You break my heart. What, have you no memories, Camille? Not a quickening of your heart for our childhood, for all that poor time past, so good and happy, so full of delightful memories? Wouldn't you like to see the path we used to take to the farm?

CAMILLE: No, not this evening.

PERDICAN: Not this evening! Well, when? Our whole life lies there.

CAMILLE: I'm not young enough to play with my dolls or old enough to be in love with the past.

PERDICAN: What do you mean?

CAMILLE: I mean that childhood memories are not to my taste.

PERDICAN: They bore you?

CAMILLE: Yes, they bore me.

PERDICAN: Poor child. I am sincerely sorry for you.

(*They go out in different directions.*
The BARON and DAME PLUCHE enter.)

BARON: You saw them, my good Pluche, and you heard them. I was expecting the sweetest harmony, but I seem to be listening to a concert where the violin is playing a hymn tune and the flute a country dance. Just think of the appalling discord such a combination would produce. Yet that is what is going on in my heart.

DAME PLUCHE: I agree. But I find it impossible to blame Camille. In my view, nothing could be in worse taste than boating parties.

BARON: Are you speaking seriously?

DAME PLUCHE: My lord, no young girl with any self-respect would venture out on rivers.

BARON: But do remember, Dame Pluche, her cousin is to marry her and besides...

DAME PLUCHE: Decency forbids the holding of a tiller and it is unseemly to leave dry land alone with a young man.

BARON: But I repeat... I tell you...

DAME PLUCHE: That is my opinion.

BARON: Are you mad? Really you'll make me say there are some expressions I don't wish... I am loath to use... You make me want to... Really if I don't restrain myself... You're a blithering fool, Pluche! I don't know what to think of you.

(*They go out.*

PERDICAN and CHORUS enter.)

PERDICAN: Good evening, my old friends. Don't you recognise me?

CHORUS: My lord, you look like a child we once loved very dearly.

PERDICAN: Wasn't it you who used to carry me on your back to cross the streams in your meadows; you made me dance on your knees; you swung me up behind you on your sturdy horses; you sometimes used to squeeze up round your table to make room for me at supper on your farm.

CHORUS: We remember, my lord. You were quite the worst young scamp and the best young fellow we ever saw.

PERDICAN: Well then, why don't you take me in your arms, instead of bowing to me like a stranger?

CHORUS: God bless you, my dear boy! Every one of us wanted to take you in his arms. But we are old, my lord, and you're a man now.

PERDICAN: Yes, it's ten years since I saw you last and in a single day everything changes under the sun. I have grown up a few feet toward heaven and you have bent down a few inches toward the grave. Your heads are white and your steps are slower. You can't lift me up from the ground as you did when I was a child. So it's for me to be your father, as you were all once mine.

CHORUS: Your return is a happier day for us than your birth. It's better to find someone you love than to kiss an unknown baby.

PERDICAN: So here is my dear valley. My walnut trees, my green paths, my little woodland spring. Here are my days gone by, still so full of life; here is the mysterious world of my childhood dreams. Home! Home! Incomprehensible word! Is man born for only one particular place, where he must build his nest and live for just a single day?

CHORUS: They tell us you're a learned man now, my lord.

PERDICAN: Yes, they've told me that too. Science is a fine thing, my children. But these trees and meadows teach, for all the world to see, the finest thing of all, the way to forget all knowledge.

CHORUS: There has been more than a change or two, while you've been away. Girls have got married and boys gone off into the army.

PERDICAN: You must tell me everything. I am expecting so much news. But really I don't want it yet. How small this fountain is. In the old days I used to think it vast. I took away in my head the idea of an ocean and a forest, but now I find a drop of water and a few blades of grass. Who is that girl singing at her window behind those trees?

CHORUS: It's Rosette, your cousin's foster sister.

PERDICAN: (*Approaching.*) Rosette, come out quickly and
join us.
(*ROSETTE enters.*)
ROSETTE: Yes, my lord.
PERDICAN: You saw me from the window, you wicked girl,
and you didn't come? Quickly, give me your hand, and
your cheeks. I must kiss you.
ROSETTE: Yes, my lord.
PERDICAN: Are you married, my dear? I was told you were.
ROSETTE: Oh, no.
PERDICAN: Why? There's not a prettier girl in the village.
We'll find you a husband, my child.
CHORUS: My lord, she says she'll never marry.
PERDICAN: Is that true, Rosette?
ROSETTE: Oh, no.
PERDICAN: Your sister Camille is here. Have you seen her?
ROSETTE: No, not yet.
PERDICAN: Go and put on your best dress and come to
supper at the castle.

Scene IV

A room in the castle.
The BARON and FATHER BLAZIUS enter.

FATHER BLAZIUS: My lord, there is something I must tell
you. The parish priest is a drunkard.
BARON: You should be ashamed of yourself. That's
impossible.
FATHER BLAZIUS: I'm sure of it. He drank three bottles of
wine at dinner.
BARON: That is excessive.
FATHER BLAZIUS: And when he left the castle, he began
walking on the flowerbeds.
BARON: On the flowerbeds? I'm amazed. That's very odd…
Drinking three bottles of wine at dinner! Walking on the
flowerbeds! I can't understand it. Why didn't he walk on
the path?
FATHER BLAZIUS: Because he was staggering.

BARON: (*Aside*.) I'm beginning to believe Bridaine was right
this morning. This fellow Blazius smells most horribly of
wine.

FATHER BLAZIUS: Besides, he ate a great deal. And his
speech was confused.

BARON: It's a fact. I noticed it too.

FATHER BLAZIUS: He let fall a few words of Latin. They
were nothing but platitudes. My lord, he is a depraved man.

BARON: (*Aside*.) Pah! The smell of this fellow Blazius is
intolerable. (*Aloud*.) You must know, sir, I have other things
to think about. I never bother myself with what people eat
or with what they drink. I am not a butler.

FATHER BLAZIUS: May it please God that I should not
displease you, my lord. Your wine is good.

BARON: There is good wine in my cellar.

(*FATHER BRIDAINE enters*.)

FATHER BRIDAINE: My lord, your son is down in the
square, talking with all the rogues in the village.

BARON: Impossible.

FATHER BRIDAINE: I've seen him with my own eyes. He's
picking up stones to play ducks and drakes.

BARON: Ducks and drakes? My head's in a whirl, my thoughts
are all confused. Don't be ridiculous, Bridaine. No one's ever
heard of a doctor of canon law playing ducks and drakes.

FATHER BRIDAINE: Look out of the window, my lord.
You'll see him with your own eyes.

BARON: (*Aside*.) Heavens above, Blazius is right. Bridaine is
staggering.

FATHER BRIDAINE: Look, my lord, there he is by the
fountain. He's holding a young girl by the arm.

BARON: A young girl! Has my son come here to debauch
my tenants? Holding her arm! And surrounded by all the
rogues of the village! I'm going out of my mind.

FATHER BRIDAINE: This calls for vengeance.

BARON: Everything's ruined! Hopelessly ruined! I am
ruined. Bridaine can't walk straight; Blazius smells most
horribly of wine; and my son's playing ducks and drakes
and seducing all the girls in the village.

ACT TWO

Scene I

A room in the castle, the next day.
FATHER BLAZIUS and PERDICAN enter.

FATHER BLAZIUS: My lord, your father is in despair.

PERDICAN: Why is that?

FATHER BLAZIUS: You are not unaware that he had planned for you to marry your cousin.

PERDICAN: Well? There's nothing I should like better.

FATHER BLAZIUS: However the Baron thinks he's noticed that your characters are not well-matched.

PERDICAN: That's unfortunate. I can't alter mine.

FATHER BLAZIUS: You're not going to make this marriage impossible?

PERDICAN: I tell you once again there's nothing I'd like better than to marry Camille. Go and find the Baron and tell him that.

FATHER BLAZIUS: My lord, I'll leave you. Here is your cousin.

(FATHER BLAZIUS goes out.
CAMILLE enters.)

PERDICAN: Up already, Camille? I still think what I told you yesterday. You're as lovely as the dawn.

CAMILLE: Let us talk seriously, Perdican. Your father wishes us to marry. I don't know what you think of it; but I believe I ought to tell you that as far as that is concerned my mind is made up.

PERDICAN: All the worse for me if you dislike me.

CAMILLE: No more than anyone else. I don't wish to marry. There is nothing in that to offend your pride.

PERDICAN: Pride is not one of my qualities. I care nothing for its joys or its pains.

CAMILLE: I have come here to receive my mother's estate. Tomorrow I return to the convent.

PERDICAN: You have behaved very frankly. Give me your
hand, let us be friends.

CAMILLE: I don't like shaking hands.

PERDICAN: (*Taking her hand.*) Give me your hand, Camille,
please. What have you to fear from me? You don't wish us
to marry? Very well then; we won't. Is that any reason for
us to hate each other? Aren't we brother and sister? When
your mother prescribed this marriage in her will, she
wished our friendship to last forever; that is all she wished.
Why should we marry? Here is your hand and here is
mine. For them to stay united till our last breath, we don't
require a priest, do we? All we need is God.

CAMILLE: I'm glad that you don't mind my refusing.

PERDICAN: I do mind, Camille. Your love would have given
me life, but your friendship will console me. Don't leave
the castle tomorrow. Yesterday you refused to walk in
the garden, because you saw in me a husband you didn't
want. Stay here a few days. Let me hope our past life is not
completely dead in your heart.

CAMILLE: I must go.

PERDICAN: Why?

CAMILLE: That is my secret.

PERDICAN: Do you love someone else?

CAMILLE: No. But I wish to go.

PERDICAN: Definitely?

CAMILLE: Yes, definitely.

PERDICAN: Well then, goodbye. I should have liked to sit
with you under the chestnut trees in the copse and talk as
friends for an hour or two. But if you don't want to, let's
say no more. Goodbye, my dear.
(*PERDICAN goes out.*
DAME PLUCHE enters.)

CAMILLE: Dame Pluche, is everything ready? Are we
leaving tomorrow? Has my guardian finished the accounts?

DAME PLUCHE: Yes, my stainless dove. The Baron called
me a blithering fool last night and I'm delighted to go.

CAMILLE: Wait. Here is a note I want you to take to
Perdican before dinner.

DAME PLUCHE: Good lord above! I can't believe it! You're writing a note to a man?

CAMILLE: I'm to be his wife, aren't I? Surely I can write to the man I'm going to marry.

DAME PLUCHE: Perdican has just left you. What can you be writing to him? The man you're going to marry, for heaven's sake! You don't mean that you've forgotten Jesus?

CAMILLE: Do what I tell you, and get everything ready for our departure.

(*They go out.*

FATHER BRIDAINE enters with SERVANTS who start to lay the table.)

FATHER BRIDAINE: Yes, it's certain he will be given the place of honour again today. This chair on the Baron's right which I have occupied for so long will be the tutor's prize. How miserable I am! An ignorant fool, a shameless drunkard, relegates me to the bottom of the table. The steward will serve him the first glass of malaga, and when the dishes reach me they'll be half cold, with the choicest morsels already taken. Oh, holy Catholic Church! I can understand that he should be given the best place yesterday; he had just arrived; it was the first time for a number of years that he'd sat at this table. Heavens, how he ate! No, not a piece of chicken will be left for me but the bones and feet. I will not tolerate this insult. Farewell, beloved chair, where I have so often collapsed when gorged to the full with succulent dishes! Farewell, bottles of glorious vintage and scent of venison cooked to perfection! Farewell, splendid banquets, noble dining room where I shall nevermore say grace! I return to my own house. I shall never again be seen here mingling with the multitude of guests. Like Caesar I would rather be first in a village than second at Rome.

(*He goes out.*)

Scene II

The village square, immediately afterwards.
ROSETTE and PERDICAN enter.

PERDICAN. As your mother's not at home, come and take a
  walk with me.
ROSETTE: Do you think it's right to give me all these kisses?
PERDICAN: What harm is there in that? I'd kiss you in front
  of your mother. Aren't you Camille's sister? Aren't I your
  brother as much as hers?
ROSETTE: Words are words and kisses are kisses. I'm
  not very clever. I realise that as soon as I want to say
  something. Fine ladies know what it means if someone
  kisses their right hand or their left. Their fathers kiss them
  on the forehead, their brothers on the cheek, and their
  lovers on the lips. But everybody kisses me on both cheeks
  and that annoys me.
PERDICAN: How pretty you are, my dear.
ROSETTE: Now you mustn't start worrying about that. How
  unhappy you are this morning. Has your marriage been
  cancelled?
PERDICAN: Everybody in the village remembers they once
  loved me. The dogs in the kennels and the trees in the
  woods remember too. But Camille remembers nothing.
  What about you, Rosette, when are you going to be
  married?
ROSETTE: Don't let's talk about that, please. Let's talk of the
  weather we're having, and those flowers over there, and
  your horses and my bonnets.
PERDICAN: Talk about anything you like, anything that can
  cross your lips without removing that lovely smile. I revere
  it more than anything on earth. (*He kisses her.*)
ROSETTE: You revere my smile, but you don't seem to
  revere my lips as far as I can see. Why look, a drop of rain
  has fallen on my hand, but the sky is clear.
PERDICAN: Forgive me.
ROSETTE: What have I done to make you weep?
  (*They go out.*)

Scene III

Inside the castle, later the same day.
FATHER BLAZIUS and the BARON enter.

FATHER BLAZIUS: My lord, I've something strange to tell you. Just now by chance I was in the kitchen, I mean the gallery; what would I be doing in the kitchen? Well, I was in the gallery. I'd found by accident a bottle of wine, I mean a glass of water; how could I have found a bottle of wine in the gallery? Well, I was in the act of drinking a glass of wine, I mean water, to pass the time, and I was looking out of the window between two vases of flowers which seemed to be in the modern style, although they were imitated from the Etruscan...

BARON: What an insufferable way of talking you've adopted, Blazius. Your speech is most peculiar.

FATHER BLAZIUS: Listen to me, my lord, give me just a moment of your attention. As I say, I was looking out of the window... Don't get impatient, for heaven's sake, the honour of the family is concerned in this.

BARON: The family? I don't understand a word. The honour of the family, Blazius? Do you realise we're thirty-seven males and almost as many females...that is, including Paris as well as the country?

FATHER BLAZIUS: Allow me to continue. While I was drinking a glass of wine, I mean water, to hasten my slow digestion, what do you think, I saw Dame Pluche pass in front of the window, out of breath.

BARON: Why out of breath, Blazius? This is most unusual.

FATHER BLAZIUS: And beside her, red with rage, your niece Camille.

BARON: Who was red with rage, my niece or Dame Pluche?

FATHER BLAZIUS: Your niece, my lord.

BARON: My niece red with rage! I've never heard of such a thing. And how do you know it was rage? She might have been red for dozens of reasons. She'd probably been chasing butterflies in the garden.

FATHER BLAZIUS: I can't say anything about that. You

may be right. But she was shouting as loudly as she could, 'Go on. Find him. Do what you're told. You're a fool. I insist.' And she beat Dame Pluche on the neck with her fan, so that with every blow the old woman leapt into the shrubbery.

BARON: The shrubbery? Well, what did the governess reply to my niece's extravagances? For that's the only way I can describe her conduct.

FATHER BLAZIUS: The governess replied, 'I won't go. I can't find him. He's chasing after village girls and shepherdesses. I'm too old to start carrying love letters. Thanks be to God I've lived a pure life till now.' And as she spoke, she crumpled up a little piece of folded paper.

BARON: I don't understand a word. My thoughts are completely confused. What reason could Dame Pluche have to crumple up a piece of folded paper and start leaping into the shrubbery? I can't believe in such monstrous behaviour.

FATHER BLAZIUS: But, my lord, don't you understand what that must mean?

BARON: No, my dear fellow, no. I understand absolutely nothing. It all seems most unruly behaviour, it's true, but as pointless as it's inexcusable.

FATHER BLAZIUS: It means that your niece is conducting a secret correspondence.

BARON: What are you saying? Remember who you're talking to. Weigh your words well, sir.

FATHER BLAZIUS: If I weighed them in the celestial balance that's to weigh my soul at the last judgement, I should not find one word that rings false. Your niece is conducting a secret correspondence.

BARON: But just think, my dear fellow. That's impossible.

FATHER BLAZIUS: Why should she give the governess a letter? Why should she cry 'Find him', while the old woman sulked and grumbled?

BARON: Who was this letter written to?

FATHER BLAZIUS: Precisely, my lord, there lies the whole kernel of the mystery. Who was this letter written to? A man who makes love to a shepherdess. Now if a man is publicly known to make love to girls who look after sheep, he may be strongly suspected of being born to look after them himself. However, it's impossible for your niece with her upbringing to be in love with such a man. That is what I say, and that is what I cannot understand, any more than you – with all respect, my lord.

BARON: Great heavens. Only this morning my niece told me she was refusing her cousin. She can't be in love with a shepherd! Let's go to my study. Since yesterday I've suffered such violent shocks, I can't collect my thoughts. (*They go out.*)

Scene IV

A woodland spring, later the same day.
PERDICAN enters, reading a note.

PERDICAN. 'Be at the little spring at twelve o'clock.' What can that mean? So very cold, so proud and hard, such a definite, cruel refusal, and after all this a rendezvous. If she wants to speak of business, why does she choose a place like this? Is it some feminine trick? This morning when I was walking with Rosette, I heard someone moving in the bushes, but I thought it was a deer. Is it a plot of some sort? (*CAMILLE enters.*)

CAMILLE: Good morning, Perdican. Rightly or wrongly, I thought you seemed sad when you left me earlier. You took my hand against my will; I have come to ask you to give me yours. I refused you a kiss; here it is. (*She kisses him.*) Just now you told me you would like to talk as friends. Sit down, let us talk. (*She sits.*)

PERDICAN: Was that a dream, or is this?

CAMILLE: You thought it strange to receive a note from me, didn't you? My moods change. But this morning you said something very true. 'As we're parting, let us part good friends.' You don't know the reason why I'm leaving and I have come to tell you. I am going to take the veil.

PERDICAN: I can't believe it! Is this you, Camille, reflected in this pool, sitting here as you used to long ago?

CAMILLE: Yes, Perdican, it is. I have come here to relive ten minutes of our past life. I seemed to you abrupt and haughty. It's quite simple; I have renounced the world. However, before I leave it, I should like to have your opinion. Do you think I'm right to become a nun?

PERDICAN: Don't ask me about that. I'll never become a monk.

CAMILLE: In the ten years we have lived apart, you have begun to experience life. I know what sort of man you are; with a heart and mind like yours you must have learned a great deal in a short time. Tell me, have you had mistresses?

PERDICAN: Why do you ask that?

CAMILLE: Answer me, please, without modesty and without conceit.

PERDICAN: I have had them.

CAMILLE: Did you love them?

PERDICAN: With all my heart.

CAMILLE: Where are they now? Do you know?

PERDICAN: Really, these are strange questions. What do you want me to tell you? I'm not their husband or their brother. They went wherever they wanted to go.

CAMILLE: There must have been one of them you loved more than the others. How long did you love the one you loved the best?

PERDICAN: You're a strange girl. Do you want to be my confessor?

CAMILLE: It's a favour I'm asking you, to answer me sincerely. You are certainly not a rake and I think you have an honest heart. You must have inspired love; you deserve it, you wouldn't have given way to a passing fancy. Answer me, please.

PERDICAN: I must say, I don't remember.

CAMILLE: Do you know any man who has loved only one woman?

PERDICAN: There are such people, certainly.

CAMILLE: Do you know one? Tell me his name.

PERDICAN: There's no name I can tell you. But I believe there are men capable of loving only once in their life.

CAMILLE: How many times can an honourable man fall in love?

PERDICAN: Do you want to make me say a litany, or are you saying a catechism?

CAMILLE: I want to learn, to know if I am right or wrong to become a nun. If I married you, wouldn't you have to answer frankly all my questions and show me your heart quite bare? I respect you highly; through your education and your nature I believe you to be superior to many other men. I am sorry you can't remember what I ask you; perhaps if I got to know you better, I should grow bolder.

PERDICAN: What are you trying to say? Tell me: I shall answer.

CAMILLE: Then answer my first question. Am I right to stay in the convent?

PERDICAN: No.

CAMILLE: Then I should do better to marry you?

PERDICAN: Yes.

CAMILLE: If your village priest breathed on a glass of water and told you it was a glass of wine, would you drink it as if it were?

PERDICAN: No.

CAMILLE: If your village priest breathed on you and told me you'd love me all your life, would I be right to believe him?

PERDICAN: Yes and no.

CAMILLE: What would you advise me to do the day I saw you didn't love me any more?

PERDICAN: Take a lover.

CAMILLE: Then what shall I do the day my lover doesn't love me any more?

PERDICAN: You'll take another.

CAMILLE: How long will that last?

PERDICAN: Till your hair is grey; and then mine will be white.

CAMILLE: Do you know what the cloister is, Perdican? Have you ever sat there for a whole day?

PERDICAN: Yes, I have.

CAMILLE: I have a friend, a sister who is only thirty years old and had an income of five hundred thousand livres at the age of fifteen. She is the loveliest and noblest creature who ever walked on earth. She was a peeress of the realm and her husband was one of the most distinguished men in France. All the noblest human qualities had flowered in her; no one has ever been lovelier or happier. Her husband deceived her; she loved another man; now she is dying of despair.

PERDICAN: That is possible.

CAMILLE: We live in the same cell and I have spent whole nights talking of her misfortunes. They have almost become mine. That is strange, isn't it? I don't know how it happens. She told me of her marriage, she painted for me the ecstasy of the first days, then the peace of others, and how finally everything vanished; in the evening she would sit by the fire and he by the window, without exchanging a single word; their love had languished and every effort to come together only ended in quarrels; then little by little a strange face came to stand between them and glide into their sorrows. When she spoke, it was myself I saw. When she said: 'Then, I was happy', my heart leapt; and when she added: 'Then, I cried', my tears flowed. But do you know something even stranger? I finished by creating for myself an imaginary life. That has lasted for four years. There's no point in explaining all the meditations and heart searching that brought this about. What I wanted to tell you, as a curiosity, is that all Louise's stories, all the fictions of my dreams, bore your likeness.

PERDICAN: My likeness? Mine?

CAMILLE: Yes; it's natural. You were the only man I had known. It's a fact; I loved you, Perdican.

PERDICAN: How old are you, Camille?

CAMILLE: Eighteen.

PERDICAN: Go on, go on. I'm listening.

CAMILLE: There are two hundred women in our convent. A few of these women will never know life and all the rest are waiting for death. More than one of them has left the convent, as I leave it now, young and full of hope. They came back soon afterwards, old and desolate. Every day one of them dies in our dormitories and every day a new one arrives to take the place of the dead on their horsehair mattress. When strangers visit us, they admire the calm and order of our house. They look with interest at the whiteness of our veils. But they ask why we lower them over our eyes. What do you think of these women, Perdican? Are they wrong or are they right?

PERDICAN: I have no idea.

CAMILLE: Some of them have advised me to remain unmarried. I'd like your opinion. Do you believe those women would have done better to take a lover and to advise me to do the same?

PERDICAN: I have no idea.

CAMILLE: You promised to answer.

PERDICAN: Obviously I'm excused. I don't believe it's you speaking.

CAMILLE: You may be right. In all these thoughts of mine there must be very silly things. It may be I've been learning a lesson and I'm only an ill-taught parrot. In the gallery there's a little picture of a monk bent over a missal; through the dark bars of his cell glides a feeble ray of sunshine; you can see an Italian inn and next to it a goatherd is dancing. Which of those men do you admire most?

PERDICAN: Neither and both. They're two men of flesh and blood. One of them's reading and the other's dancing. I see nothing else. You are right to become a nun.

CAMILLE: Just now you told me no.

PERDICAN: Did I say 'No'? Perhaps I did.

CAMILLE: And so that is what you advise?

PERDICAN: And so you believe in nothing?

CAMILLE: Raise your head, Perdican. What kind of man believes in nothing?

PERDICAN: (*Rising.*) Here is one. I don't believe in immortal
    life. My dear, the nuns have given you their experience,
    but believe me it won't be yours. You won't die without
    loving.

CAMILLE: I want to love, but I don't want to suffer. I want to
    love with an eternal love and make vows that will not be
    broken. Here is my lover. (*She shows her crucifix.*)

PERDICAN: That lover does not exclude others.

CAMILLE: For me at least it will exclude them. Don't smile,
    Perdican. For ten years I haven't seen you and I leave
    tomorrow. After another ten years, if we meet, we'll talk
    of this again. I didn't want to remain in your memory as
    a cold statue, because lack of feeling can lead to the point
    I have reached. Listen to me. Return to life; and as long
    as you are happy, as long as you love, as one can love on
    earth, forget your sister Camille. But if it ever happens
    to you to be forgotten, or to forget, if the angel of hope
    abandons you, then when you're alone with a void in your
    heart, think of me. I shall pray for you.

PERDICAN: You are proud. Be careful.

CAMILLE: Why?

PERDICAN: You are eighteen and you don't believe in love?

CAMILLE: Do you believe in it? You? Here you are bent
    before me on knees that have worn themselves out on
    the carpets of mistresses whose names you don't even
    remember. You've wept tears of joy and tears of despair.
    But you knew the water in the springs is more constant
    than your tears and it would always be there to bathe your
    swollen eyelids. You behave as young men always do, you
    smile when you're told of women who are desolate. You
    don't think anyone can die of love, but you live, you have
    loved. Well, what is the world? I'd have thought you'd
    heartily despise the women who take you, such as you are,
    and chase away their last lover to welcome you in their
    arms with someone else's kisses on their lips. Just now I
    asked you if you'd ever loved and you answered like a
    traveller who's asked if he has ever been in Germany or
    Italy and says 'Yes, I've been there'; then he thinks of going

to Switzerland or the first country that comes into his mind.
Is your love a coin to pass from hand to hand till death?
No, it's not even a coin. The smallest piece of gold is worth
more than you and keeps its likeness in whatever hands it
passes.

PERDICAN: How beautiful you are, when your eyes flash.

CAMILLE: Yes, I am beautiful, I know. Flattery won't teach
me anything. When the cold nun cuts off my hair, she
may perhaps grow pale at the mutilation she is wreaking.
But my hair will not be made into rings and chains to be
sported in boudoirs. Not one hair will be missing from my
head when the iron passes over it. I want a single stroke of
the scissors. Then when the priest blesses me and puts on
my finger the golden ring of my celestial husband, the lock
of hair which I give him will serve him as a mantle.

PERDICAN: Yes, you are really angry.

CAMILLE: I was wrong to speak. My whole life is on my lips.
Oh, Perdican, don't smile. It's so sad, it breaks my heart.

PERDICAN: Poor child, I've let you speak. Now I should like
to say a word in reply. You told me of a nun who seems
to have had a dismal influence on you. You say she was
deceived, she herself deceived her husband, and she is in
despair. Are you sure that if her husband or her lover came
back to stretch out his hand through the convent grille, she
would not stretch out her own to take it?

CAMILLE: What did you say? I didn't understand.

PERDICAN: Are you sure that if her husband or her lover
came back to tell her to suffer once more, she would
answer 'No'?

CAMILLE: I believe so.

PERDICAN: There are two hundred women in your convent
and the majority of them in the depths of their hearts have
the deepest wounds. They have made you feel them, they
have coloured your girlish thoughts with drops of their
blood. They have lived, haven't they? And they have
shown you with horror the road they have travelled. You
have crossed yourself before their scars as you would
before the wounds of Christ. They have given you a place

in their gloomy processions and you squeeze up against their skinny bodies with religious terror when you see a man go by. Are you sure that if that man was the one who deceived them, and made them weep and suffer, the man they're cursing as they pray to God, are you sure that at the sight of him they wouldn't break their chains to run toward their past miseries and press their bleeding breasts against the dagger that stabbed them? Oh, my child! Do you know the dreams of these women who tell you not to dream? Do you know what name they're murmuring as the sobs on their lips make the Host tremble when it's given to them? These women sit next to you with shaking heads to pour into your ear their withered old age, they sound the tocsin of their despair in the ruins of your youth and make your bright red blood feel the coldness of their tomb. But do you know what they are?

CAMILLE: You frighten me. You are angry too.

PERDICAN: Do you know what these nuns are, you wretched girl? These women represent to you the love of men as a lie, but do they know there is something still worse, the lie of divine love? Do they know what a sin they're committing to come and whisper these women's words into the ear of a young girl? Oh, how well they've taught you! Yes, this is what I expected when you stopped before our old aunt's portrait. You wanted to leave without shaking my hand. You didn't wish to see this little copse or this spring which looks at us and weeps. You were denying the days of your childhood and the plaster mask the nuns have placed on your cheeks refused me a brother's kiss. But your heart was beating. It couldn't read, it had forgotten its lesson, so you came back to sit on the grass and here we are. All right. Camille, these women have spoken well. They have put you on the right road. It will have cost me my life's happiness, but tell them from me, 'Heaven is not for them'.

CAMILLE: Nor for me, you mean?

PERDICAN: Goodbye, Camille. Go back to your convent. And when they recall these dreadful stories that have

poisoned your mind, tell them what I am going to say
to you now. All men are liars, false, gossips, hypocrites;
proud or cowardly, despicable and sensual. All women are
faithless, artful, vain, inquisitive, and depraved. The world
is just a bottomless sewer, where shapeless beasts writhe
and crawl on mountains of mire. But in this world there
is one thing holy and sublime; that is the union of two of
these imperfect, frightful creatures. We are often deceived
in love, often hurt, often unhappy. But we love. And when
we are on the edge of the grave, we turn round to look
back and say, 'I have often suffered, sometimes made
mistakes, but I have loved. It is I who have lived, not some
artificial being created by my pride and my despair.'
(*He goes out.*)

ACT THREE

Scene I

A room in the castle, the next day.
The BARON and FATHER BLAZIUS enter.

BARON: Apart from your drunkenness, Father Blazius, you're a rogue. My servants saw you secretly enter the cellar, and when you're convicted of stealing my wine in the most pitiful manner, you think to justify yourself by accusing my niece of conducting a secret correspondence.

FATHER BLAZIUS: But, my lord, do please remember…

BARON: Get out, sir, and never let me see you again. It's beyond all reason to behave as you have done, and my position forces me never to forgive you for the rest of my life. (*The BARON goes out. FATHER BLAZIUS follows. PERDICAN enters.*)

PERDICAN: I should so like to know if I'm in love. First of all, this manner of asking questions is rather cavalier for a girl of eighteen. Then the ideas these nuns have planted in her head will be difficult to root out. Besides she's due to leave today. Devil take it, I love her, that's certain. After all, who knows? Perhaps she was repeating a lesson and anyway it's plain she doesn't care for me. And I don't mind if she is pretty, that doesn't prevent her being much too decided in her ways and sharp in her manner. All I have to do is to think no more about it. It's plain I don't love her. She certainly is pretty. But why can't I get yesterday's conversation out of my mind? It's a fact, I've been talking nonsense all night. Now where was I going? Ah yes, to the village. (*Goes out.*)

Scene II

The village square, immediately afterwards.
FATHER BRIDAINE enters.

FATHER BRIDAINE: What are they doing now? Ah me,

it's twelve o'clock. They are sitting down to dinner. What are they eating? What are they not eating? I saw the cook crossing the square with an enormous turkey. The kitchen maid was carrying truffles and a basket of grapes.
(*FATHER BLAZIUS enters.*)

FATHER BLAZIUS: Who could have foreseen this disgrace? Here I am, turned out of the castle and of course the dining room. I shall never again drink wine from that cellar.

FATHER BRIDAINE: I shall never again smell those glorious dishes. I shall never again warm my ample stomach at the fire of that noble hearth.

FATHER BLAZIUS: Why did such fatal curiosity make me listen to Dame Pluche's conversation with his niece? Why did I report to the Baron everything I saw?

FATHER BRIDAINE: Why have pride and vanity made me quit that splendid table where I was so warmly welcomed? What did it matter if I was on the right or on the left?

FATHER BLAZIUS: Ah me, I was drunk, I must admit, when I behaved so foolishly.

FATHER BRIDAINE: Ah me, the wine had gone to my head, when I acted so imprudently.

FATHER BLAZIUS: I think I see the priest.

FATHER BRIDAINE: It's the tutor in person.

FATHER BLAZIUS: Oh, oh, my dear sir, what are you doing here?

FATHER BRIDAINE: I'm going to dinner. Aren't you coming?

FATHER BLAZIUS: Not today. Oh, Father Bridaine, intercede on my behalf. The Baron has turned me out. I falsely accused Camille of having a secret correspondence but as God's my witness, I saw, or thought I saw, Dame Pluche in the shrubbery. My dear sir, I'm ruined.

FATHER BRIDAINE: What's that you're telling me?

FATHER BLAZIUS: The truth, the truth. I'm in complete disgrace for stealing a bottle of wine.

FATHER BRIDAINE: What are you saying, sir, about stolen bottles and correspondence in a shrubbery?

FATHER BLAZIUS: I beg you to plead my cause. I'm an

honest man, my lord Bridaine. Oh, worthy lord Bridaine, I am your servant.

FATHER BRIDAINE: (*Aside.*) What good fortune! Am I dreaming? So I shall once again be sitting on you, happy, happy chair.

FATHER BLAZIUS: I'd be so grateful if you'd listen to my story. Do please excuse me, my worthy lord, my dear, dear sir.

FATHER BRIDAINE: That is impossible, sir. It has struck twelve and I am going to dinner. If the Baron complains about you, that is your business. I shall certainly not intercede for a drunkard. (*Aside.*) Quick, let us fly to the gate. Oh, my beloved stomach, extend yourself to capacity. (*FATHER BRIDAINE goes out, running.*)

FATHER BLAZIUS: Wretched Pluche, I'll make you pay for this. Yes, you're the cause of my disgrace, shameless woman, vilest go-between, it's through you I'm ruined. Oh, holy University of Paris! I've been called a drunkard! I'm ruined if I can't seize a letter and prove to the Baron that his niece has a secret correspondence. I saw her this morning writing at her desk. Patience, here comes Pluche again.
(*DAME PLUCHE enters, carrying a letter.*)
Pluche, give me that letter.

DAME PLUCHE: What does this mean? It's a letter from my mistress. I'm going to send it off in the village.

FATHER BLAZIUS: Give it to me or I'll kill you.

DAME PLUCHE: Me? Kill me? Mary, Jesus, saints and martyrs!

FATHER BLAZIUS: Yes, Pluche, kill you. Give me that letter.
(*They fight.*
PERDICAN enters.)

PERDICAN: What's happening? What are you doing, Blazius? Why are you assaulting this woman?

DAME PLUCHE: Give me back the letter. He took it from me, my lord. I demand justice.

FATHER BLAZIUS: She's a go-between, my lord. It's a love letter.

DAME PLUCHE: It's a letter from Camille, my lord, from your betrothed.

FATHER BLAZIUS: It's a love letter to a shepherd boy.

DAME PLUCHE: You're a liar, Father. And I'm happy to tell you so.

PERDICAN: Give me this letter. I don't understand a word you're saying, but as I'm going to marry Camille, I take upon myself the right to read it. (*He reads.*) 'To Sister Louise, at the convent of…' (*Aside.*) What dreadful curiosity seizes me in spite of myself? My heart beats so strongly, I don't know what I feel. You may go, Dame Pluche. You're a respectable woman and Father Blazius is a fool. Go to dinner. I will see that this letter's delivered.

(*DAME PLUCHE and FATHER BLAZIUS go out.*)

It's wrong to open a letter, I know that too well to do it. What can Camille be saying to this sister? Can I be in love? But what hold has this strange girl obtained over me to make my hand tremble at seeing this address? How odd! In fighting with Dame Pluche, Blazius has broken the seal. Is it wrong to unfold the paper? After all, I shan't change anything. (*He opens the letter and reads.*) 'I am leaving today, my dear, and everything has happened as I expected. It's a terrible thing, but this young man is heartbroken. He will never be consoled for losing me. But I have done everything I could to make him hate me. God will forgive me for reducing him to despair by my refusal. But, my dear, what could I do? Pray for me. We shall see each other again tomorrow and always. All my love to you, my dearest heart, Camille.'

I can't believe it. Camille wrote this? It's me she's talking about! I am in despair at her refusal! By God, we'll see if that's true. What is there to be ashamed of in being in love? She has done everything she could to make me hate her, she says, and I'm heartbroken. What purpose can she have in inventing such a story? So it's true what I thought last night? Oh, women! This poor girl may be very pious. With the greatest joy she gives herself to God, but she resolved and decreed to leave me in despair. It was settled between these two good friends before she left the convent. It was decided that Camille would see her cousin, they would want to make him marry her, she'd refuse, and he'd be miserable. How very interesting, a young girl sacrifices her cousin's happiness to God! No, no, Camille, I don't love you, I'm not in despair, I'm not heartbroken, and I'll prove it to you. Yes, you'll know I love someone else before you leave here. Hey, there, fellow!

(*A PEASANT enters.*)

Go up to the castle and tell them in the kitchen to give this letter to Camille. (*He writes.*)

PEASANT: Yes, my lord. (*Goes out.*)

PERDICAN: Now then. I'm in despair, am I? Hey there, Rosette, Rosette! (*He knocks at her door.*)

(*ROSETTE opens the door.*)

ROSETTE: It's you, my lord! Come in, my mother's here.

PERDICAN: Put on your prettiest bonnet, Rosette, and come with me.

ROSETTE: Wherever to?

PERDICAN: I'm going to tell you. Ask your mother's permission; but hurry.

ROSETTE: Yes, my lord.

(*ROSETTE goes into the house.*)

PERDICAN: I've asked Camille for another rendezvous and I'm sure she'll come. But by heaven she won't find what she expects to find. I'm going to make love to Rosette in front of Camille herself.

Scene III

The woodland spring.
CAMILLE and the PEASANT enter.

PEASANT: I was going to the castle with this letter for you. Should I give it to you now or leave it in the kitchen as Perdican told me?

CAMILLE: Give it to me.

PEASANT: If you'd rather I took it to the castle, it's no trouble.

CAMILLE: I tell you to give it me.

PEASANT: As you wish. (*He gives her the letter.*)

CAMILLE: Here. Take this for your pains.

PEASANT: Many thanks. I'll go, shall I?

CAMILLE: If you want to.

PEASANT: I'll go, I'll go. (*Goes out.*)

CAMILLE: (*Reading.*) Perdican asks me to say goodbye to him, before I go, at the little spring where I made him come yesterday. What can he have to say to me? But here is the spring and I am ready. Should I grant him this second meeting? Oh! (*She hides behind a tree.*) Here he comes with Rosette. I suppose he'll leave her. I'm glad I shan't seem the first to arrive.

(*PERDICAN and ROSETTE enter and sit down. CAMILLE is hidden.*)

What does this mean? He makes her sit down next to him? Has he asked me to meet him here, so he can talk to someone else? I'm curious to know what he'll say to her.

PERDICAN: (*Aloud, so that CAMILLE shall hear.*) I love you, Rosette. You're the one person in the world who hasn't forgotten the lovely days gone by. Only you remember the life of long ago. Take part in my new life. Here is the pledge of our love. (*He puts his chain around her neck.*)

ROSETTE: You're giving me your gold chain?

PERDICAN: Now look at this ring. Get up, come to the pool. Do you see us both in the water, leaning on each other's arm? Do you see your lovely eyes next to mine, your hand in my hand? Watch it all disappear. (*He throws his ring in the water.*) See how our image has vanished? Here it is, coming slowly back. The troubled water resumes its calm. It still trembles. Great black circles rise to the surface. Be patient, we shall soon be there once more. I can already see your arms entwined again in mine. One more minute and not a single wrinkle will remain on your pretty face. Look. It was a ring Camille gave me.

CAMILLE: (*Aside.*) He threw my ring in the water.

PERDICAN: Do you know what love is, Rosette? Listen. The wind is silent. The morning rain rolls in pearls off the dry leaves, but the sun is giving them new life. By the light of heaven, by this sun you see above, I love you. You wish me well, don't you? Your youth has not been withered? The dregs of a faded blood have not been filtered into your pure, bright scarlet? You don't want to become a nun. Here you are, young and lovely, in the arms of a young man. Oh, Rosette, Rosette, do you know what love is?

ROSETTE: Oh, my lord, I'll love you as best I can.

PERDICAN: Yes, as best you can. And although you've never been to school, you'll love me better than these pale statues fashioned by the nuns, who have a head instead of a heart, and leave their cloisters to come and spread through life the damp atmosphere of their cells. You know nothing. You can't read in a book the prayer your mother teaches you, as her mother once taught it to her. You don't even understand the words you're repeating when you kneel at the foot of your bed. But you understand well enough that you're praying and that is all that God requires.

ROSETTE: The things you say, my lord.

PERDICAN: You can't read. But you know what these woods and meadows are saying, these warm streams, these lovely fields ripe with harvest, the whole of nature splendid in its youth. You recognise all these thousands of brothers and me as one of them. Get to your feet. You shall be my wife and we will take root together in the sap of the all-powerful world.

(*PERDICAN and ROSETTE go out.*)

Scene IV

The village square, later the same day.
CHORUS enters.

CHORUS: Something strange is happening at the castle. Camille has refused to marry Perdican. She should return today to her convent. But I believe her noble cousin has been consoling himself with Rosette. I fear the poor girl doesn't know the danger she runs in listening to the speeches of a young and gallant gentleman.

(*DAME PLUCHE enters.*)

DAME PLUCHE: Quick, quick, saddle my mule.

CHORUS: Will you leave us like a passing dream, oh
venerable dame? Are you going so soon to straddle once
more that wretched beast which does so hate to carry you?

DAME PLUCHE: Thanks be to God, dear rabble, I shall not
die here.

CHORUS: Die far away then, Pluche, my sweet. Die
unknown in some insanitary cellar. We shall offer up
prayers for your respected resurrection.

DAME PLUCHE: Here comes my mistress.

(*CAMILLE enters.*)

Camille dear, everything is ready for our departure. The
Baron has finished the accounts and my mule is saddled.

CAMILLE: Go to the devil and take your mule with you. I
shan't leave here today. (*Goes out.*)

CHORUS: What does this mean? Dame Pluche grows pale
with fright. Her false hair tries hard to stand on end, her
lungs whistle loudly, her fingers stretch and claw.

DAME PLUCHE: Beloved Jesus! She used bad language!
(*Goes out.*)

(*The BARON enters, followed by FATHER BRIDAINE.*)

FATHER BRIDAINE: My lord, I must speak to you most
urgently. Your son is making love to a girl from the village.

BARON: Don't be absurd, my dear fellow.

FATHER BRIDAINE: I distinctly saw him walking in the
woods with her, arm in arm. He was whispering in her ear
and promising to marry her.

BARON: This is monstrous.

FATHER BRIDAINE: Be convinced of it. He has given her
a considerable present and the child has shown it to her
mother.

BARON: Oh, great heavens! Considerable, Bridaine? In what
way was it considerable?

FATHER BRIDAINE: In its value and its meaning. It's his
gold chain.

BARON: Let us go to my study. I don't know what to think.
(*They go out.*)

Scene V

A room in the castle, later the same day.
CAMILLE and DAME PLUCHE enter.

CAMILLE. He took my letter, you say?

DAME PLUCHE: Yes, my child. He undertook to have it delivered.

CAMILLE: Dame Pluche, be so good as to go and tell Perdican that I'm waiting for him here. (*DAME PLUCHE goes out.*) He read my letter, that's certain. The scene he staged in the wood was in revenge, like his love for Rosette. He wanted to show me he loved someone else and pretend not to care in spite of being angry. Would he by any chance be in love with me? (*She raises a curtain.*) Are you there, Rosette?
(*ROSETTE appears.*)

ROSETTE: Yes. May I come in?

CAMILLE: Listen to me, my child. Perdican has made love to you, hasn't he?

ROSETTE: (*Sadly.*) Yes, he has.

CAMILLE: What do you think of all he told you this morning?

ROSETTE: This morning? Why, where?

CAMILLE: Don't play the hypocrite. This morning, at the spring, in the copse.

ROSETTE: So you saw me?

CAMILLE: Poor little innocent! No, I didn't see you. He made fine speeches, didn't he? I'm sure he promised to marry you.

ROSETTE: How do you know that?

CAMILLE: What does it matter how I know? Do you believe in his promises, Rosette?

ROSETTE: Why shouldn't I? You mean he'd deceive me? Why should he?

CAMILLE: Perdican won't marry you, my dear.

ROSETTE: I don't know anything about that.

CAMILLE: You love him, poor child. He won't marry you. As for proof, I'm going to give it to you. Go back behind this curtain. You have only to listen and come when I call you. (*ROSETTE goes out.*) I thought I'd do an act of revenge; but will it be an act of kindness? The poor girl is deeply in love with him.

(*PERDICAN enters.*)

Good afternoon, Perdican. Sit down.

PERDICAN: What a lovely dress, Camille. Who are you angry with?

CAMILLE: You, perhaps. I'm sorry I couldn't come to the rendezvous you gave me. Was there something you wanted to talk about?

PERDICAN: (*Aside.*) I must say that's a pretty big little lie for a stainless lamb. I saw her behind a tree listening to our conversation. (*Aloud.*) All I have to say to you is goodbye, Camille. I thought you had gone. But your horse is in the stable and you don't look as though you're dressed for travel.

CAMILLE: I like argument. I am not sure I wouldn't like to quarrel with you again.

PERDICAN: What's the point of quarrelling when reconciliation is impossible? The pleasure of a dispute lies in making peace.

CAMILLE: Are you convinced I don't want to do that?

PERDICAN: Don't joke. I'm not feeling strong enough to answer you.

CAMILLE: I should like to be made love to. I don't know if it's because I have a new dress, but I want to enjoy myself. You suggested we should go down to the village. Let us go, I should like to. Let's take the boat. I want to dine in the open air or walk in the forest. Will there be a moon this evening? How strange, you aren't wearing the ring I gave you.

PERDICAN: I've lost it.

CAMILLE: Then that is how I found it. Look, Perdican, here it is.

PERDICAN: I can't believe it. Where did you find it?

CAMILLE: You are looking to see if my hands are wet, aren't you? It's a fact, I spoiled my convent dress in taking this little children's plaything out of the spring. That is why I'm wearing another, and I tell you it has changed me. So put this on your finger.

PERDICAN: You took this ring from the water? Am I dreaming? You're here! You're putting it on my finger! Oh, Camille, why do you give me back this sad pledge of a happiness that no longer exists? Say something. Why are you going? Why are you staying? Why from one hour to the next do you change appearance and colour, like the stone of this ring at each ray of sunshine?

CAMILLE: Do you understand women, Perdican? Are you sure of their inconstancy? Do you know if they really change their thoughts when they sometimes change their language? Some people say they don't. No doubt we must often play a part, often lie. You see I'm being frank. But are you sure that a woman lies with her whole being when she lies with her tongue? Have you considered the nature of this feeble, violent creature, how strictly she is judged, the principles that are imposed upon her? And who knows whether this little brainless being, forced by the world to deceive, can't take pleasure in so doing, and sometimes lie for amusement, as she lies for necessity?

PERDICAN: I don't understand any of this. I never lie. I love you, Camille, that's all I know.

CAMILLE: You say you love me and you never lie?

PERDICAN: Never.

CAMILLE: Yet here is someone who says it happens to you occasionally.

(*She raises the curtain. ROSETTE can be seen on a chair, unconscious.*)

How will you answer this child, Perdican, when she asks you to account for your words? If you never lie, how did she happen to faint when she heard you say you loved me? I leave you with her. Try to revive her. (*She wishes to go out.*)

PERDICAN: One moment, Camille, listen to me.

CAMILLE: What do you want to say? It's Rosette you must speak to. I don't love you. I didn't take this poor girl out of spite from her cottage to make her a bait, a plaything. I didn't recite to her ardent phrases addressed to someone else. I didn't pretend to throw away for her sake the souvenir of a cherished friendship. I didn't put my chain round her neck. I didn't tell her I'd marry her.

PERDICAN: Listen to me, listen to me.

CAMILLE: You smiled just now, didn't you, when I told you I couldn't go to the spring? Very well then. Yes, I was there and I heard everything. But God is my witness, I wouldn't wish to have spoken as you did. What will you do with this girl now, when she comes in tears with your burning kisses on her lips to show you how you've wounded her? You wanted to revenge yourself on me, didn't you, to punish me for the letter I wrote to the convent? At any price you wanted to deal some blow which could strike me, and you didn't care if your poisoned arrow pierced this girl, provided it hit me standing behind her. I prided myself I'd inspired in you some love, I'd leave you feeling some regret. And that wounded your noble pride? Very well then. Allow me to tell you, you love me, do you hear? But you shall marry this girl or you're nothing but a coward.

PERDICAN: Yes, I shall marry her.

CAMILLE: And you will do well to.

PERDICAN: Very well, and much better than marrying you. What is it that makes you so heated? This child has fainted. We must bring her to and all we need for that is a little vinegar. You wanted to prove I'd lied once in my life. That may be so, but I think it impudent of you to decide which time it was. Come and help me to revive Rosette.

(*They go out.*)

Scene VI

A room in the castle, a little later.
The BARON and CAMILLE enter.

BARON. If that happens, I shall go out of my mind.

CAMILLE: Use your authority.

BARON: I shall go out of my mind and refuse my consent. That much is certain.

CAMILLE: You must speak to him and make him listen to reason.

BARON: This will throw me into despair for the whole season; I shan't be able to appear once at court. It's a marriage out of all proportion. No one's ever heard tell of marrying a cousin's foster sister. That passes every kind of bounds.

CAMILLE: Have him sent for, tell him clearly you don't like this marriage. Believe me, it's a sudden whim; he won't resist.

BARON: I shall wear black all winter, you may take that for granted.

CAMILLE: But speak to him, for heaven's sake. It's a desperate impulse. Perhaps it's too late already. If he's said he'll do it, he will.

BARON: I shall shut myself up to abandon myself to my grief. If he asks for me, tell him I have shut myself up and I'm abandoning myself to my grief at seeing him marry a nameless girl. (*Goes out.*)

CAMILLE: Shan't I ever find a man of courage? Really, when you look for one, it's frightening how alone you are. (*PERDICAN enters.*)
Well, Perdican, when is the wedding to be?

PERDICAN: As soon as possible. I've already spoken to the notary, the priest, and all the village.

CAMILLE: Then you definitely intend to marry Rosette?

PERDICAN: Certainly.

CAMILLE: What will your father say?

PERDICAN: Whatever he likes. I want to marry this girl. It's an idea I owe to you and I'm keeping to it. Do I have to tell you again the ties that join her birth and mine? She is young and pretty and she loves me. That's more than we need, to be three times happy. Whether she's intelligent or whether she isn't, I could have found worse. Let people complain and laugh. I wash my hands of the matter.

CAMILLE: There's nothing to laugh at in that. You do well to marry her. But there is one thing that makes me sorry for you; people will say you have done it out of spite.

PERDICAN: You are sorry about that? Oh no, you're not.

CAMILLE: Yes, I am really sorry for you. It's bad for a young man, if he can't resist a moment of spite.

PERDICAN: Then be sorry. As far as I'm concerned, it's all the same to me.

CAMILLE: You can't be serious. She's a nobody.

PERDICAN: Then she'll be somebody, when she's my wife.

CAMILLE: She will bore you before the notary has put on his new coat and shoes to come here. You will lose all appetite at the wedding breakfast.

PERDICAN: You'll see I shan't. You don't know me. When a woman is sweet and sensitive, young and good and lovely, I'm capable of being content with that, yes, it's a fact, to the point of not caring whether she can speak Latin.

CAMILLE: It's a pity so much money has been spent in teaching it to you. That's three thousand crowns wasted.

PERDICAN: Yes. They'd have done better to give them to the poor.

CAMILLE: You will be doing that, at least to the poor in spirit.

PERDICAN: And they will give me in exchange the Kingdom of Heaven; for it is theirs.

CAMILLE: How long will this little joke last?

PERDICAN: What little joke?

CAMILLE: Your marriage to Rosette.

PERDICAN: Not very long. God didn't make man a very lasting work. Thirty or forty years at the most.

CAMILLE: I look forward to dancing at your wedding!

PERDICAN: Now listen, Camille, that bantering tone is quite unseasonable.

CAMILLE: I like it too much to leave it.

PERDICAN: Then I'll leave you. I've had enough of this just now.

CAMILLE: Are you going to see your bride?

PERDICAN: Yes, right away.

CAMILLE: Then give me your arm. I'll go with you.

(*ROSETTE enters.*)

PERDICAN: There you are, my dear. Come with me, I want you to meet my father.

ROSETTE: My lord, I've come to ask you a favour. Everyone I've spoken to in the village this morning tells me you're in love with your cousin and you only made love to me to amuse you both. They all make fun of me when I go by; I shall never be able to find a husband after being the laughing-stock of the whole village. Allow me to give you back the chain you gave me and let me live in peace with my mother.

CAMILLE: You're a good girl, Rosette. Keep the chain. I give it to you and my cousin will take mine in its place. Don't worry about a husband, I undertake to find you one.

PERDICAN: That's not difficult, I must say. Come, Rosette, let me take you to my father.

CAMILLE: Why? There's no point.

PERDICAN: Yes, you're right. My father would receive us badly. This first moment of surprise he is feeling must be allowed to pass. Come with me, we'll go back to the village. I find it amusing they say I don't love you when I'm going to marry you. By God, we'll make them hold their tongues.

(*He goes out with ROSETTE.*)

CAMILLE: What's happening inside me? He took her away so calmly. How strange this is! I think I feel faint. Does he really mean to marry her? Hey, there! Dame Pluche! Dame Pluche! Is there no one here?

(*A SERVANT enters.*)

Run after Perdican. Tell him to come back here. I want to talk to him. (*The SERVANT goes out.*) But what is all this? I'm exhausted, my feet won't support me.

(*PERDICAN enters.*)

PERDICAN: You sent for me, Camille?

CAMILLE: No. No.

PERDICAN: You are really very pale. What do you want to say? You called me back to speak to me?

CAMILLE: No, no. Oh God! (*Goes out.*)

Scene VII

The castle chapel, immediately afterward.
CAMILLE enters and throws herself down at the foot of the altar.

CAMILLE. Oh God, have You abandoned me? When I came here, you know I swore to be faithful to You. When I refused to become the bride of another, I thought I was speaking sincerely before You and my conscience. You know that, Father, so why don't You want me any more? Oh, why do You make truth itself lie? Why am I so weak? Oh, I can't pray any more.
(*PERDICAN enters.*)

PERDICAN: Oh, why did pride have to come between this girl and me? There she is, pale and frightened, pressing her heart and face on the unfeeling stones. She could have loved me; we were born for each other. Oh, what did pride do to our lips, when our hands were about to join?

CAMILLE: Who has followed me? Who is speaking over there? Is that you, Perdican?

PERDICAN: What fools we are! We love each other. What dream did we create, Camille? What vain words and miserable stupidities have passed like a blighted wind between us? Which of us wanted to deceive the other? Oh, this life itself is such a painful dream. Why should we mingle our own dreams with it? Oh, God, happiness is so rare a pearl in this ocean here on earth. But You gave it to us, You plucked this priceless jewel from the depths of the abyss, and we're such spoiled children, we made a plaything of it. Of course vanity and gossip and anger had to come between us. Of course we had to do wrong because we're men. Oh, what fools we are! We love each other. (*He takes her in his arms.*)

CAMILLE: Yes, Perdican, we love each other. Let me feel it on your heart. God is watching us, but He will not be offended. He wants me to love you; for fifteen years He has known it.

PERDICAN: My darling, you belong to me. (*He kisses her.*)
(*A great cry is heard from behind the altar.*)

CAMILLE: That is Rosette's voice.

PERDICAN: How can she be here? I left her on the stairs, when you sent for me. She must have followed me without my noticing.

CAMILLE: Come to the gallery. That is where the cry came from.

PERDICAN: I don't know what I feel. I think my hands are stained with blood.

CAMILLE: Poor child, she must have been watching us. She has fainted again. Let us go and help her. Oh, how cruel this all is!

PERDICAN: No, I will not go there. I feel a mortal cold that paralyses me. Go and try to bring her round. (*CAMILLE goes out.*) I beseech you, God; do not make me a murderer. You see what is happening. We are two foolish children and we have played with life and death. But our hearts are pure. Do not kill Rosette! God, be just! I will find her a husband; I will redeem my fault. She is young; she shall be rich, she shall be happy. Do not do this thing, oh God! You can still bless four of your children.

(*CAMILLE re-enters.*)

Well, Camille, what is it?

CAMILLE: She is dead. Goodbye, Perdican.

THE CANDLESTICK
(Le Chandelier)

Characters

ANDRÉ, an elderly country lawyer

JACQUELINE, his young wife

CLAVAROCHE, a cavalry officer

FREDERICK, a clerk

FORTUNIO, a clerk

WILLIAM, a clerk

MADELEINE, Jacqueline's maid

PETER, a gardener

SERVANT

The action takes place in André's house and garden in a small French provincial town.

This translation of *The Candlestick* was first transmitted by the
BBC Third Programme on Tuesday 3 August 1965, with the
following cast:

ANDRÉ, Willoughby Goddard

JACQUELINE, Susannah York

CLAVAROCHE, Joss Ackland

FREDERICK, Alan Haines

FORTUNIO, Gordon Gardner

WILLIAM, Nigel Graham

MADELEINE, Jane Wenham

PETER, Bruce Beeby

SERVANT, Bruce Beeby

Produced by Charles Lefeaux

ACT ONE

Scene I

JACQUELINE's bedroom, early morning.
JACQUELINE is in bed. ANDRÉ enters in a dressing gown, holding a candlestick.

ANDRÉ: Hey there! Ho, Jacqueline! Hey, hallo, Jacqueline! What a sleepy girl! Hey, hey, wake up! Hallo, hallo, get up, Jacqueline! She sleeps so soundly! Hallo, hallo, hallo, hey, hey, hey! It's me, André, your husband. I've something serious to talk about. Hey, hey, pst, pst, hm, brm, brm, pst! Jacqueline, are you dead? If you don't wake up this minute, I'll crown you with the water jug.

JACQUELINE: What's the matter, darling?

ANDRÉ: Bless my soul, it's about time. Will you stop stretching your arms? It's all very well to go on sleeping. Now listen, I want to talk to you. Last night, Frederick, my clerk…

JACQUELINE: Good heavens, it's not yet daylight. Have you gone mad, to wake me up in this stupid way? Do please get back to bed. Are you ill?

ANDRÉ: I'm not mad or ill; and I know just what I'm about in waking you up. I want to talk to you now. Just listen to me first and then answer my questions. This is what happened to Frederick, my clerk: you know him, of course…

JACQUELINE: What's the time, please?

ANDRÉ: Six o'clock. Pay attention to what I'm saying. It's not a pleasant subject and no laughing matter. My honour, and yours, perhaps our whole life together, depend on the explanation I'm going to get from you. This very night Frederick, my clerk, saw…

JACQUELINE: My dear, if you're ill, you should have told me earlier. Isn't it my duty to look after you and take good care of you?

ANDRÉ: I'm quite well, I tell you. Are you in a mood to listen?

JACQUELINE: Good heavens, you frighten me. Have we been robbed?

ANDRÉ: No, we have not been robbed. Now sit quietly and listen as hard as you can. Frederick, my clerk, has just woken me to give me some work he had to finish during the night. While he was in my office...

JACQUELINE: Mother of God, I see it all. You've had a quarrel at the café.

ANDRÉ: No. No. I've had no quarrel, nothing's happened to me. Will you listen? I tell you, Frederick, my clerk, saw a man creep through your window this very night. For heaven's sake, woman, are you deaf?

JACQUELINE: Will you please draw the curtains?

ANDRÉ: There! You can yawn after dinner, you usually do. Now take care, Jacqueline. I'm an easy-tempered man and I've looked after you well. I made up my mind to come here and treat you gently. And you can see that's what I'm doing, because before I condemn you I'm willing to discuss the matter and give you a chance to defend yourself and explain everything. If you refuse, take care. There's a garrison in town and, God forgive me, you see any number of officers. I've had my suspicions for a long time and your silence will only confirm them.

JACQUELINE: Oh, my dear, you don't love me any more. Your using kind words won't hide the coldness that's replaced all the love you had for me. It wasn't like this in the past. You never used to speak in this way. Then you wouldn't have condemned me on one chance remark without hearing what I had to say. At one single chance remark, two years of peace and love and happiness wouldn't have vanished like shadows. No, it's jealousy driving you on. For a long time you've been cold and indifferent. What use would evidence be? Innocence itself would be guilty to you. You can't love me any more to accuse me like this.

ANDRÉ: That's all very fine, Jacqueline, but it's not the point. Frederick, my clerk, saw a man…

JACQUELINE: For heaven's sake, I heard you. Do you think I'm an idiot to go on repeating it like this? It's tiring me out; I can't stand it.

ANDRÉ: Then why don't you answer?

JACQUELINE: (*In tears.*) Oh dear, I'm so miserable! What's going to happen to me? I can see you've decided to kill me. You'll do just what you want. You're a man and I'm a woman. Strength is on your side. I'm resigned, it's what I expected. You'll seize the first excuse to justify your violence. There's nothing left for me now but to go into a convent, in a desert if there is one. And all I'll have to keep in the depths of my heart is the memory of the happy times that used to be.

ANDRÉ: For the love of God and the holy saints, woman, are you making fun of me?

JACQUELINE: Really, are you serious?

ANDRÉ: Am I serious? By the Holy Sabbath, I'm losing my patience. I don't know why I don't take you to court.

JACQUELINE: You? Take me to court?

ANDRÉ: Yes, me. Take you to court. Having to deal with a mule like this is enough to drive a man mad. I've never heard of anyone so stubborn.

JACQUELINE: (*Jumping out of bed.*) Did you see a man climb through the window? Did you see it, yes or no?

ANDRÉ: I didn't see it with my own eyes.

JACQUELINE: You didn't see it with your own eyes and you want to take me to court?

ANDRÉ: Yes, by heaven, if you don't answer.

JACQUELINE: Do you know something my grandmother learned from hers? When a husband trusts his wife, he keeps to himself any evil gossip he hears. Then, when he's sure of his facts, he only has to mention them to her. If he has any suspicions, they're removed. If he lacks proof, nothing's said. If he can't show he's right, then he's wrong. There. Come now, let's go.

ANDRÉ: So that's the way you take it?

JACQUELINE: Yes it is. Go on, I'll follow.

ANDRÉ: Where do you want me to go at this time of night?

JACQUELINE: To court.

ANDRÉ: To court? But Jacqueline…

JACQUELINE: Go on, go on. If a man makes threats, he mustn't make them in vain.

ANDRÉ: Come, come now, calm yourself a little.

JACQUELINE: No. You want to take me to court and I want to go there right away.

ANDRÉ: What will you say in your defence? You might as well tell me now.

JACQUELINE: No. I'll say nothing here.

ANDRÉ: Why?

JACQUELINE: Because I want to go to court.

ANDRÉ: You're driving me out of my mind. It's like a dream. Eternal Lord, Creator of the World, I'm going mad.

JACQUELINE: Come along.

ANDRÉ: What, what! It can't be true. Now listen to me. I was in bed, asleep, and as God's my witness in full possession of my senses. Frederick, my clerk, a boy of eighteen who's never in his life said an ill word of anyone, the most honest boy in the world, has just spent the night copying an inventory and sees a man come in through the window. He tells me, I take my dressing gown, I come to see you in a friendly way, I ask you in all kindliness to explain what it means, and you insult me. You behave so furiously, you finish up by jumping out of bed and seizing me by the throat. No, I can't believe it. It will be a week before I'm capable of adding up two columns of figures. Jacqueline, my dearest, how can you treat me this way?

JACQUELINE: Well, really! You are a poor fellow.

ANDRÉ: After all, my darling, what makes you answer me like this? Do you think I really believe you're deceiving me? Good heavens, a single word would be enough. Why won't you say it? Perhaps it was a thief who crept in through the window. This isn't one of the safest districts: we'd do well to move. I don't a bit like all these soldiers, my lovely one, my precious. When we go out for a walk or to the theatre or a ball or even in our own home, they never leave us. I can't say a word to you without bruising myself on their epaulettes or tripping up on an enormous sword. They might well be impertinent enough to climb up to our windows. I can see that you don't know anything about it: you don't encourage them. But those wretches are capable of anything. Come then, give me your hand. Are you angry, Jacqueline?

JACQUELINE: Of course I'm angry. Threatening to take me to court! My mother will have something to say, when she hears about it.

ANDRÉ: Oh, my dear, don't tell her. What's the point of letting other people know about our little misunderstandings? They're just tiny clouds that pass across the sky for a second and then leave it quieter and clearer than it was before.

JACQUELINE: That's better. Give me your hand.

ANDRÉ: Don't I know you love me? Don't I trust you implicitly? After all, this window Frederick was talking about doesn't lead directly into your room. If you cross the verandah, there's a way into the kitchen garden. I shouldn't be surprised if old Thomas next door hadn't come to steal our peaches. Come now; don't fret yourself. Tonight I'll put the gardener there as a sentry and a mantrap on the path. We'll have a good laugh about this tomorrow.

JACQUELINE: I'm tired to death. What a ridiculous hour to wake me up!

ANDRÉ: Get back to bed, my darling. I'm going, I'll leave you. There now, goodbye, we won't think any more about it. You see, my dear, I don't make the slightest search of your room. I haven't opened a cupboard. I accept your word. I think I love you a hundred times more than I did before, through suspecting you wrongly and finding you innocent. I'll soon make everything all right. We'll go off to the country and I'll give you a little present. Goodbye, goodbye. There! You see, there's nothing like explaining things properly. It always leads to complete understanding.

(*He goes out. JACQUELINE opens a wardrobe in which CLAVAROCHE can be seen.*)

CLAVAROCHE: (*Coming out of the wardrobe.*) Ouch.

JACQUELINE: Quick, come out. My husband's furious. Someone's seen you, but you weren't recognised. What was it like in there?

CLAVAROCHE: Wonderful.

JACQUELINE: There's no time to lose. What are we going to do? We must meet without anyone knowing. How can we? The gardener will be out there tonight. I'm not sure of my maid. We can't possibly go anywhere else; in a small town like this, everyone knows everything. You're covered with dust. Are you limping?

CLAVAROCHE: I've cracked my knee and my skull too. The hilt of my sword went right through my ribs. Pah! I look as though I'd come out of a mill.

JACQUELINE: Burn my letters as soon as you get home. If anyone finds them, I'm ruined. Frederick, one of the clerks, saw you go by. I'll make him pay for it. What can we do? How? Say something. You're as pale as death.

CLAVAROCHE: I hadn't got into a comfortable position when you slammed the door. For a whole hour I've been doubled up like a natural history specimen in a jar of spirit.

JACQUELINE: We must think. What shall we do?

CLAVAROCHE: It's all right. There couldn't be anything easier.

JACQUELINE: Well, how?

CLAVAROCHE: I've no idea. But it's quite simple. You don't think this is the first time, do you? I'm exhausted. Give me a glass of water.

JACQUELINE: (*Pointing to a table.*) There. I think the best plan would be to meet at the farm.

CLAVAROCHE: These husbands! What inconvenient brutes they are when they wake up. This uniform's in a pretty state. I shall look fine on parade. (*He drinks.*) Damn it, with all that dust I needed the devil's own strength to avoid sneezing. Have you a brush here?

JACQUELINE: On my dressing table. Over there.

CLAVAROCHE: (*Brushing his hair.*) What's the use of going to the farm? All in all, your husband's a fairly mild fellow. Does he make a habit of these nocturnal appearances?

JACQUELINE: No, thank goodness. It's still making me tremble. Remember, with all these ideas he's got into his head now, his suspicions are going to fall on you.

CLAVAROCHE: Why me?

JACQUELINE: Why? I don't know... I think it's bound to happen. You see, truth is a strange thing, rather like a ghost. You know it's there without being able to put your finger on it.

CLAVAROCHE: (*Adjusting his uniform.*) Bah, it's only grandparents and policemen who say everything gets known. And they have the very good reason that if it doesn't, they're unconscious of it, so for them it doesn't exist. It sounds as though I'm saying something silly, but if you think, you'll see it's true.

JACQUELINE: Whatever you say. My hands are trembling. I'm so frightened, it's worse than torture.

CLAVAROCHE: Be patient. We'll arrange everything.

JACQUELINE: How? Tell me. It's getting light.

CLAVAROCHE: Good lord, what a mad little thing you are. You're pretty as a picture, when you're frightened like this. Let's think a little. Sit down there and we'll sort it all out. The damage has been repaired, I'm almost presentable. What an uncomfortable wardrobe you have. I don't envy your clothes.

JACQUELINE: Don't laugh. It terrifies me.

CLAVAROCHE: Now listen, my dear, let me tell you my principles. When you come across the mischievous sort of brute that's known as a jealous husband...

JACQUELINE: Really! Have some respect for me.

CLAVAROCHE: Have I shocked you? (*He kisses her hand.*)

JACQUELINE: Do at least speak more quietly.

CLAVAROCHE: There are three certain ways of avoiding all difficulties. The first is to part. We don't exactly want that.

JACQUELINE: You'll make me die of fright.

CLAVAROCHE: The second, and undoubtedly the best, is not to take any precautions and if necessary…

JACQUELINE: Well, what?

CLAVAROCHE: No, that won't do either. Your husband's not a military man, we must keep our sword in its scabbard. There remains the third way. That's to find a candlestick.

JACQUELINE: A candlestick? What do you mean?

CLAVAROCHE: In the regiment that's what we call a good-looking fellow, who's made to carry a shawl or a parasol when necessary. When a lady gets up to dance, he solemnly sits on her chair as he follows her round with a melancholy eye and plays with her fan. At the theatre he gives her his arm, when she leaves her box, and proudly sets down her glass on the nearest table, when she's finished drinking. If anyone admires the lady, he gets angry. If they insult her, he fights them. A cushion's missing from the sofa: he runs off to find it, because he knows the house and everyone in it; he's part of the furniture, he can find his way down every passage without a light. Is there a gala she wants to go to? He's shaved at dawn and on the steps by noon, to reserve chairs with his gloves. Ask him why he's turned himself into a shadow, he can't say, he doesn't know. It isn't because the lady encourages him occasionally with a smile, or, when she waltzes, gives him the tips of her fingers which he lovingly clasps. He's like those noble lords who have an honorary post and come to court on great occasions: but the private apartments are closed to them and beyond their reach. In short his privileges cease at the point where the real ones start. He has everything one can see in a woman, and nothing one wants. Behind this convenient dummy hides the happy man of mystery; the other serves as a screen for everything that happens confidentially. If the husband's jealous, it's of him. Any rumours are about him. He comes and goes and worries; they let him, it's his job. And all the while the discreet lover and his very innocent friend are covered by an impenetrable veil, so they can laugh at him and all inquisitive people.

JACQUELINE: I can't help laughing, though I scarcely feel like it. Why call this man a candlestick?

CLAVAROCHE: Because he holds a candle to throw light on himself and leave the real lover in shadow.

JACQUELINE: Yes, yes, I see.

CLAVAROCHE: Look, my dear, can't you find some kind friend to play this important part? After all, it's not without its rewards. Try to think of someone. (*He looks at his watch.*) Seven o'clock! I must go. I'm on duty today.

JACQUELINE: Really I don't know anyone here. Besides, it's so deceitful, I wouldn't be able to carry it through. To encourage some young man, rouse his hopes, perhaps make him seriously fall in love with me; and then laugh at him. It's a wicked thing to do.

CLAVAROCHE: Would you rather I lost you? In our situation, don't you see we must divert suspicion at any cost?

JACQUELINE: Why make it fall on someone else?

CLAVAROCHE: It must fall somewhere. The suspicions of a jealous husband, my dear, can't hover in space like swallows. They must come to earth sooner or later and the safest way is to prepare a nest for them.

JACQUELINE: No, I definitely can't. Anyway, I'd have to compromise myself, wouldn't I?

CLAVAROCHE: Are you joking? You'll still be able to prove your innocence, if you ever have to. Because a man's in love with you, it doesn't mean he's your lover.

JACQUELINE: I know. But...

CLAVAROCHE: (*Going to the window.*) Look. In your own garden. Do you see those three young men sitting under a tree? Your husband's clerks. I leave it to you to choose among them. When I return, one of them must be madly in love with you.

JACQUELINE: How could they be? I've never said a word to them.

CLAVAROCHE: You're a daughter of Eve, aren't you? Come, Jacqueline, say you will.

JACQUELINE: Don't rely on it. I won't promise anything.

CLAVAROCHE: Give me your hand. Thank you. Goodbye, my frightened little girl. You're young and beautiful and a little in love…aren't you? To work! Just a cast of your net!

JACQUELINE: You're bold, my dear.

CLAVAROCHE: Bold and proud. Proud to have you and bold to keep you.

Scene II

The garden at the back of the house, immediately afterwards. On the left, a door leads into the office.

FORTUNIO, FREDERICK, and WILLIAM are talking.

FREDERICK: My dear fellow, I assure you. Every word is true.

FORTUNIO: It's really very odd. The whole thing's most extraordinary.

FREDERICK: Anyway, don't let's go on gossiping about it. You'll get me sacked.

FORTUNIO: Very peculiar, and very wonderful. Whoever he is, he's a lucky man.

FREDERICK: Promise to say nothing about it. The master made me swear to.

WILLIAM: We won't breathe a word to man, woman, or child.

FORTUNIO: It makes my heart leap to know such things can happen. Frederick, you really did see it?

FREDERICK: Yes, I did. Don't keep on asking me.

FORTUNIO: You heard someone walking softly?

FREDERICK: Creeping along behind the wall.

FORTUNIO: And tap gently at the window?

FREDERICK: Like a grain of sand underfoot.

FORTUNIO: Then on the wall the shadow of a man passing through the gate?

FREDERICK: In a cloak, like a ghost.

FORTUNIO: And a hand behind the shutter?

FREDERICK: Trembling like a leaf.

FORTUNIO: A light in the gallery, then a kiss and a few distant steps?

FREDERICK: Then silence; the curtains were drawn and the light disappeared.

FORTUNIO: If I'd been you, I'd have waited till daylight.

WILLIAM: Are you in love with Jacqueline? You'll have a hard time there.

FORTUNIO: William, I swear I've never looked her in the face. I'd never dare to be in love with her, even in a dream. I met her once at a ball: I didn't touch her hand, she didn't speak to me. I've no idea what she does or what she thinks, except that she takes a walk here in the afternoon and I've rubbed the dirt off our window to see her stroll down the path.

WILLIAM: If you're not in love with her, why did you say you'd have waited? The best thing was what Frederick did; go and tell the master.

FORTUNIO: Frederick did what he thought best. Let Romeo have his Juliet. I'd rather be the lark that warned them of the danger.

WILLIAM: Don't be such a fool. What good can it do you if Jacqueline has a lover? It's probably one of the garrison officers.

FORTUNIO: I wish I'd been in the office. I wish I'd seen it all.

WILLIAM: Well, well, the bookseller's been poisoning your mind with his novels. Where will they lead you in the end? Just back to earth again. Or are you by any chance hoping it will be your turn next? Yes, that's it. Our fine gentleman imagines that one of these days she'll start thinking of him. Poor fellow! You don't know our provincial beauties. Black-coated men like us can't hope for anything so exalted. They only fancy a uniform and once they've tried one, what do they care if the garrison changes? All soldiers are alike. If you love one, you love a hundred. Only the badges are different. Apart from that, there's always the same curl of a moustache, the same messroom manners, the same talk, and the same pleasure. They're all made to a single model. Women can change from one to another without noticing.

FORTUNIO: There's no talking with you. You spend all your spare time watching people play bowls.

WILLIAM: While you're all alone at your window with your nose buried in your flowers. A fine difference that is! With your romantic ideas, you're only fit for a straitjacket. Come on, let's go in. What are you thinking about? It's time for work.

FORTUNIO: I wish I'd been in the office last night with Frederick.

(*They go into the office.*
JACQUELINE and MADELEINE enter.)

JACQUELINE: The plums will be good this year and the peaches are coming along.

MADELEINE: Don't you mind the wind, madam? It's not very warm this morning.

JACQUELINE: Really, in the two years I've lived in this house, I don't think I've been twice in this part of the garden. Look at the honeysuckle. How charming that pergola is with the clematis.

MADELEINE: Besides, madam, you haven't got a hat. You wouldn't bring one.

JACQUELINE: By the way, who are those young men in there? I may be wrong, but I thought they were looking at us. They were here just now.

MADELEINE: You must know them. They're the master's clerks.

JACQUELINE: Oh, so you know them, do you, Madeleine? You blushed as you said that.

MADELEINE: Me, madam? Why should I? I know them because I see them every day. Yes, every day. Of course I know them.

JACQUELINE: Come now. Admit you blushed. And really, why shouldn't you? As far as I can see from here, they're not at all bad-looking. Tell me, which one do you like best? Take me into your confidence. You're a pretty girl, Madeleine; what harm is there in these young men courting you?

MADELEINE: I don't say there is any harm. They're good

young fellows and they come from respectable families. Do you see that short, fair one? There's not a girl in town who'd turn up her nose at him.

JACQUELINE: (*Going toward the office.*) Which do you mean? The one who's sharpening his pen?

MADELEINE: Oh, no. That's Frederick, a big yokel who never opens his mouth.

JACQUELINE: Then it's the other one writing?

MADELEINE: Oh, dear me, no. That's William. He's a good steady fellow, but his hair's so straight he hasn't much luck when he wants to go dancing on Sundays.

JACQUELINE: Who do you mean, then? I don't think there's anyone else in the office.

MADELEINE: Don't you see that neat young man with the well-brushed hair, near the window? Look, he's searching in a drawer. That's Fortunio.

JACQUELINE: Oh, yes, I see him now. Yes, not at all bad-looking, with that air of innocence. Watch out, Madeleine, that's the sort of angel who ruins young girls. So he goes courting everyone in town, does he, with those blue eyes of his? Well, Madeleine, that's no reason for casting your own eyes down and looking so particular. Really, you could do a lot worse. So he can dance and make conversation, can he?

MADELEINE: With all respect, madam, if I thought he was in love with someone here, it wouldn't be with a maid like me. If you'd turned round when you were walking in the garden, you'd have seen him more than once, with his arms crossed and his pen behind his ear, staring at you as hard as he could.

JACQUELINE: Are you joking, girl? Remember who you're talking to.

MADELEINE: A cat may look at a king and some people say the king doesn't mind being looked at by the cat. He's not such a fool, this boy, and his father's a rich jeweller. I can't see any insult in watching people take a walk.

JACQUELINE: Who told you he was looking at me? I don't suppose he took you into his confidence?

MADELEINE: Come now, madam, when a young man turns his head, you scarcely have to be a woman to guess where he's looking. If he took me into his confidence, I'd only learn what I know already.

JACQUELINE: I'm feeling cold. Go and fetch me a shawl; I've had enough of your ideas.

(*MADELEINE goes out.*)

Isn't that the gardener I can see over there? Hullo, Peter, come here.

(*PETER enters.*)

PETER: You called, madam?

JACQUELINE: Yes. Go in there and ask for a clerk called Fortunio. Tell him to come here. I want to speak to him.

(*FORTUNIO enters.*)

PETER: Here he comes. Excuse me, sir. Madam would like to have a word with you. (*Goes out.*)

FORTUNIO: Of course there must be some mistake, madam, but I've just been told you were asking for me.

JACQUELINE: Sit down; there's no mistake. You find me, sir, very embarrassed, very worried. I don't really know how to tell you what I want to ask you or why I've approached you.

FORTUNIO: I'm only the third clerk. If it's important business, William's there, our chief clerk. Would you like me to call him?

JACQUELINE: Why, no. If it were business, I'd speak to my husband, wouldn't I?

FORTUNIO: Is there anything I can do for you? Please speak frankly. I may be young, but I'd willingly give my life to serve you.

JACQUELINE: That's gallantly and valiantly spoken. But if I'm not mistaken, you don't know me.

FORTUNIO: A star that shines on the horizon doesn't know the people who look at it. But it is known to the humblest shepherd on the hills.

JACQUELINE: There's a secret I want to tell you, but I'm hesitating for two reasons. First, you could betray me.

Secondly, just by doing me this service, you might think
badly of me.

FORTUNIO: Can you test me in some way? Do please
believe in me.

JACQUELINE: But, as you say, you're very young. Even
though you believed in yourself, you might not always pass
the test.

FORTUNIO: I know my inmost feelings will pass any test.

JACQUELINE: Necessity leaves me no alternative. See that
no one's listening.

FORTUNIO: No one. The garden's empty and I've shut the
office door.

JACQUELINE: No, I definitely can't tell you. Forgive my
approaching you like this. It must never be mentioned
again.

FORTUNIO: I'm sorry. That makes me most unhappy. But of
course it's as you wish.

JACQUELINE: You see, the position I'm in is really absurd. I
need – can I tell you? – not exactly a friend, but a friend's
help. I cannot make up my mind. I was walking in the
garden looking at the peaches; and, as I say, I don't know
why, I saw you at the window and suddenly decided to
send for you.

FORTUNIO: I don't know why fate has favoured me like this,
but please let me take advantage of it. I can only repeat
what I've said already: I'd willingly give my life for you.

JACQUELINE: Don't repeat it too often. It's the way to make
me say nothing.

FORTUNIO: Why? It's what I really feel.

JACQUELINE: Why? Why? You understand nothing, I don't
want to think about it. No. What I have to ask you can't
lead to anything as serious as that, thank heavens. It's
nothing, a trifle. You're just a boy, aren't you? You think
I'm pretty perhaps and you pay me a few compliments
lightly, out of gallantry. And that's the way I take them; it's
quite simple. Any man in your position would have said as
much.

FORTUNIO: I always tell the truth. I know I am just a boy
and you may not believe what I've said. God can judge it.

JACQUELINE: Well done. You know your part and you'll
keep to it. That's enough of that. Bring up that chair and sit
down.

FORTUNIO: Very well. As you ask me.

JACQUELINE: Excuse my asking a question you may think
odd. Madeleine, my maid, tells me your father's a jeweller.
He must have connections with the shops in town.

FORTUNIO: Yes, I can say that nearly all those of any
standing know our place.

JACQUELINE: So you must go there sometimes. They must
know you.

FORTUNIO: Yes, if that can help you at all.

JACQUELINE: A friend of mine has a husband who's jealous
and a miser. She's not without money, but she can't use it.
Her pleasures, her tastes, her jewellery, her caprices if you
like (what woman is without them?) – they're all regulated
and controlled. It's not that she can't afford to spend large
sums. But every month, every week almost, she has to
calculate and argue about everything she's bought. So
with all her wealth she leads a very restricted life. She's
poorer than her bank account, her money's no use to her.
Clothes and jewellery mean a lot to a woman, you know.
So at all costs she has had to use a scheme of some sort.
Her tradesmen's accounts only show trivial expenses,
which her husband calls 'of prime importance', and they're
paid openly. But at certain agreed times, certain other
secret accounts show a few trifles that the woman calls
'of secondary importance', which they are: only warped
minds could call them superfluous. So everything works
wonderfully. Everybody's happy. The husband's sure of his
receipts, but doesn't know enough about clothes to guess
he hasn't paid for everything he sees on his wife's back.

FORTUNIO: I don't see much harm in that.

JACQUELINE: Now this is what happens. The husband gets
suspicious and finally notices, not too many clothes, but
too little money. He threatens the servants, examines the

cashbox and scolds the tradesmen. The poor wife hasn't
lost a franc; but like Tantalus she finds herself consumed
from morning to night by a thirst – for clothes. No more
confidants, no more secret accounts, no more unknown
expenses. But this thirst torments her, she must at all
cost satisfy it. She needs a young man, clever, above all
discreet, and with a position high enough not to arouse
any suspicion. He must be willing to visit the shops and
buy as if for himself the things she needs and desires. In
particular he must have access to her house, to be able to
come and go in safety. He must have good taste obviously
and know how to buy intelligently. It might be fortunate if
there were some attractive girl people might think he was
paying attentions to. You aren't in this position, I suppose?
That would justify everything. Then everyone would think
it was this girl you were buying for. That's the sort of man
we have to find.

FORTUNIO: Tell your friend I'm at her disposal. I'll serve
her as best I can.

JACQUELINE: If that could be arranged, you understand,
then you see, don't you, that in order to have free access to
the house as I mentioned, the confidant must be more than
a servant. You understand he must be able to appear in the
drawing room. You understand discretion is so difficult a
virtue that the lady would of course be grateful. Apart from
goodwill, a little tact would not be amiss. One evening,
take this evening for example if it's fine, he must be able
to find the door unlocked and bring a bracelet furtively,
boldly, like a smuggler. An air of mystery must never
betray his skill. He must be prudent, quick, and cunning.
He must remember an old proverb that brings success to
those who follow it: 'Fortune favours the brave'.

FORTUNIO: Do please let me help you.

JACQUELINE: Once all these conditions are fulfilled and I
can be sure of his silence, I'll be able to tell this confidant
the name of the lady. Then he'll receive a purse and have
no doubts how to use it. Quickly, I can see Madeleine

bringing my coat. Be careful and discreet. Goodbye. I'm the lady; you're the friend. The purse is under the chair.
(*She goes out.*)

(*WILLIAM and FREDERICK appear at the office window.*)

WILLIAM: Hallo, Fortunio! The master's calling you.

FREDERICK: Your desk's piled high with work. What are you doing out there?

FORTUNIO: Eh? What is it? What do you want?

WILLIAM: We're telling you, the master's asking for you.

FREDERICK: Come here; you're wanted. What's the fellow dreaming about?

FORTUNIO: It's really very odd; the whole thing's most extraordinary.
(*He goes into the office.*)

ACT TWO

The dining room, the next evening. A table is laid for dinner.
WILLIAM and FREDERICK are talking.

WILLIAM. Fortunio doesn't seem to have stayed long in the office.

FREDERICK: There's a party tonight; he's been invited.

WILLIAM: Yes; so all the work's left to us. My right hand's paralysed.

FREDERICK: He's only the third clerk. They could have asked us too.

WILLIAM: After all, he's a good fellow. There's not much harm in it.

FREDERICK: No. But there wouldn't have been any more if they'd included us.

WILLIAM: What a smell of cooking! They're making such a noise, you can't hear yourself speak.

FREDERICK: I think they're going to dance. I saw some violins.

WILLIAM: The devil take all that work! I won't do any more today.

FREDERICK: Do you know, I've an idea there's something of a mystery here.

WILLIAM: Bah. How can there be?

FREDERICK: Yes, yes. It's not as simple as you think. If I wanted to gossip…

WILLIAM: Don't be afraid, I won't say anything.

FREDERICK: You remember the other night I saw a man climb up to the window. Who it was, no one knew. But today, this evening, I saw something, as true as I'm standing on this very spot; and what that something was, I do know.

WILLIAM: What was it? Tell me.

FREDERICK: As it was getting dark, I saw Jacqueline open the garden gate. A man was behind her; he crept along by the wall, and kissed her hand. Then he ran off and I heard him say, 'Don't worry, I'll be back soon'.

WILLIAM: No! I don't believe it.

FREDERICK: I saw it as plain as I can see you now.

WILLIAM: If that's so, I know what I'd do in your place. I'd warn the master, like last time; no doubt about it.

FREDERICK: I'm not too sure. With a man like him, it's dangerous. He changes his mind every day.

WILLIAM: What a row they're making! Crash, the doors! Bang, the plates and dishes! Clang, the knives and forks! I think someone's singing.

FREDERICK: It's the captain. He's just arrived.

WILLIAM: Well, as we haven't been invited, let's take a stroll and talk in comfort. When the master's enjoying himself like this, the least we can do is have a little rest ourselves. (*They go out.*

CLAVAROCHE and a SERVANT enter.)

CLAVAROCHE: No one here yet?

SERVANT: No, sir.

CLAVAROCHE: All right, I'll wait. (*Servant goes out.*) Frankly, it would be a sad business if you ever fell seriously in love with these beauties. On the whole, it's too tiresome having a love affair. Sooner or later, in the most delightful spot, a maid will come tapping at the door and force you to take to your heels. A woman, who'd ruin herself for you, surrenders just one ear and in the middle of the most passionate raptures suddenly locks you in the wardrobe. Sooner or later you're home again, stretched out on a sofa, exhausted by all the manoeuvring, and a hastily sent messenger arrives to remind you she adores you and she's ten miles off. You immediately send for barber and valet. You hurry, you run: then the opportunity's vanished, her husband's come home. It's pouring with rain and you have to dance attendance for an hour at least. Do you think you might be ill or not in the mood? Impossible. Sun and frost and storm, all the uncertainties and all the dangers have made you tough. The difficulty lies in having the privilege of increasing the pleasure, and the east wind would be angry, if it thought that by cutting your face it wasn't warming your heart. Why is Cupid always shown

with wings and a bow and arrow? We'd do better to paint
him chasing a wild goose in a weatherproof coat, with a
full-bottomed wig to keep his neck warm. What besotted
fools men are to deprive themselves of a good free meal
in barracks, to go chasing…well, what, for heaven's sake?
The shadow of their pride. (*He goes toward a mirror.*) But
garrison duty lasts six months. You can't always go to the
café; provincial theatres are boring: you glance in the
mirror and see no point in looking your best for nothing.
Jacqueline has a good figure. So one's patient and puts up
with everything without finding it too difficult.
(*JACQUELINE enters.*)
Well, my dear, what have you done? Did you follow my
advice? Are we out of danger?

JACQUELINE: Yes.

CLAVAROCHE: How did you manage? Do tell me. Is one of
the clerks responsible for our safety?

JACQUELINE: Yes.

CLAVAROCHE: You're incomparable. There isn't a cleverer
woman on earth. You made this young man come up to
your boudoir, is that it? I can just see him with his hands
clasped, twisting his hat in his fingers. What story did you
tell him to succeed so quickly?

JACQUELINE: The first one that came into my head. I can't
remember.

CLAVAROCHE: What fools we are, when you women want
to make fools of us. Well, what does your husband think?
Has the storm that threatened us struck the lightning
conductor? Is it beginning to swerve aside?

JACQUELINE: Yes.

CLAVAROCHE: We shall have some fun. I'll enjoy myself
watching this little comedy, observing the cues and the
action, even playing a part in it myself. Tell me, has
this humble slave fallen in love with you already, since
yesterday? I'm sure I saw him as I came in; a busy-looking
face and clothes to match. Is he already at his post? Does
he do all his necessary duties in the right manner? Has he

risked a few words of timid love and respectful tenderness? Are you satisfied with him?

JACQUELINE: Yes.

CLAVAROCHE: With all these services to come, have you given him something on account? Have these lovely flashing eyes let him guess that he's allowed to sigh for them? Has he obtained some mark of favour? Tell me frankly how far you've got. Have your eyes met? Have you started to cast your spell? The least you can do is to give him some encouragement for all he's doing for us.

JACQUELINE: Yes

CLAVAROCHE: What's the matter? You're daydreaming; you're only half answering.

JACQUELINE: I did what you told me.

CLAVAROCHE: Are you sorry?

JACQUELINE: No.

CLAVAROCHE: You look worried. There's something on your mind.

JACQUELINE: No.

CLAVAROCHE: You don't think there's anything serious in a joke like this? Come now, there's nothing to it.

JACQUELINE: If people knew what has happened, why would they think that I've done wrong and you perhaps right?

CLAVAROCHE: Why, it's a game, there's nothing to it. Don't you love me, Jacqueline?

JACQUELINE: Yes.

CLAVAROCHE: Well then, what's worrying you? Haven't you done this to preserve our love?

JACQUELINE: Yes.

CLAVAROCHE: I promise you it amuses me. I don't take it too much to heart.

ANDRÉ: (*Off.*) Close the door behind you.

JACQUELINE: Sh! It's nearly dinner-time, my husband's coming.

CLAVAROCHE: Is this our man with him?

JACQUELINE: Yes. My husband invited him. He's spending the evening here.

(*ANDRÉ and FORTUNIO enter.*)

ANDRÉ: No, today I won't listen to a single word of business. I want everyone to be gay and dance; there must be nothing but laughter. I'm overjoyed, I'm floating on a wave of happiness and all I want is a good dinner.

CLAVAROCHE: I can see you're in a good humour, sir.

ANDRÉ: I must tell you all what happened to me yesterday. It's unbelievable. I suspected my wife unjustly. I had a mantrap set in front of the garden gate and this morning I found the cat in it. It's only fair, I deserve it. But I want to do justice to Jacqueline. You must all of you know we've made friends and she's forgiven me.

JACQUELINE: It's all right, I've no ill feelings. Please don't say any more about it.

ANDRÉ: No, I want everyone to know. I've told them all in town. Talking of town, I bought a little figure of Cupid to stand on the mantelpiece as a token of our reconciliation. Then every time I look at it, I'll love my wife a hundred times more than I did before. It will guarantee me against not trusting her in the future.

CLAVAROCHE: That's the action of a generous husband, sir. It's typical of you.

ANDRÉ: Thank you, Captain. Will you have dinner with us?

CLAVAROCHE: With pleasure. I see a place is laid for me.

(*They sit down to dinner.*)

ANDRÉ: We're having a little party here today, you're very welcome.

CLAVAROCHE: I'm highly honoured.

ANDRÉ: I want to introduce you to a new guest. It's one of my clerks. Ha, ha. The pen is mightier than the sword. No offence, Captain. He's an intelligent boy. He's paying court to my wife.

CLAVAROCHE: May I ask your name, sir? I'm delighted to meet you.

ANDRÉ: Fortunio. It's a lucky name. To tell the truth, he's been working in my office for more than a year now and I never noticed what an excellent fellow he was. I even believe, without Jacqueline, I'd never have thought of it.

His writing's not too neat; and some of his figures are not above reproach. But my wife needs him for some little business of hers and she's delighted with his keenness. It's their secret. We husbands mustn't stick our noses in there. A pleasant guest in a small town like this is quite a rarity, so he's become one of the family. I pray the Lord he enjoys himself. We'll do our best for hun.

FORTUNIO: I'll do all I can to be worthy of it.

ANDRÉ: (*To CLAVAROCHE.*) As you know, my work keeps me in the office during the week. I'm not sorry Jacqueline's going to amuse herself without me, as she intends to. She sometimes needs a companion to take a walk with. The doctor wants her to go out more, the fresh air will do her good. This boy knows all the news and reads aloud very well. What's more he comes from a good family, they've brought him up properly. He's an escort for my wife and I ask your friendship for him.

CLAVAROCHE: My dear sir, my friendship is entirely at your service. It's something you've earned; you can dispose of it as you wish.

FORTUNIO: The captain's very kind. I don't know how to thank him.

CLAVAROCHE: I'll be honoured, if you'll count me as a friend.

ANDRÉ: Excellent. That's wonderful. Hurrah for happiness! (*He drinks.*)

CLAVAROCHE: (*Aside to JACQUELINE.*) If things go on like this, we'll only have to deal with this clerk of yours.

JACQUELINE: I did what you told me.

ANDRÉ: I'm feeling remarkably happy.

CLAVAROCHE: Come, Fortunio, fill the lady's glass.

FORTUNIO: With pleasure, Captain. I drink your health.

CLAVAROCHE: For shame, that's not very gallant of you. To my charming neighbour.

ANDRÉ: Yes. To my wife. Captain, I'm delighted you find this wine to your liking. (*Sings.*) 'Friends, drink deep and never cease…'

JACQUELINE: Do be quiet.

CLAVAROCHE: That song's a little out of date. Why don't you sing, Fortunio?

ANDRÉ: Can he sing? Why, what do you mean 'out of date'? I wrote it myself for my own wedding.

FORTUNIO: If our hostess would like me to.

ANDRÉ: Ha, ha, the boy knows his manners.

JACQUELINE: Very well then; do sing, please.

CLAVAROCHE: One moment. Have a biscuit, before you start. It will clear your throat and improve your voice.

ANDRÉ: He will have his little joke.

FORTUNIO: No thank you, it would choke me.

CLAVAROCHE: No, no. Ask our hostess to give you one. I'm sure that from her white hand it would be far too delicate for that. (*Looking under the table.*) Good heavens, what's this? (*To JACQUELINE.*) Your feet on the floor! You must have a footstool.

FORTUNIO: (*Rising.*) There's one over there. (*He places it under JACQUELINE's feet.*)

CLAVAROCHE: Well done. I thought you were going to let me do that. If a young man's paying court to a lady he shouldn't let anyone anticipate him.

ANDRÉ: Oh, the boy will go far. You've only to breathe a word…

CLAVAROCHE: Now do sing, please. We're all attention.

FORTUNIO: I daren't in front of experts. I don't know any after-dinner songs.

CLAVAROCHE: A lady's asked you to; you can't refuse.

FORTUNIO: Then I'll do the best I can.

CLAVAROCHE: Haven't you started writing poetry to your lady? Now's your opportunity.

ANDRÉ: Quiet, quiet. Let him sing.

CLAVAROCHE: It must be a love song, mustn't it, Fortunio? Nothing else, please. (*To JACQUELINE.*) Do ask him to sing us a love song. We couldn't survive without one.

JACQUELINE: Please, Fortunio.

FORTUNIO: (*Sings.*)
> I love a lady of renown
>> And virtuous fame.

But would not for a princely crown
  Tell you her name.

To serve her for eternity
  My soul aspires.
I swear that I would gladly die,
  If she desires.

I'd go through all the fires of hell
  And brave the flame.
If I were tortured, I'd not tell
  My lady's name.

ANDRÉ: The young rogue's really in love, like he says; there are tears in his eyes. Come, my boy, have a drink to put you right. What young barmaid's put you in this sad state?

CLAVAROCHE: Surely his ambitions aren't as lowly as that. I thought his song was aimed rather higher. (*To JACQUELINE.*) What do you think? Give us your opinion.

JACQUELINE: It was very nice. Let's go and have coffee. (*They all rise.*)

ANDRÉ: Ah yes, coffee. Another glass of wine, Captain, before we go.

JACQUELINE: (*Aside to FORTUNIO.*) Have you got it?

FORTUNIO: Yes.

JACQUELINE: Wait for me here. I'll be back in a moment.

ANDRÉ: Your health, Captain. No, no, to my wife. Jacqueline, your health. 'Friends, drink deep and never cease…'

(*ANDRÉ goes out, singing, together with CLAVAROCHE. JACQUELINE follows.*)

FORTUNIO: There's not a happier man alive. Jacqueline loves me, I'm sure of it. With all the signs she's given, I couldn't possibly make a mistake. Here I am, welcomed, feasted, absolutely pampered in the house. And when she goes out, I escort her. What charm! What a smile! When her eyes fasten on me, I don't know what's happening. Happiness seems to seize me by the throat. It's all I can do not to take her in my arms. The more I think, the more I weigh it up, every sign, every mark of favour, it's certain. She loves me, she loves me. I'd be an absolute fool if I pretended not to see it. Just now when I sang, how her eyes sparkled. Ah, here she is!

(*JACQUELINE enters.*)

JACQUELINE: Fortunio, are you there?

FORTUNIO: Yes. Here is what you asked for. (*He gives her a small parcel.*)

JACQUELINE: You're a man of your word. I'm very pleased with you.

FORTUNIO: I don't know how to say what I feel. One look from your eyes has changed my existence. I only live to serve you.

JACQUELINE: That was a charming song you gave us at dinner. Who did you write it for? Will you let me have a copy?

FORTUNIO: It was written for you. I'm hopelessly in love with you. My life is at your service.

JACQUELINE: Really! I thought your song forbade you to say who you were in love with.

FORTUNIO: Jacqueline, take pity on me. It isn't only since yesterday that I've been suffering like this. For two years I've followed your every footstep. For two years, perhaps without your even knowing I existed, you've never left the house, your slightest shadow hasn't appeared on the blinds, you haven't opened your window, without my being there to see you. I could never come near you, but your beauty belonged to me, as the sun belongs to us all. I watched out for it, I breathed it in, I lived in your shadow. If you passed the morning on the terrace, I came back in the evening to kiss its stones. If I overheard a few words from your lips, I repeated them for a whole day. I learned by heart the songs you played on the piano. Everything you loved, I loved too. I see you're smiling. I swear I'm speaking the truth. I love you so much it almost kills me.

JACQUELINE: I'm not smiling because you say you've been in love with me for two years, but because I'm thinking it will be two days tomorrow...

FORTUNIO: I swear I'll never see you again, if I'm not

speaking the truth. For two whole years I've only lived for you.

JACQUELINE: What exactly have you got in mind?

FORTUNIO: My mind is full of fear and misery and hope. I don't know if I'm living or dying. How I ever dared speak to you, I can't imagine. I've lost my reason. I'm in love. I'm in agony. You must know and have some pity.

JACQUELINE: You've made love to dozens of girls. I know as well as if I'd seen you.

FORTUNIO: You're joking. Whoever told you that?

JACQUELINE: Yes, yes, you go out dancing and you dine down by the river.

FORTUNIO: With my friends on a Sunday. What's wrong with that?

JACQUELINE: No, I don't believe a word you're saying. I don't wish to believe it.

FORTUNIO: How can you possibly think I'm lying?

JACQUELINE: I told you yesterday, it's to be expected. You're young. At your age, a man's heart is full and he's not a miser with his kisses.

FORTUNIO: What can I do to convince you? Do please tell me.

JACQUELINE: What a charming question! Well, you must prove it.

FORTUNIO: How can anyone prove they're in love? Here I am in front of you. Every beat of my heart makes me want to take you in my arms. What made me tell you, was this crushing agony I've been fighting for two years and can't repress any longer. But you remain cold and unbelieving. I can't make you feel a spark of the fire that's consuming me. You even say I'm not suffering when I'm ready to die in front of you. This is crueller than contempt or indifference or a plain 'No', and I don't deserve it.

JACQUELINE: Sh! Someone's coming. I believe you, I love you. We mustn't be seen together. Go down by the back stairs and come back to the hall. I'll meet you there. (*Goes out.*)

FORTUNIO: She loves me. Jacqueline loves me. But she

goes away and leaves me like this. No, I can't go down yet.
Someone's coming. They've stopped her. They're coming
here. Quick, I must go. (*He tries a door.*) It's locked. What
can I do? If I use the other door, I'll meet them.

CLAVAROCHE: (*Offstage.*) Come along, just for a moment.

FORTUNIO: The captain's with her! (*He hides behind a
curtain.*)

(*CLAVAROCHE and JACQUELINE enter.*)

CLAVAROCHE: Damn it all, I've been looking for you
everywhere. What were you doing alone?

JACQUELINE: (*Aside.*) Thank heavens, Fortunio's gone.

CLAVAROCHE: You left me in a tête-à-tête that was really
unbearable. What can I possibly talk to André about, I ask
you? Besides, you left us alone just when your husband's
admirable wine should make it doubly precious to talk to
his delightful wife.

FORTUNIO: (*Hidden.*) How extraordinary. What can he
mean?

CLAVAROCHE: Let's see. Is this the bracelet? By the way,
what are you going to do with it? Give it away to someone?

JACQUELINE: You know it's our little plan.

CLAVAROCHE: It's a gold one. If you mean to use the same
scheme every day, our game will very soon end by not
being worth... By the way, that was an entertaining dinner
party. What an odd face our young initiate has.

FORTUNIO: (*As before.*) Initiate? Into what? Does he mean
me?

CLAVAROCHE: The bracelet's lovely; and valuable. That
was an extraordinary idea of yours.

FORTUNIO: (*As before.*) Ah, he must be in her confidence
too.

CLAVAROCHE: How the poor boy trembled when he
raised his glass. He amused me with the footstool. It was a
pleasure to see him.

FORTUNIO: (*As before.*) He does mean me; it's about this
evening's dinner.

CLAVAROCHE: I suppose you'll send this back to the
jeweller he got it from?

FORTUNIO: (*As before.*) Send it back! Why on earth should she?

CLAVAROCHE: His song in particular enchanted me. André was right. God forgive me, he really did have tears in his eyes.

FORTUNIO: (*As before.*) I daren't even think or try to understand. Is it a dream? Who is this fellow Clavaroche?

CLAVAROCHE: Besides it's no use pushing matters any further. What's the good of an inconvenient third person, if there won't be any more suspicions? These husbands never fail to adore their wives' lovers. Look what's happened! As soon as he trusts you completely, you must blow out the candle.

JACQUELINE: Who can tell what may happen? With a character like his, you can never be sure. We must keep a way of getting us out of any embarrassment.

FORTUNIO: (*As before.*) If they make a plaything out of me, there must be a motive. It's all a puzzle.

CLAVAROCHE: I'd get rid of him.

JACQUELINE: As you wish. I'm not thinking of myself. When the trouble starts, you don't think it will he be my choice, do you? The storm might easily break tomorrow, or this evening, or in half an hour even. We can't be too sure of this calm lasting.

CLAVAROCHE: You think so?

FORTUNIO: (*As before.*) Well I'm damned!

JACQUELINE: I thought I heard someone.

CLAVAROCHE: It's your husband.

(*ANDRÉ enters, rather drunk.*)

ANDRÉ: Captain, Captain, where have you got to? Well, are you going to let me have my coffee on my own? What about our game of cards?

CLAVAROCHE: (*Aside.*) This is rather amusing.

ANDRÉ: Yesterday he trumped my queen.

CLAVAROCHE: Do you want to play now?

ANDRÉ: Yes, I want my revenge.

CLAVAROCHE: Come along then.

(*ANDRÉ, CLAVAROCHE and JACQUELINE go out.*)

FORTUNIO: Good God above! He's her lover.

ACT THREE

Scene I

JACQUELINE's bedroom, the following afternoon.
JACQUELINE is seated. MADELEINE enters.

MADELEINE. Madam, you're in danger. When I was in
the hall just now, I heard the master talking to one of his
clerks. As far as I could gather, it's something about an
ambush they're planning for tonight.

JACQUELINE: An ambush? Where? What for?

MADELEINE: In the office. The clerk said that last night
he saw you, yes you, madam, and a man with you, in the
garden. Then the master swore he'd catch you and take
you to court.

JACQUELINE: You're sure about this, Madeleine?

MADELEINE: You'll do as you like, madam. I haven't the
honour of being in your confidence. But that doesn't
prevent my doing you a service. I've my work waiting for
me.

JACQUELINE: You were right to tell me, you can rely on
my not being ungrateful. Have you seen Fortunio this
morning? Where is he? I must speak to him.

MADELEINE: He didn't come to the office. I rather think
the gardener's seen him. But they're worried. They were
looking for him just now all over the place.

JACQUELINE: Go and try to find him.
(*MADELEINE goes out.*
CLAVAROCHE enters.)

CLAVAROCHE: What the devil's going on here? I think I've
some right to André's friendship, but when he met me just
now, he ignored me. The clerks are looking at me out of
the corners of their eyes and I'm not even sure the dog
won't snap at my heels. What's happened, for heaven's
sake? Why are your guests so ill-treated?

JACQUELINE: We've nothing to laugh at. What I expected

has happened. It's serious. This is the time for deeds, not words.

CLAVAROCHE: Deeds? What do you mean?

JACQUELINE: Those wretched clerks have been up to their spying again, they've seen us, André knows, he's going to hide in the office, we're in the greatest danger.

CLAVAROCHE: Is that all that's worrying you?

JACQUELINE: Are you mad? How can you possibly joke about it?

CLAVAROCHE: Because nothing could be easier than getting us out of this. You say your husband's furious? Well, let him shout; what does it matter? He wants to set a trap for us? Let him, nothing could be better. The clerks are in it? Why not? The whole town too, if it amuses them. They want to surprise my lovely Jacqueline and her very humble servant? Well, they can, if they like, I won't stop them. What do you see in that to bother us?

JACQUELINE: I don't understand a word you're saying.

CLAVAROCHE: Get Fortunio to come here. Where's this young man got to? Why, here we are in danger and the idiot abandons us. Come now, send for him at once.

JACQUELINE: I thought of that. But no one knows where he is. He hasn't been seen this morning.

CLAVAROCHE: I don't believe it. He must be hidden somewhere in your petticoats. You've forgotten him in a wardrobe and your maid's hooked him on a coat-hanger by mistake.

JACQUELINE: How can he be any use to us? I asked where he was, without really knowing why myself. On thinking it over, I don't see what good he can do.

CLAVAROCHE: Don't you see I'm getting ready to make the greatest of all sacrifices for him? Nothing less than giving him all a lover's privileges – for this evening.

JACQUELINE: This evening? What do you mean?

CLAVAROCHE: All I mean is that our worthy André and his good clerks shouldn't pass an unprofitable night in the open air. We must deliver someone to them.

JACQUELINE: You can't do that. It's a horrible idea.

CLAVAROCHE: Why horrible? Nothing could be more innocent. If you can't find Fortunio, you'll write him a note. You'll make him come here this evening, by inviting him secretly. He arrives, the clerks surprise him and André collars him. What would you like to happen then? You'll come down in your nightdress and ask in the most natural way in the world why they're making so much noise. They'll explain. André will be furious and ask you why his young clerk's creeping about in the garden. You'll blush a little at first, then you'll admit quite sincerely everything it suits you to admit, that this boy goes shopping for you and brings you jewellery in secret; in short, the simple truth. What's so frightening about that?

JACQUELINE: No one will believe me. It's not very likely I'd make midnight assignations to pay my bills.

CLAVAROCHE: People always believe what's true. Truth has an accent it's impossible not to recognise. Honest hearts never mistake it. Isn't it a fact that you're employing this young man to do your shopping for you?

JACQUELINE: Yes.

CLAVAROCHE: Well then. As it's what you do, it's what you'll say; they'll see it plain enough. Let him have the proof in his pocket. A jewel case like yesterday, the first thing he finds, that will be enough. Now, here's a pencil.

JACQUELINE: You can't do it. It's a deliberate trick.

CLAVAROCHE: (*Giving her a pencil and paper.*) Please write this: 'Twelve o'clock tonight in the garden'.

JACQUELINE: It's sending this boy into a trap. It's delivering him up to the enemy.

CLAVAROCHE: Don't sign, there's no need. (*He takes the paper.*) Frankly, my dear, it will be chilly tonight, you'd do better to stay in your room. Let this young man have a little stroll on his own and take advantage of the fine weather. I agree they'll find it difficult to believe he's come about your shopping. If they question you, you'd do better to say you knew nothing about the whole business.

JACQUELINE: This note will prove I did.

CLAVAROCHE: Nonsense. Do you think we gallant lovers

are going to show a husband his wife's letters? Besides, you
can see your hand must have been trembling, the writing's
almost disguised. Yes, I'll give this letter to the gardener.
Fortunio will have it right away. For heaven's sake, don't
be frightened. (*Goes out.*)

JACQUELINE: No, I won't do it. Who knows what sort
of revenge a man like André might think up, once he
resorts to violence? I won't send this young man into
such dreadful danger. Clavaroche is quite without pity.
Everything's a battlefield to him; he's ruthless. What's the
point of exposing Fortunio to danger, when it's just as easy
to expose nobody at all? I can understand that in this way
all suspicions would vanish. But it's a wrong way, I won't
use it. No, it distresses me, I don't like it. I don't want this
boy to be ill-treated. As he says he loves me, well, all right.
I won't return evil for good.

(*FORTUNIO enters.*)

FORTUNIO: You sent for me?

JACQUELINE: Yes. You should have received a note from
me. Have you read it?

FORTUNIO: I've received it and read it. You can make what
use you like of me.

JACQUELINE: It's not necessary, I've changed my mind.
Tear it up and don't let's say any more about it.

FORTUNIO: Is there anything else I can do for you?

JACQUELINE: (*Aside.*) How odd, he doesn't insist. (*Aloud.*)
No, I don't need you. I asked you for your song.

FORTUNIO: Here it is. Have you any other orders?

JACQUELINE: No. No, I don't think I have. What's the
matter? You look so pale.

FORTUNIO: If you don't want me any more, please let me
go.

JACQUELINE: I like your song very much. That little tune is
as naïve as you are, and the words are charming.

FORTUNIO: You're too kind.

JACQUELINE: Why, yes. At first I had this idea of sending
for you. Then I thought it over; it was mad of me. I

listened to you too quickly. Come now, sing me your little ballad.

FORTUNIO: I'm sorry, I can't now.

JACQUELINE: Well, why not? Are you ill or is it just some silly idea? I'm almost inclined to make you sing, whether you want to or not. Have I no rights in this song now? (*She puts it on the piano.*)

FORTUNIO: It's not that I don't want to. I can't stay any longer; your husband's waiting for me.

JACQUELINE: I rather like the thought of your getting into trouble. Sit down there and sing.

FORTUNIO: If you insist, I must obey. (*He sits down at the piano.*)

JACQUELINE: Well, what are you thinking about? Are you waiting for an audience?

FORTUNIO: I don't feel well. Let me go.

JACQUELINE: First of all sing, then we'll see if you feel well and if I'll let you go. Sing, I tell you. I wish it. You won't? Well now, what's the boy doing? Come, if you sing I'll let you kiss the tips of my fingers.

FORTUNIO: Stop, Jacqueline, listen to me. You'd have done better to tell me, I'd have agreed to everything.

JACQUELINE: What are you saying? What are you talking about?

FORTUNIO: Yes, you'd have done better to tell me. I swear I'd have done everything you wanted.

JACQUELINE: Everything I wanted? What do you mean?

FORTUNIO: Jacqueline, Jacqueline, you must love him very much. It must hurt you to lie and joke in this heartless way.

JACQUELINE: Me? Joke? What makes you think that?

FORTUNIO: Please don't lie to me any more. That's enough. I know everything.

JACQUELINE: Well really, what do you know?

FORTUNIO: I was in the dining room yesterday when you were talking to Clavaroche.

JACQUELINE: Is that true? You were there?

FORTUNIO: Yes, I was. For heaven's sake, don't say another word about it.

(A pause.)

JACQUELINE: As you know everything, sir, it only remains for me to ask you to say nothing. The wrongs I've done you I feel so deeply I don't even want to try to excuse them. Any other person could perhaps understand and excuse, if, not forgive, the conduct I've been forced to adopt. Unfortunately you're too interested to judge it kindly. I'm resigned and waiting.

FORTUNIO: Don't be afraid of anything. I'd cut off my right hand rather than hurt you.

JACQUELINE: Your word is enough, I've no right to doubt it. The talk we had yesterday may perhaps need an explanation. As I can't justify everything, I'd better keep silent. Let me believe I have only hurt your pride. If that is so, these two days can be forgotten. We'll talk about it later.

FORTUNIO: I shall never want to discuss it again.

JACQUELINE: As you wish; I must do whatever you say. However, if I'm not to see you again, there are a few words I must add. As regards you and me, I'm not afraid, as you've promised to say nothing. There is someone else. If he continues to visit this house, the consequences could be unfortunate.

FORTUNIO: I've nothing to say about that.

JACQUELINE: Please listen to me. As you realise, a quarrel between you would ruin me. I'll do all I can to prevent it Anything you demand, I'll submit to without a word. Don't go without considering this. Dictate your own conditions. Must this person leave here for a time? Shall he apologise to you? Whatever you decide will be accepted by me as a favour and him as a duty. I'm asking you this because I can remember certain jokes he made. What do you want? Tell me.

FORTUNIO: There's nothing I want. You love him. Live in peace as long as he loves you.

JACQUELINE: Thank you for those two promises. Is there anything else you wish me to do? You have only to say.

FORTUNIO: Nothing. Goodbye. Don't be afraid. You'll

never have reason to complain of me. (*He takes his music and goes toward the door.*)

JACQUELINE: Ah, Fortunio, leave me that.

FORTUNIO: What will you do with it? In the ten minutes you've been speaking to me, you haven't uttered a word that came from your heart. It was all about your excuses, your sacrifices, your reparations! Your Clavaroche and his crazy vanity! And my pride! You think you've wounded my pride? You think that what hurts me is to have been made a fool of and be teased at a dinner party? That's not all I remember. When I told you I loved you, did you think I had no feelings? When I told you of my two years of suffering, did you think I was acting as you were? You break my heart, you say you're sorry and that's how you leave me. You've been forced, you say, to do wrong, and you apologise. You blush, you turn away. You pity me because I'm hurt. You can see me, you know what you've done. This is how you cure the wound you've inflicted. It's in my heart, Jacqueline, you've only to stretch out your hand. I swear that if you'd wanted it, however shameful it may be to say so, when you'll even laugh at it, I'd have agreed to anything. God, I feel faint, I can't move. (*He leans on a table.*)

JACQUELINE: Poor boy. I am very much to blame.

FORTUNIO: Keep these attentions for him. I'm not worthy of them; they weren't made for me. I'm not witty or clever; I'd never be able to invent some deep-laid plot when it was wanted. I was fool enough to think you loved me. Yes, because you smiled at me and your hand trembled in mine; because your eyes seemed to seek mine and your lips opened and uttered a little sigh; yes, I admit it, I created a dream; I thought that was how women behaved when they loved you. What a fool! Was it on some parade that your smile congratulated me on the beauty of my horse? Was it the sun flashing on my helmet that dazzled your eyes? I came out of a dark room where for two years I'd followed your walks in the garden. I was just a poor clerk who dared to look in silence. That's the way to be in love.

JACQUELINE: Poor boy.

FORTUNIO: Yes, poor boy. Say it again. I don't know if I'm awake or dreaming, and in spite of everything whether you don't love me. Since last night, I've thought over what my eyes have seen and my ears have heard, and wondered if it were possible. Even now, you tell me, I feel it, I'm suffering, I'm dying and I can't believe it or understand it either. What have I done, Jacqueline? How can you behave like this without loving me or hating me, without knowing me or ever having met me? Everybody loves you; you're good and kind and believe in God, you've never… Oh God, I'm accusing you, when I love you more than life itself. Jacqueline, forgive me.

JACQUELINE: Calm yourself. Come now, calm yourself.

FORTUNIO: All I'm fit for now is to give up my life to your service and whatever work you care to give me. I dare to complain, but you chose me. I was going to have a place in your life. Your lovely radiant face was beginning to shine on me. I was going to live… Must I lose you, Jacqueline? Have I done something wrong, to make you chase me away? Then why won't you go on pretending to love me? (*He falls unconscious.*)

JACQUELINE: (*Running to him.*) Good heavens, what have I done? Fortunio, Fortunio!

FORTUNIO: Who are you? Let me get up.

JACQUELINE: Lean on me. Come to the window. Do please lean on me. Please, Fortunio.

FORTUNIO: It's nothing. I'm all right now.

JACQUELINE: Do you hate me so much, you can't even bear to have me near you?

FORTUNIO: I feel better, thank you.

JACQUELINE: I have done you a great wrong.

FORTUNIO: They were asking for me when I came up. Goodbye, madam, you may rely on me.

JACQUELINE: Shall I see you again?

FORTUNIO: If you wish.

JACQUELINE: Will you come up to the drawing room this evening?

FORTUNIO: If you want me to.

JACQUELINE: You're going? Just one more minute.

FORTUNIO: I can't stay. Goodbye! Goodbye! (*Goes out.*)

JACQUELINE: (*Calls.*) Fortunio. Listen to me.
(*FORTUNIO enters.*)

FORTUNIO: What do you want, Jacqueline?

JACQUELINE: Listen to me, I must speak to you. I don't want to apologise; I don't want to go back over anything; I don't want to justify myself. You are good and honest and sincere. I have been false and disloyal. I can't leave you like this.

FORTUNIO: I forgive you with all my heart.

JACQUELINE: No, you're hurt, the harm is done. Where are you going? What do you want to do? Knowing everything as you did, how could you come back here?

FORTUNIO: You sent for me.

JACQUELINE: But you came to tell me I should see you at this rendezvous. Would you have been there?

FORTUNIO: Yes, if it would have helped you, and I confess I thought it would.

JACQUELINE: What do you mean 'help' me?

FORTUNIO: Madeleine told me something.

JACQUELINE: Then you knew, but you were coming to the garden?

FORTUNIO: The first words I ever said to you were that I'd willingly give my life for you, and the second that I always told the truth.

JACQUELINE: You knew, but you were coming. Do you realise what you're saying? It was a trap.

FORTUNIO: I knew everything.

JACQUELINE: You'd have been caught, killed perhaps, dragged off to prison, I don't know. It's horrible to think about.

FORTUNIO: I knew everything.

JACQUELINE: You knew everything? You knew everything?

You were listening yesterday, weren't you? You knew
everything then, didn't you?

FORTUNIO: Yes.

JACQUELINE: You knew I'd lied and cheated, I'd tricked
you, I might kill you? You knew I loved Clavaroche and
he could make me do whatever he wanted? That I was
playing a part? That here yesterday I was making a fool
of you? That I'm cowardly and contemptible? That I was
exposing you to death for my own pleasure? You knew
everything? You were sure? Well…well…what do you
know now?

FORTUNIO: Jacqueline, I think… I know…

JACQUELINE: Do you know I love you, you silly boy? And
if you don't forgive me, I shall die? And I'm asking you on
my knees?

FORTUNIO: Jacqueline!

Scene II

The same, the next evening.
JACQUELINE and FORTUNIO are talking.
ANDRÉ and CLAVAROCHE enter.

ANDRÉ. Come along, Captain. Thank heavens, here we all
are, happy, reunited, and friends again. If ever I doubt my
wife in the future, let me be poisoned by my own wine.

CLAVAROCHE: (*Aside to JACQUELINE.*) I tell you once
again, this clerk of yours annoys me. Will you please get
rid of him?

JACQUELINE: (*Aside.*) I did what you told me.

ANDRÉ: When I think I spent last night in the office
catching my death of cold through being so confoundedly
suspicious, I don't know what sort of a fool to call myself.

CLAVAROCHE: (*Aside.*) If that clerk of yours doesn't leave
the house immediately, then I will.

JACQUELINE: (*Aside.*) I did what you told me.

ANDRÉ: I've told everybody: justice must be done in this
house. The whole town will know what kind of a man
I am. To make amends, from now on I'll never suspect

anything again, whatever happens. Let's go and have dinner. Fortunio, you can sing us your song and we'll drink to your love affairs. And I'll give you a song. (*He sings.*) 'Friend, drink deep and never cease...'

FORTUNIO: That song's a little out of date. Why don't you sing, Captain?

A DIVERSION
(Un Caprice)

Characters

FLORA

COUNT DE CHAVIGNY, her husband

MADAME DE LÉRY

FOOTMAN

Scene: Flora's boudoir in Paris.

A Diversion

FLORA is alone, working at a net purse.

FLORA: One more stitch and I've finished. (*She sings.*)
(*FOOTMAN enters.*)
Has a parcel come from the jeweller's?
FOOTMAN: No madam not yet.
FLORA: How infuriating. Send someone again. At once.
(*FOOTMAN goes out.*) I should have bought the first tassels
I saw. It's eight o'clock. He's dressing. I know he'll be
here before it's ready. That will make it another day late.
Making a purse in secret for one's husband! Most people
would think that a little over-romantic. After being married
for one year! Charlotte, now, what would she say if she
knew? And he, what will he think? He will laugh perhaps
at the secrecy, but he won't laugh at the gift. Why this
secrecy, in fact? I don't know. But I don't believe I'd have
worked with such pleasure in front of him. It would have
been like saying, 'See how much I think of you'. It would
look like a reproach. But if I show it him finished, he'll
then say to himself that I've thought of him.
(*FOOTMAN enters.*)
FOOTMAN: This has come from the jeweller's, madam. (*He
gives her a small parcel.*)
FLORA: (*She sits again*). At last. Let me know as soon as the
Count leaves his room.
(*FOOTMAN goes out.*)
Now, my dear little purse, we're going to give you the final
touches. Let's see how pretty you'll look with these tassels.
Not bad. How will you be received now? Will you reveal
all the pleasure that's gone into your making, all the care
that's been taken of you? You're not expected, you know.
You were only meant to be seen in your full finery. Would
a kiss make you happier? (*She kisses the purse and stops.*) Poor
little thing. You're not worth very much. I could buy you
in a shop for twenty francs. Then why does it make me sad
to part with you? When you were started, you were to be

finished as quickly as possible. Ah, I was happier then than I am now. But it only took a fortnight. Only a fortnight, can that be right? Yes, that's all. And how much has happened in that time! Are we going to be too late, I wonder? Why do I think such things? Someone's coming. It's he. He still loves me.

(*FOOTMAN enters.*)

FOOTMAN: Here is the Count, madam.

FLORA: Heavens, I've only sewed one tassel and forgotten the other. What a fool I am! I still shan't be able to give it to him today. Ask him to wait a minute, a second only, in the drawing room. Quickly, before he comes.

FOOTMAN: Here he is, madam.

(*FOOTMAN goes out.*
FLORA hides the purse.
CHAVIGNY enters.)

CHAVIGNY: Good evening, my dear. Do I disturb you?

FLORA: Me, Henry? What a question.

CHAVIGNY: You look worried, as though there's something on your mind. When I come into your room, I always forget I'm your husband and throw open the door too quickly.

FLORA: That sounds rather wicked. But as it also sounds rather charming, it won't stop me kissing you. (*She kisses him.*) Who do you think you are then, when you forget you're my husband?

CHAVIGNY: Your lover, my darling. Am I wrong?

FLORA: Lover and beloved, you're not wrong. (*Aside.*) I'd like to give him the purse just as it is.

CHAVIGNY: Why are you dressed like that? Aren't you going out?

FLORA: No. I wanted… I was hoping perhaps…

CHAVIGNY: Hoping? Why, what's the matter?

FLORA: Are you going to the ball? You look magnificent.

CHAVIGNY: Not very. I don't know if it's my fault or my tailor's, but I don't seem to have the figure I used to.

FLORA: Faithless creature! You don't give a thought to me when you admire yourself in the mirror.

CHAVIGNY: Bah! Well, who then? Do you think I'm going to the ball for the sake of dancing? I promise you I shall find it utterly boring. I don't know why I bother to get involved.

FLORA: Oh, well… But do stay, please. We'll be all alone and I'll tell you…

CHAVIGNY: Your clock must be fast. It can't be as late as that.

FLORA: No one goes to a ball at this hour, whatever the clock says. We've only just finished dinner.

CHAVIGNY: I ordered the carriage. I've a call to make.

FLORA: Oh, that's different. I… I didn't know… I thought…

CHAVIGNY: Well?

FLORA: I imagined…after what you said… But the clock's quite right. It's only eight. Please stay for a few minutes. I've a little surprise for you.

CHAVIGNY: You know, my dear, I leave you free to go out whenever you choose. You will agree it's right to do the same for me. What is this surprise you have?

FLORA: Nothing. I never used the word.

CHAVIGNY: I'm sorry, I thought I heard you. Have you those Strauss waltzes? Lend them to me if you're not using them.

FLORA: There they are. Do you want them now?

CHAVIGNY: Yes, if you don't mind. I've been asked for them for the last day or two. I shan't need them for long.

FLORA: Are they for Madame de Blainville?

CHAVIGNY: (*Taking the waltzes.*) I beg your pardon. Did you mention Madame de Blainville?

FLORA: I? No, I didn't.

CHAVIGNY: This time I did hear you. (*He sits.*) What did you say about Madame de Blainville?

FLORA: I thought my waltzes were for her.

CHAVIGNY: And why did you think that?

FLORA: Because…because she likes them.

CHAVIGNY: She does. And so do I. And so do you, I think. There's one in particular. How does it go? I've forgotten… What is it called?

FLORA: I don't know if I can remember. (*She sits at the piano and plays.*)

CHAVIGNY: That's it. It's charming, divine, and you play it like an angel or, rather, like a real musician.

FLORA: As well as she does, Henry?

CHAVIGNY: Who? Madame de Blainville? You seem to be obsessed with her.

FLORA: Not particularly. If I were a man, she's not the sort of woman I'd lose my head about.

CHAVIGNY: (*Rising.*) And you would be quite right. A man should never lose his head, about a woman or a waltz.

FLORA: Were you intending to gamble this evening, my dear?

CHAVIGNY: What an idea. One may play, but one doesn't start out with the intention of doing so.

FLORA: Have you enough money on you?

CHAVIGNY: I think so. Do you need any?

FLORA: I? Good heavens, why should I?

CHAVIGNY: Why not? I may throw open your door too quickly, but I don't open your desk at all. Perhaps I'm doubly wrong.

FLORA: That's not true. It's not so very long since I noticed you'd opened it and given me far too much money.

CHAVIGNY: Not too much, my dear, as long as there are any poor people in this world. I know how you spend your money and I only ask you to let me make my own gifts to charity through you.

FLORA: Dear Henry, how noble and good you are. Tell me something. Do you remember you once had some small debt to pay and complained about not having a purse?

CHAVIGNY: When was that? Oh, of course. The fact is that when one's out, it's impossible to rely on one's pockets; they're useless.

FLORA: Would you like a red purse with a black net?

CHAVIGNY: No, I hate red. Good lord, that reminds me, I received a new purse yesterday. It's a present. What do you think of it? Is it in good taste? (*He takes a purse from his pocket.*)

FLORA: Let me see it.

CHAVIGNY: Take it. (*He gives it to her. She looks at it, then gives it back.*)

FLORA: It's very pretty. What colour is it?

CHAVIGNY: (*Laughing.*) What colour? You ask the funniest questions.

FLORA: I'm sorry... I meant... Who gave it to you?

CHAVIGNY: This is too amusing. Really, your absent-mindedness is adorable.

(*FOOTMAN enters.*)

FOOTMAN: Madame de Léry.

FLORA: I told them to say I was out.

CHAVIGNY: No, no, let her come in. Why not see her?

FLORA: Very well. (*FOOTMAN goes out.*) Now, about this purse... Am I allowed to know who gave it to you?

(*MADAME DE LÉRY enters.*)

CHAVIGNY: Come in, come in, please. You couldn't have arrived at a better time. Flora has just made an absent-minded remark that's worth its weight in gold. Just imagine, I show her this purse...

MADAME DE LÉRY: Oh, how nice! Let me see it.

CHAVIGNY: I show her this purse. She looks at it, feels it, turns it over, and as she gives it back, what do you think she says? She asks me what colour it is.

MADAME DE LÉRY: Well, it's blue.

CHAVIGNY: Yes, it's blue. Of course it is. And that's precisely the point. Can you imagine anyone asking such a thing?

MADAME DE LÉRY: It's perfect. Good evening, Flora, my dear. Aren't you coming to the embassy?

FLORA: No, I thought I'd stay at home.

CHAVIGNY: But my little story doesn't amuse you?

MADAME DE LÉRY: Of course it does. Now, who made this purse? Oh, I recognise it, Madame de Blainville! Well, you're really not going?

CHAVIGNY: (*Sharply.*) How do you recognise it, may I ask?

MADAME DE LÉRY: Because it's blue. I've seen her carrying it around for ages. It's taken seven years to make and you can imagine how often it's changed its destination in that time. It's theoretically belonged to three people to my knowledge. It's a treasure you have there, my dear Count. You've come into quite an inheritance.

CHAVIGNY: Anyone would think there was only one purse in the world.

MADAME DE LÉRY: No, but there's only one blue one. To begin with, I detest blue. It doesn't mean anything, it's a stupid colour. I can't be mistaken about a thing like that; it's enough to have seen it once. I loathe blue just as much as I adore mauve.

FLORA: Blue's the colour of constancy.

MADAME DE LÉRY: Nonsense, it's the colour for baby boys. I only looked in for a moment. You see, I'm in full dress. You have to arrive early at a party like this. There'll be such a crowd, I'll probably break a rib. But why aren't you coming? I wouldn't miss it for the world.

FLORA: I didn't intend to and it's too late now.

MADAME DE LÉRY: Nonsense, you've plenty of time. Look, my dear, I'll ring the bell. Ask for a dress. We'll put your husband out of the room, with his little present. I'll do your hair myself, put a couple of sprays of flowers on top, and then whisk you off in my carriage. There, the whole thing's settled.

FLORA: Not this evening. I'm definitely not going out.

MADAME DE LÉRY: 'Definitely'? Have you made up your mind? My dear Count, why don't you take her?

CHAVIGNY: (*Drily.*) I never meddle in other people's affairs.

MADAME DE LÉRY: No, you stay out in the cold and turn blue apparently. Listen then, I'll tell you what I'll do. Give me a cup of tea and I'll stay here.

FLORA: How kind of you, Charlotte dear! But no, I won't deprive the ball of its queen. Go and have a waltz for me and come back at eleven o'clock if you want to. We'll chat here by the fire on our own, as Henry's deserting us.

CHAVIGNY: I? Not at all. I don't know if I'm going out.

MADAME DE LÉRY: Well then, it's settled, I'll leave you.

By the way, have you heard about my troubles? I've been robbed.

FLORA: What do you mean?

MADAME DE LÉRY: Four dresses, my dear, four divine dresses which were sent me from London, lost because of the customs. If you'd seen them! It's enough to make one weep. There was a pink and a purple. I'll never get anything like them again.

FLORA: I am so sorry. Have they been confiscated?

MADAME DE LÉRY: Nothing of the sort. If that were all, I'd scream till they gave them back, but this is criminal. Here I am, naked for the season. Believe it or not, they've ripped my gowns to pieces. They've thrust those testing spikes of theirs all over the place through the boxes and made holes in every dress big enough to put your fist through. That's the news they served me up for lunch yesterday.

CHAVIGNY: There wasn't a blue one among them, by any chance?

MADAME DE LÉRY: No, sir, there was not. Goodbye, Flora my dear. I'll just make a fleeting appearance. I think I'm in the middle of my twelfth cold this winter; now I'm going to catch the thirteenth. As soon as I can, I'll rush back here to your fireside and we'll have a little chat about customs officials and dressmakers, eh? No, I'm rather melancholy, we'll be sentimental. Well, it doesn't matter. Goodbye, my azure gentleman. If you see me out, I shan't come back. (*Goes out.*)

CHAVIGNY: What a scatterbrained woman that is. You choose your friends very carefully.

FLORA: It was you who had her shown in.

CHAVIGNY: I'm sure you think Madame de Blainville made me that purse.

FLORA: No, as you say she didn't.

CHAVIGNY: I'm sure you think so.

FLORA: What makes you so sure?

CHAVIGNY: Because I know you too well. You always echo Madame de Léry. Only a fool could think such a thing.

FLORA: That's a compliment I scarcely deserve.

CHAVIGNY: Oh yes. And I'd much rather you were honest about it instead of prevaricating.

FLORA: But if I don't think so, I can't pretend to, just to seem sincere.

CHAVIGNY: I tell you, you do think so. It's written all over your face.

FLORA: If I must say so to satisfy you, very well, I will. I think so.

CHAVIGNY: You do? And if it were true, what harm would there be?

FLORA: None, and for that reason I don't see why you should deny it.

CHAVIGNY: I don't deny it. She did make it. Good night. I may come back later to take tea with your friend.

FLORA: Henry, don't leave me like this.

CHAVIGNY: What do you mean 'like this'? Are we angry with each other? It all seems very simple to me. Someone makes me a purse and I use it. You ask me who and I tell you. There's nothing less like a quarrel.

FLORA: And if I asked you for the purse, would you give it to me?

CHAVIGNY: Possibly. But what would you do with it?

FLORA: That doesn't matter. I do ask you for it.

CHAVIGNY: You don't mean to use it, I suppose? I should like to know what you'll do with it.

FLORA: I do mean to use it.

CHAVIGNY: How very amusing! You'll use a purse made by Madame de Blainville?

FLORA: Why not? You do.

CHAVIGNY: Admirable logic. But I'm not a woman.

FLORA: Very well. If I don't use it, I'll throw it on the fire.

CHAVIGNY: Ah, at last you're being honest. Well, equally honestly, I'll keep it, if you'll let me.

FLORA: You're free to do so, of course. But I tell you it makes me most unhappy to think you'll show it to everyone and they'll all know who made it for you.

CHAVIGNY: Show it to everyone? One would think it was a trophy!

FLORA: Listen to me, please, and give me your hand. Do you love me, Henry? Tell me.

CHAVIGNY: I love you and I'm listening to you.

FLORA: I promise I'm not jealous. But if you give me this purse as a favour, I'll thank you with all my heart. It's a small exchange I'm proposing and I think, at least I hope, that you won't find you lose anything by it.

CHAVIGNY: Let's see this exchange. What have you got?

FLORA: I'll tell you if you insist. But if you take my word and give me the purse first, it will make me very happy.

CHAVIGNY: I never take anyone's word.

FLORA: Henry, please.

CHAVIGNY: No.

FLORA: Well then, I beg you on my knees. (*She kneels.*)

CHAVIGNY: Get up, Flora, please. You know I hate that sort of thing. I cannot stand anyone going down on their knees and I understand less than ever why you should do it now. It's too much to insist on such childishness. If you seriously demanded it, I'd throw the purse on the fire myself without any question of an exchange. Come now, get up and don't let's talk any more about it. Goodbye. I'll be back later. (*Goes out.*)

FLORA: Since I can't burn the other one, it will have to be my own. (*She goes to her desk and takes out the purse which she made.*) Poor little thing, I kissed you just now. And do you remember what I said? We did arrive too late, you see. He doesn't want you and he doesn't want me any more either. (*She goes toward the fire.*) How foolish to indulge in dreams. They never come true. Why is there such an attraction, an irresistible charm in forming a plan? Why is there so much pleasure in secretly carrying it out? What good does it all do? It only ends in tears. Well, what does fate require? What sacrifices and prayers are needed to realise successfully the simplest wish, the most paltry hope? You were quite right, Henry, to say that what I was demanding was childishness, but it meant so much to me. And you, whether you're proud or unfaithful, it wouldn't have cost you much to take part in such childishness. He doesn't love me any more, he doesn't love me. He loves you, Madame de Blainville. (*She weeps.*) Come now, I mustn't think about it any more. Let's throw on the fire this silly toy which hadn't the sense to arrive in time. If I'd given it to him this evening, he would probably have lost it tomorrow. Yes, of course he would. He'd have left my purse lying on a table somewhere deliberately, but he'll always use hers. Yes, now at this very moment, he's gambling and pulling it out with pride. I can see it lying on the cloth, bulging with the money he's won. I'm so unhappy. I'm jealous; and that was all I needed to make me angry. (*She goes to throw the purse on the fire and stops.*) But why should I destroy my own work like this? In this little fragile net lie two weeks of my life; its bright colours are still unfaded. I like it, I want to keep it. Yes, I'll finish it and wear it next to my heart. It will do me at the same time both good and harm. It will remind me of my own love for him, but also his forgetfulness, his caprices. And who knows, one day perhaps he may come back for it. (*She sits and sews on the tassel.*)

MADAME DE LÉRY: (*Off.*) No one about? What does that mean? It's like coming into a museum. (*She opens the door and laughingly announces.*) Madame de Léry!
(*MADAME DE LÉRY enters.*
FLORA rises.)
Good evening once again, my dear. Have you no servants in this house? I've been running all over the place trying to find one. I'm exhausted. (*She sits.*)

FLORA: Take off your furs.

MADAME DE LÉRY: In a moment, I'm frozen. Do you like this old fox? They say it's Ethiopian marten or something. My husband brought it me from Holland. But frankly I think it's hideous. I'll wear it three times to be polite and then give it to my maid.

FLORA: But a maid couldn't wear that.

MADAME DE LÉRY: Quite right. I'll turn it into a rug.

FLORA: Well, was it a beautiful ball?

MADAME DE LÉRY: Good heavens, the ball! But I haven't been. You'll never believe what's happened.

FLORA: You never went?

MADAME DE LÉRY: Yes, I went, but I never got there. It will make you die with laughter. Just imagine, the queue, the queue... (*She bursts out laughing.*) Does that sort of thing frighten you?

FLORA: Oh, yes. I hate a crowd of carriages.

MADAME DE LÉRY: It's worse when you're alone. I kept on shouting to the coachman on the box to drive on, but he didn't move. I was in such a temper I nearly climbed up to give him a box on the ears. You feel such a fool sitting there in a ball dress staring at a streaming windowpane. Because apart from everything else, it was pouring with rain. I amused myself for half an hour watching the passers-by splashing about and then I decided to come back. There's my ball for you. This fire is delicious. I feel I'm coming back to life again.

(*FLORA rings.*
FOOTMAN enters.)

FLORA: Some tea.

(*FOOTMAN goes out.*)

MADAME DE LÉRY: Your husband has gone out, has he?

FLORA: Yes, I think he's going to the ball. And he'll be more determined than you.

MADAME DE LÉRY: I don't think he exactly likes me – between ourselves, of course.

FLORA: You're wrong, I promise you. He's often told me he thinks you're one of the prettiest women in Paris.

MADAME DE LÉRY: Really? That's very charming. But I deserve it, as I've a very high opinion of him too. Can you lend me a pin?

FLORA: There's a box next to you.

MADAME DE LÉRY: The dresses that Palmira woman makes. You can never feel the shoulders and you think the whole time that everything's going to fall down. Did she make those sleeves of yours?

FLORA: Yes.

MADAME DE LÉRY: Very pretty, very pretty indeed! Definitely there's nothing like straight sleeves, but it's taken me a long time to come round to them. Besides you mustn't be too fat to wear them or you look like a grasshopper with an enormous body and tiny feet and hands.

FLORA: What a charming thought.

(*FOOTMAN enters with the tea. He places it on a table and goes out.*)

MADAME DE LÉRY: But isn't it true? Look at Mademoiselle Saint-Ange. But of course you mustn't be too thin either or there's nothing left at all. Everybody's talking about the Marquise d'Ermont. But to me she looks like a gallows. She has a lovely face I agree, but she's just a Madonna on the end of a flagstaff.

FLORA: (*Laughing.*) Can I give you some tea, my dear?

MADAME DE LÉRY: Nothing but hot water, with a dash of tea and a wisp of milk.

FLORA: (*Pouring the tea.*) Are you going to Madame d'Egly's tomorrow? I'll take you if you like.

MADAME DE LÉRY: Now there's another of them! With all those curls and lanky legs, she looks to me like one of those long-handled brooms you use for dusting picture rails. Well of course I'm going. (*She drinks.*) No, I can't. I'm going to a concert.

FLORA: (*Aside.*) She really is a little odd.

MADAME DE LÉRY: Look at me, please.

FLORA: Why?

MADAME DE LÉRY: Look me straight in the face.

FLORA: What's so extraordinary about me?

MADAME DE LÉRY: Yes, I was right, your eyes are red; you've just been crying, it's as clear as daylight. Why, what's happened, Flora, my dear?

FLORA: Nothing, I promise. What do you want to have happened?

MADAME DE LÉRY: I've no idea, but you've just been crying. I'm disturbing you. I'll go.

FLORA: Indeed you're not. Do please stay.

MADAME DE LÉRY: Do you mean it? I'll stay if you like, but you're going to tell me what's the matter. (*FLORA *shakes her head.*) No? Then I'll go. If I'm no use to you, I must be upsetting you, although I don't mean to.

FLORA: Please stay. Your being here means a great deal to me. You're so amusing that if I did have any worries, I'd soon forget them.

MADAME DE LÉRY: Look, my dear, I'm very fond of you. You may think I'm frivolous, but no one could be more serious about serious matters. I don't understand how anyone can joke about affairs of the heart and that's why people think I haven't got one. But I know what it is to be hurt, I learned when I was quite young. And I know what it means to be able to talk about one's troubles. So if you feel you can tell me yours, then please do. I'm not saying this out of curiosity.

FLORA: You're very kind and I know you mean well. But I can't tell you.

MADAME DE LÉRY: Good heavens, yes, of course. The blue purse! It was dreadfully stupid of me to mention Madame de Blainville. It struck me as I left the house. Is your husband running after her?

(*FLORA rises and, not being able to reply, turns away and puts her handkerchief to her eyes.*)

Is that really so?

(*A pause.*

FLORA walks up and down a little, then sits at the other end of the room.

MADAME DE LÉRY seems to be thinking. She rises and approaches FLORA who puts out her hand.)

You know, my dear, that dentists tell you to shout when they hurt you. Well, I tell you now, 'Cry as much as you can'. Tears are always a relief.

FLORA: Oh, heavens!

MADAME DE LÉRY: But the whole thing's unbelievable. Nobody could be in love with Madame de Blainville. She's nothing but a middle-aged flirt without brains or beauty. She's not worth your little finger. No one leaves an angel for a devil.

FLORA: (*Sobbing.*) I know he loves her, I know it.

MADAME DE LÉRY: No, my child, it's impossible. It's a diversion, an idle fancy. I know your husband better than he thinks. He may be a little naughty, but he's not wicked. It's only a whim. Did you cry in front of him?

FLORA: Oh no!

MADAME DE LÉRY: Well done. I wouldn't be surprised if he'd have been rather pleased.

FLORA: Pleased? Pleased to see me in tears?

MADAME DE LÉRY: Heavens, yes. I may be only twenty-five, but I know a lot about life. How did all this happen?

FLORA: Well... I don't know...

MADAME DE LÉRY: Tell me. Are you frightened of me? I'll reassure you at once. If it will make it easier, I'll prove I trust you and make you trust me. Is that necessary? I'll do it. What would you like to know about me?

FLORA: You're the best friend I have. I'll tell you everything and trust you completely. It's nothing very serious, but I'm so hasty and I get carried away. I've been secretly making a little purse for my husband and I meant to give it to him this evening. For a fortnight, I've hardly seen him; he spends every day with Madame de Blainville. I thought that giving him this purse would reproach him mildly for his absence and show him he was leaving me alone. But just as I was going to give it to him, he pulled out the other one.

MADAME DE LÉRY: But that's nothing to cry about.

FLORA: Oh, yes, it is. I did something very silly. I asked him for the other purse.

MADAME DE LÉRY: That wasn't very wise.

FLORA: I know, Charlotte; and he refused...and then...oh, I'm so ashamed..

MADAME DE LÉRY: Well?

FLORA: Well, I asked him on my knees. I wanted him to make this little sacrifice for me and I'd have given him my purse in exchange for hers. I asked him... I begged him...

MADAME DE LÉRY: And he did nothing. Naturally. You poor thing. He's not worthy of you.

FLORA: I'll never believe that, in spite of everything.

MADAME DE LÉRY: You're right. I'm expressing myself
   badly. He is worthy of you and he loves you, but he's a
   man and he's proud. What a pity it all is! Where is your
   purse?

FLORA: Here, on the table.

MADAME DE LÉRY: (*Taking the purse.*) This one? But my
   dear, it's ten times prettier than hers. To begin with it's
   not blue and anyway it's charming. Let me have it and I'll
   guarantee to make him like it.

FLORA: If only you could!

MADAME DE LÉRY: To be like this after one year of
   marriage! It's unheard of. There must be some witchcraft
   behind it. That Blainville woman and her indigo, I hate her
   from top to toe. Anyway her eyes have almost dropped
   down to her chin. Flora, will you do something? It won't
   cost anything to try. Will your husband come in to see you
   this evening?

FLORA: I've no idea.

MADAME DE LÉRY: What was the situation when he left?

FLORA: I was very sad and he was very severe.

MADAME DE LÉRY: He'll come. Are you brave? When I
   have an idea, I warn you, I must carry it out quickly. Don't
   worry, I'll succeed.

FLORA: Tell me what to do and I'll do it.

MADAME DE LÉRY: Get dressed as quickly as you can
   and go down to my carriage. I don't want to send you to
   the ball, but when you get back, you must look as though
   you've been there. Drive wherever you like, the Invalides,
   the Bastille, anywhere. It won't be very amusing, but you
   might as well try to keep awake there as here. Do you
   agree? Now, wrap up your purse in this piece of paper
   and I'll address it. There. Now, at the first corner, tell my
   coachman to stop. Then ask the footman to bring this little
   parcel back here, give it to the first servant he sees and go
   away at once without saying anything.

FLORA: Do at least say what you want to do.

MADAME DE LÉRY: My dear child, it's impossible to say

what I want to do, I can only see if it's possible to do it. For the last time, do you trust me?

FLORA: Utterly and completely, if it will make him love me.

MADAME DE LÉRY: Hurry. There's a carriage.

FLORA: It's he. I hear his voice on the steps.

MADAME DE LÉRY: You must go. Is there a back staircase?

FLORA: Yes, thank heavens. But look at my hair. How could anyone think I've been to a ball?

MADAME DE LÉRY: (*Taking the spray of flowers from her head, and giving them to FLORA.*) Here. You can put them on in the carriage.

(*FLORA goes out.*)

On her knees! A woman like that on her knees! And this gentleman takes no notice. Poor child, to have to ask him as a favour to accept her purse in exchange for a present from Madame de Blainville. How hard-hearted men are! Heavens, we're much better creatures.

(*She sits and takes a magazine from the table. A moment later there is a knock at the door.*)

Come in.

(*CHAVIGNY enters.*)

(*Absent-mindedly, as she reads.*) Good evening. Would you like some tea?

CHAVIGNY: No, thank you. I never take it. (*He sits and looks about the room.*)

MADAME DE LÉRY: Was the ball amusing?

CHAVIGNY: So-so. Weren't you there?

MADAME DE LÉRY: Now that's not a very gallant question. No, I wasn't. But I sent Flora. You seem surprised she's not here.

CHAVIGNY: You're joking, I presume.

MADAME DE LÉRY: I beg your pardon? I'm sorry, I'm reading such an interesting article.

(*A pause. CHAVIGNY rises and walks restlessly to and fro.*)

CHAVIGNY: Has Flora really gone to the ball?

MADAME DE LÉRY: Of course. As you see, I'm waiting for her.

CHAVIGNY: How odd! She didn't want to, when you first suggested it.

MADAME DE LÉRY: She evidently changed her mind.

CHAVIGNY: Why didn't she go with you?

MADAME DE LÉRY: Because I didn't care about it any more.

CHAVIGNY: She had no carriage.

MADAME DE LÉRY: No, I lent her mine. Have you read this?

CHAVIGNY: What?

MADAME DE LÉRY: This magazine. There's a very good article by George Sand about orangutans.

CHAVIGNY: About what?

MADAME DE LÉRY: Orangutans. No, I'm wrong, it's not by her, it's the next column. How very amusing.

CHAVIGNY: I simply can't understand this idea of going to the ball without telling me. I could at least have brought her back.

MADAME DE LÉRY: Do you like George Sand's novels?

CHAVIGNY: No, I don't. But if she's there, why didn't I see her?

MADAME DE LÉRY: What, George Sand? I didn't know you knew her.

CHAVIGNY: Are you making fun of me?

MADAME DE LÉRY: Perhaps. It depends what you're talking about.

CHAVIGNY: My wife.

MADAME DE LÉRY: Did you ask me to look after her?

CHAVIGNY: Quite right. I'm being very silly. I'll go and look for her.

MADAME DE LÉRY: Nonsense, you'll get stuck in the queue.

CHAVIGNY: True enough. I might just as well wait...so I shall. (*He sits down near the fire.*)

MADAME DE LÉRY: (*Stops reading.*) You know, my dear Count, you surprise me. I thought I heard you say you left Flora perfectly free to go where she wished.

CHAVIGNY: I do. You see the proof of it.

MADAME DE LÉRY: I don't see it at all. You look furious.

CHAVIGNY: I? How absurd. Not in the least.

MADAME DE LÉRY: You keep on getting up. I must confess I thought you quite a different sort of person. Seriously, I wouldn't have lent Flora my carriage, if I'd known you'd be like this.

CHAVIGNY: But I assure you it seems quite natural to me; I'm grateful to you for lending it to her.

MADAME DE LÉRY: No, no, you're not grateful. I assure you, you're furious. Frankly, I think that one of her reasons for going was to join you.

CHAVIGNY: How very likely, after she refused to go with me.

MADAME DE LÉRY: Yes, that's what I told her. But we women are like that. First we don't want to, then we do. Are you definitely not having any tea?

CHAVIGNY: No, it disagrees with me.

MADAME DE LÉRY: Well, give me some.

CHAVIGNY: I beg your pardon?

MADAME DE LÉRY: Give me some. (*CHAVIGNY rises and pours out a cup of tea which he offers her.*) That's right. Put it down there. Have we a government this evening?

CHAVIGNY: I've no idea.

MADAME DE LÉRY: What odd sort of hotels these governments are. People come in and go out, without knowing why. It's like a puppet show.

CHAVIGNY: Drink your tea. It's nearly cold already.

MADAME DE LÉRY: There's not enough sugar. Give me another lump or two.

CHAVIGNY: As you wish. It's not worth drinking.

MADAME DE LÉRY: Good. Now a little more milk.

CHAVIGNY: Is that all right?

MADAME DE LÉRY: A drop of hot water now. Finished? give it to me.

CHAVIGNY: (*Giving it to her.*) Here you are. But it's not worth drinking.

MADAME DE LÉRY: Really? Are you sure?

CHAVIGNY: There's no doubt about it.

MADAME DE LÉRY: Well, why isn't it worth drinking?

CHAVIGNY: Because it's cold and too sweet.

MADAME DE LÉRY: Well, if it isn't worth drinking, throw it away.

(*CHAVIGNY takes the cup.*
MADAME DE LÉRY looks at him and laughs.)

Heavens, you do amuse me. I've never seen anyone look so disagreeable.

(*CHAVIGNY impatiently empties the cup into the fire, then strides up and down the room.*)

CHAVIGNY: (*Angrily.*) It's true, I'm just a fool.

MADAME DE LÉRY: I've never before seen you jealous, but you're behaving like Othello.

CHAVIGNY: I am not. I cannot stand anyone being embarrassed or embarrassing other people. Why should I be jealous?

MADAME DE LÉRY: From pride. Like all husbands.

CHAVIGNY: What a feminine remark! You only say that because it's what people always say. The world is very hard on us poor husbands.

MADAME DE LÉRY: Not as hard as on us poor wives.

CHAVIGNY: Good lord, yes. Everything's relative. Can we allow our wives to live on the same footing as ourselves? Obviously not. There are hundreds of things which are very serious for them, but mean nothing to a man.

MADAME DE LÉRY: Yes. A love affair, for example.

CHAVIGNY: Why not? Well then, yes, a love affair. Certainly a man can have one, but a woman…

MADAME DE LÉRY: Sometimes has one too. Do you think a dress is a talisman which saves her?

CHAVIGNY: It's a barrier which should prevent her.

MADAME DE LÉRY: At least it shouldn't be a veil which assists her. There's someone coming. It must be Flora.

CHAVIGNY: It can't be. It's not twelve yet.

(*FOOTMAN enters and gives CHAVIGNY a small parcel.*)

What is it? What do you want?

FOOTMAN: This has just been brought for you, sir. (*Goes out.*)

(*CHAVIGNY unwraps the parcel, which contains FLORA's purse.*)

MADAME DE LÉRY: Is that another present for you? At this time of night, that's a little peculiar.

CHAVIGNY: What the devil does this mean? Hey, John! Hey, there! Who brought this parcel?

(*FOOTMAN enters.*)

FOOTMAN: Sir?

CHAVIGNY: Who brought this parcel?

FOOTMAN: The concierge just gave it me, sir.

CHAVIGNY: Isn't there anything with it? No letter?

FOOTMAN: No, sir.

CHAVIGNY: Has the concierge had it for long?

FOOTMAN: No, sir, it's just been given to him.

CHAVIGNY: Who gave it to him?

FOOTMAN: He doesn't know, sir.

CHAVIGNY: He doesn't know? Are you out of your mind? Was it a man or a woman?

FOOTMAN: A servant in livery, but he doesn't know him.

CHAVIGNY: Is this servant still here?

FOOTMAN: No, sir, he left at once.

CHAVIGNY: Without a word?

FOOTMAN: Yes, sir.

CHAVIGNY: All right.

(*FOOTMAN goes out.*)

MADAME DE LÉRY: You're getting spoiled, my dear Count. It won't be the fault of these ladies if you lose your money.

CHAVIGNY: I'll be hanged if I understand a word of it.

MADAME DE LÉRY: Come now, stop pretending.

CHAVIGNY: No, I give you my word of honour, I've no idea. It must be a mistake.

MADAME DE LÉRY: Isn't your name on the wrapping?

CHAVIGNY: Of course, yes, you're right. That's odd, I know the writing.

MADAME DE LÉRY: May I see?

CHAVIGNY: Perhaps I'm being indiscreet to show it to you. But so much the worse for whoever wrote it. You know, I'm sure I've seen that writing somewhere.

MADAME DE LÉRY: I'm sure I have, too.

CHAVIGNY: Wait a moment… No, I'm wrong. What sort of writing is it?

MADAME DE LÉRY: It's a beautiful hand. There's no doubt that it's a very well-educated lady.

CHAVIGNY: You seem to know who it is.

MADAME DE LÉRY: (*With feigned embarrassment.*) I? Of course not.

(*CHAVIGNY looks at her with surprise, then continues to walk up and down.*)

What were we talking about? Oh, love affairs, I think it was. This little red herring has come at the right moment.

CHAVIGNY: You're in the secret. Admit it.

MADAME DE LÉRY: There are some people who can't do anything. If I were you, I'd have guessed by now.

CHAVIGNY: Come, be frank. Tell me who it is.

MADAME DE LÉRY: I would say it's Madame de Blainville.

CHAVIGNY: You're quite pitiless. Do you realise we shall soon be quarrelling?

MADAME DE LÉRY: I should welcome it. But not on this occasion.

CHAVIGNY: You won't help me solve the problem?

MADAME DE LÉRY: What a delightful task! Forget all about it. I would say it isn't your sort of problem. You'll think about it later, if only out of politeness.

CHAVIGNY: Is there any more tea? I should like a cup.

MADAME DE LÉRY: I'll make you some. You see I'm always your humble servant.

CHAVIGNY: The more I think, the more impossible it seems.

MADAME DE LÉRY: Oh really, have you made up your mind to think of nothing but that purse? I'm going to leave you – to your thoughts.

CHAVIGNY: It's simply that I'm astounded.

MADAME DE LÉRY: I tell you it's Madame de Blainville. She's been thinking about the colour of her purse and sent you another in repentance. Or, better still: she wants to tempt you and see if you'll use this one or hers.

CHAVIGNY: I'll certainly use this one. It's the only way to know who made it.

MADAME DE LÉRY: I don't understand. It's too deep for me.

CHAVIGNY: I imagine the person who sent it me will see it in my hand tomorrow. Do you think I'd make a mistake?

MADAME DE LÉRY: (*Laughing.*) This is too much. I don't care.

CHAVIGNY: It wouldn't by any chance be you?

(*A pause.*)

MADAME DE LÉRY: Here is your tea made with my own white hand and it will be better than the tea you made me just now. Do stop staring at me as if I were an anonymous letter.

CHAVIGNY: It is you. It's a joke. There's some kind of plot.

MADAME DE LÉRY: It's a well-made little plot.

CHAVIGNY: Admit that it's you.

MADAME DE LÉRY: No.

CHAVIGNY: I beg you.

MADAME DE LÉRY: Enough.

CHAVIGNY: I beseech you.

MADAME DE LÉRY: Ask me on your knees and I'll tell you.

CHAVIGNY: On my knees? As much as you like.

MADAME DE LÉRY: Well, go on then.

CHAVIGNY: Seriously? (*He kneels laughingly at her feet.*)

MADAME DE LÉRY: (*Drily.*) I like that position, it suits you admirably. But I advise you to get up before I'm completely captivated.

CHAVIGNY: (*Rising.*) So you won't say anything. Is that right?

MADAME DE LÉRY: Have you the blue purse there?

CHAVIGNY: I don't know. I think so.

MADAME DE LÉRY: I think so too. Give it to me and I'll tell you who made the other.

CHAVIGNY: Then you do know?

MADAME DE LÉRY: Yes, I know.

CHAVIGNY: Is it a woman?

MADAME DE LÉRY: If it were a man, I don't see…

220

CHAVIGNY: I mean, is it a pretty woman?

MADAME DE LÉRY: It's a woman who in your opinion is one of the prettiest in Paris.

CHAVIGNY: Dark or fair?

MADAME DE LÉRY: Blue.

CHAVIGNY: What letter does her name begin with?

MADAME DE LÉRY: Don't you want this exchange of mine? Give me Madame de Blainville's purse.

CHAVIGNY: Is she tall or short?

MADAME DE LÉRY: Give me the purse.

CHAVIGNY: Just tell me if she has a tiny foot.

MADAME DE LÉRY: Your money or your life!

CHAVIGNY: Will you tell me her name if I give you the purse?

MADAME DE LÉRY: Yes.

CHAVIGNY: (*Taking out the blue purse.*) Your word of honour?

MADAME DE LÉRY: My word of honour.

(*CHAVIGNY seems to hesitate.*
MADAME DE LÉRY stretches out her hand.
CHAVIGNY looks at her attentively. Suddenly he sits down next to her.)

CHAVIGNY: (*Gaily.*) Let us talk about love affairs. You do agree that a woman can have one?

MADAME DE LÉRY: Have you the right to ask?

CHAVIGNY: Not exactly. But it can happen that a married man has two ways of speaking and, up to a certain point, two ways of behaving.

MADAME DE LÉRY: Well! And has this exchange of ours been cancelled? I thought it was all settled.

CHAVIGNY: A married man is nonetheless a man. The wedding ceremony doesn't change him, but it sometimes forces him to play a part and say certain lines. In this world, when people speak to you, it's only a question of knowing who they're addressing, the real or the conventional, the person or the part.

MADAME DE LÉRY: I understand a choice has to be made. But how does the audience understand?

CHAVIGNY: I don't think that for an intelligent audience, that would take long or be difficult.

MADAME DE LÉRY: Don't you want to know this famous name? Come now, give me that purse.

CHAVIGNY: An intelligent woman, for example, would not, in my opinion, make a mistake about the real character of a man. An intelligent woman knows so many things. She would see at first sight…

MADAME DE LÉRY: Are you definitely going to keep that purse?

CHAVIGNY: You seem to care a great deal about it. But isn't it true that an intelligent woman should make allowance for the husband and so of course the man? What has happened to your hair? It was wreathed in flowers earlier tonight.

MADAME DE LÉRY: Yes, they were hurting me, I took them off to be more comfortable. Heavens, my hair's coming down. (*She rises and adjusts her hair in front of the mirror.*)

CHAVIGNY: You have the prettiest figure in the world. An intelligent woman like you…

MADAME DE LÉRY: An intelligent woman like me gives herself to the devil when she has to deal with an intelligent man like you.

CHAVIGNY: Never mind. I'm a pretty good sort of devil.

MADAME DE LÉRY: But not for me, at least in my opinion.

CHAVIGNY: Obviously someone must have wronged me.

MADAME DE LÉRY: And what precisely does that mean?

CHAVIGNY: It means that if I don't attract you, there must be someone else who prevents me attracting you.

MADAME DE LÉRY: That's very polite and modest, but you're wrong. No one attracts me and I wish to attract no one.

CHAVIGNY: At your age and with eyes like that, I don't believe you.

MADAME DE LÉRY: It happens to be the simple truth.

CHAVIGNY: If I did believe you, it would give me a very bad opinion of men.

MADAME DE LÉRY: I'll make you believe it very easily. I am vain enough to wish to have no master.

CHAVIGNY: Nor a servant either?

MADAME DE LÉRY: Servants or masters, you're nothing but tyrants.

CHAVIGNY: (*Rising.*) That is true enough and I will admit in that respect I've always detested the way men behave. I don't know where they get this habit of inflicting themselves on women. It only results in them getting themselves hated.

MADAME DE LÉRY: Do you sincerely think that?

CHAVIGNY: Very sincerely. Because you've amused a woman tonight, I don't understand why you should think you have the right to take advantage of it tomorrow.

MADAME DE LÉRY: But it happens to be the first chapter in the history of the world.

CHAVIGNY: Yes. And if men were sensible about it, women wouldn't be so cautious.

MADAME DE LÉRY: That is possible. The liaisons of today are in fact marriages, and when it's a question of a wedding day, that is something worth thinking about.

CHAVIGNY: Of course you're right. And tell me, why is it so? Why is there so much play-acting and so little frankness? When a pretty woman wants to put her trust in a man of honour, shouldn't she be able to find one? All men are fools.

MADAME DE LÉRY: That is very much to the point.

CHAVIGNY: But let us suppose there exists by chance a man who is not like the other fools. And let us suppose that an opportunity occurs of being frank, without misgivings or danger or fear of an indiscretion. (*He takes her hand.*) Let us suppose he says to a woman, 'We are alone; you are young and lovely; and I have the greatest respect for your heart and your intelligence. A thousand obstacles divide us, a thousand sorrows await us, if we try to meet again tomorrow. Your pride will tolerate no yoke and your prudence no bond; you have nothing to fear from either. You are asked for no promise or obligation or sacrifice;

nothing but a smile from those perfect lips and a look from those lovely eyes. Smile while this door is closed; your liberty lies on the threshold; you will find it as soon as you leave this room. What is offered you is not pleasure without love, but love without pain or bitterness. It's a diversion, a love affair if you like, as that's what we're talking about; not the blind love of the senses, but that of the heart, which is born in a moment and whose memory is everlasting.'

MADAME DE LÉRY: You were talking to me of play-acting. But I think that at times your part would be rather a dangerous one. I would like to have a diversion before replying to your little speech. And this seems to be the moment, as that was your theme. Have you a pack of cards?

CHAVIGNY: Yes, in this drawer. What do you want them for?

MADAME DE LÉRY: Give them to me. I have a little idea which you must humour, unless you want to contradict your own argument. (*She takes a card from the pack.*) Tell me, is this card red or black?

CHAVIGNY: What game are we playing?

MADAME DE LÉRY: The game is forfeits.

CHAVIGNY: Very well. Red.

MADAME DE LÉRY: It's the knave of spades. You've lost. Give me that blue purse.

CHAVIGNY: With all my heart. But I'll keep the red one, and although its colour has made me lose, I'll never blame it. For I know as well as you whose hand it was that made it.

MADAME DE LÉRY: And is this hand big or small?

CHAVIGNY: It's charming and soft as silk.

MADAME DE LÉRY: Will you allow it to satisfy a little pang of jealousy? (*She throws the blue purse into the fire.*)

CHAVIGNY: Charlotte, I adore you.

(*MADAME DE LÉRY watches the purse burning, then approaches CHAVIGNY.*)

MADAME DE LÉRY: (*Tenderly.*) Then you're no longer in love with Madame de Blainville?

CHAVIGNY: Good God, I've never loved her.

MADAME DE LÉRY: Nor I, my dear Count.

CHAVIGNY: But who can have told you I even thought about that woman? I'd never ask of her one moment of happiness. And she'd never give it to me.

MADAME DE LÉRY: Nor I, my dear Count. You have just made a little sacrifice for me and it's very gallant of you. But I won't deceive you. The red purse was not made by me.

CHAVIGNY: Is that true? Then who did make it?

MADAME DE LÉRY: It was a lovelier hand than mine. Be so good as to think for a moment and then explain this little enigma. You have just made me a very charming and beautifully worded declaration. You knelt down on both knees; and remember there's no carpet. I asked you for the blue purse and you allowed me to burn it. Tell me now, who am I to deserve all that? What do you find in me that's so extraordinary? I'm not bad-looking, it's true, I'm young, and I certainly have a tiny foot. But after all, that's not so rare. What we have proved to each other is that I am a flirt and you are a rake, simply because it's midnight and we're alone together. It's a fine exploit to record in our memoirs. And that is all, isn't it? What you have given me with a laugh, without costing you a single regret, this insignificant sacrifice which you've made for the sake of an even more insignificant diversion, is something you have refused to the only woman who loves you, the only woman you love.

(*A carriage is heard.*)

CHAVIGNY: But who can have told you all this?

MADAME DE LÉRY: Speak more quietly. There she is now, and there is the carriage come to fetch me. I have no time to draw a moral from this, but you are a man of heart and your heart will do it for you. If you find that Flora's eyes are red, wipe them with this little purse; her tears will recognise it. Yes, it is your wife who has spent two weeks making it. Goodbye. You may hate me now, but tomorrow you will have some feelings of friendship for me, and believe me, this is better than a diversion. But if that is what you really need, then here is Flora, and she, I hope, will make you forget another diversion that no one in the world, not even she, will ever know.

(FLORA enters.

MADAME DE LÉRY goes toward her and kisses her.

CLAVIGNY watches them, then goes and takes the flowers from FLORA's head and gives them to MADAME DE LÉRY.)

CHAVIGNY: Charlotte, I apologise. But she will know…and I shall never forget that it's a young priest who preaches the best sermons.

A DOOR MUST BE OPEN OR SHUT
(Il faut qu'une porte soit
ouverte ou fermée)

Characters

THE MARQUISE

THE BARON

Scene: A small drawing room in Paris.

This translation of *A Door Must be Open or Shut* was first transmitted by the BBC Third Programme in September 1955, with the following cast:

THE MARQUISE, Irene Worth

THE BARON, Hugh Burden

A Door Must be Open or Shut

THE MARQUISE is seated on a sofa near the fire, embroidering on a tambour.
THE BARON enters and bows.

THE BARON: I don't know when I'll cure myself of my
    clumsiness, but I'm so appallingly absent-minded. I find
    it quite impossible to remember which is your at-home
    day and every time I want to see you it never fails to be a
    Tuesday.

THE MARQUISE: Have you something to say to me?

THE BARON: No. But even if I had, I couldn't say it, because
    it's purely chance that you're alone and in five minutes the
    room will be invaded by a host of your intimate friends,
    who I warn you will make me leave immediately.

THE MARQUISE: It's true, today is my at-home day, but
    really I don't know why I have one. However, it's the
    fashion and there is of course a reason for it. Our mothers
    never had one, because in those days society was so small.
    But now when one's at home, one's at home to all Paris.
    And at the present time all Paris really is the whole of
    Paris, including the suburbs. A solution had to be found, so
    we all have our own days. It's the only way to see people
    as little as possible, and when you say 'I'm at home on
    Tuesdays', what you mean is 'The rest of the week leave
    me in peace'.

THE BARON: The more wrong of me to come this afternoon,
    as you allow me to see you on other days.

THE MARQUISE: Resign yourself to it and sit down there. If
    you're in a good mood, you can talk. If not, just get warm.
    I don't expect many people today and we're going to have
    a little magic-lantern show. What's the matter? You seem
    to…

THE BARON: What?

THE MARQUISE: It's so uncomplimentary to me I hardly
    like to say.

THE BARON: All right, I'll tell you. Before coming here, I was a little…

THE MARQUISE: What? It's my turn to ask.

THE BARON: Will you be angry if I tell you?

THE MARQUISE: Tonight I am going to a ball and must look my best. I cannot get angry beforehand.

THE BARON: Very well. I was a little bored. I don't know what's the matter. It's a sickness that's fashionable, like your receptions. I've been bored since midday. I've paid four calls and found no one at home. I ought to dine with friends. For no reason at all I've said I can't go. There's no theatre this evening. I came out in icy weather. I've seen nothing but red noses and blue cheeks. I don't know what to do. I'm as dull as a three-volume novel.

THE MARQUISE: I feel the same. I am bored to tears. It's probably this weather.

THE BARON: It's a fact the weather is detestable. Winter's a disease. But some people see a dry road and a blue sky, and though an icy wind almost cuts their ears off, they call it a beautiful frost. You might as well talk of a beautiful attack of gout. I don't appreciate that sort of beauty.

THE MARQUISE: I more than agree with you. But I think my boredom comes not so much from the air outside, cold as it is, but rather from the air which other people breathe. Perhaps we're just growing old. I'm almost thirty and I'm losing my zest for life.

THE BARON: I've never had that zest and what frightens me is I may acquire it. As one grows old, one gets either dull or mad and I've a horrible fear of dying sane.

THE MARQUISE: Ring for the footman to put a log on the fire. Your ideas are freezing me.

(*A bell is heard outside.*)

THE BARON: It's not worth it. There's the front-door bell, your cavalcade's beginning to arrive.

THE MARQUISE: Let's see who the advance guard will be. Do please try to stay.

THE BARON: No, I'm definitely going.

THE MARQUISE: Where?

THE BARON: I've no idea. (*He rises, bows, and opens the door.*) Goodbye, Marquise, till Thursday evening.

THE MARQUISE: Why Thursday?

THE BARON: (*Standing, holding the door handle.*) Isn't it your day for the opera? I was going to come to your box.

THE MARQUISE: I don't want you to. You're too disagreeable. Besides, I'm taking Monsieur Camus.

THE BARON: Monsieur Camus, your neighbour in the country?

THE MARQUISE: Yes. He sold me some hay with such courtesy that I want to repay his politeness.

THE BARON: That's typical of you. The most boring man in the world. He should eat his hay himself. By the way do you know what people are saying?

THE MARQUISE: No. But no one's coming. Who can have rung?

THE BARON: (*Looking out of the window.*) Nobody. A young girl, I think, with a cardboard box, heaven knows, a laundress. There she is on the steps, talking to your maids.

THE MARQUISE: 'Heaven knows'! How very polite! It's my new hat. Well then, what are people saying about me and Monsieur Camus? Do shut the door; there's a horrible draught.

THE BARON: (*Shutting the door.*) They say you're thinking of remarrying, that Monsieur Camus is a millionaire and he calls on you frequently.

THE MARQUISE: Really! Is that all? And you tell me quite simply to my face?

THE BARON: I tell you because people are talking about it.

THE MARQUISE: That's a fine reason! Do I tell you everything that's said about you?

THE BARON: About me? What could be said about me that can't be repeated?

THE MARQUISE: According to you everything can be repeated, as you inform me I'm about to announce my engagement to Monsieur Camus. What is said about you is quite as serious, because unfortunately it seems to be true.

THE BARON: Well, what is it? You frighten me.

THE MARQUISE: A further proof there's no mistake.

THE BARON: Explain what you mean, please.

THE MARQUISE: Oh no. They're your private affairs.

THE BARON: (*Sitting down again.*) I beseech you, Marquise. I ask you as a favour. You're the person whose opinion I value most in the world.

THE MARQUISE: One of the persons, you mean.

THE BARON: No. The person whose esteem, whose regard, whose…

THE MARQUISE: Oh, heavens, you're going to make a speech.

THE BARON: I am not. If you don't understand, it's because you don't wish to understand.

THE MARQUISE: Understand what?

THE BARON: You know perfectly well.

THE MARQUISE: I only know what people tell me.

THE BARON: You make fun of everything. But seriously, how can I possibly see you almost every day for more than a year, you with your wit, your grace, your beauty…

THE MARQUISE: Heavens, it's worse than a speech, it's a declaration of love. Do at least warn me. Is that right? Or is it just a sort of New Year greeting?

THE BARON: And if it were right?

THE MARQUISE: Oh, that's just what I don't want this afternoon. I've told you I'm going to a ball tonight and someone's bound to make love to me there. My health doesn't permit me that kind of thing twice in one day.

THE BARON: You're really very discouraging. I shall be delighted when you find yourself in my situation.

THE MARQUISE: So shall I. I swear to you there are times when I'd give a large sum of money to feel just a little sad. Wait now, I did, when my hair was being done only a moment ago. I sighed from the depths of my soul in despair at having nothing to think about.

THE BARON: Come, come, it will happen to you one day.

THE MARQUISE: It's quite possible; we're all mortal. I may

234

be a sensible woman, but whose fault is that? I promise you I don't try to be.

THE BARON: You don't want anyone to pay court to you?

THE MARQUISE: No. I'm very good-natured, but that is too ridiculous. Tell me, you're a level-headed person, what does that expression mean, to pay court to a woman?

THE BARON: It means you like her and you're delighted to tell her so.

THE MARQUISE: Very good. But this woman, does she like the fact that you like her? You think I'm beautiful, I imagine, and it amuses you to tell me so. Well, what follows? What does that prove? Is that any reason why I should love you? I take it that if I like someone, it's not because I am beautiful. What's the point of these compliments? You men think the way to make a woman love you is to stand in front of her, look her up and down through an eyeglass as if she were a dummy in a shop window, and say to her very pleasantly, 'Madame, I think you're charming'. Add a few hackneyed phrases and a bouquet of flowers, and that's what you call paying court to her. Rubbish! How can an intelligent man enjoy such nonsense? It puts me in a rage to think of it.

THE BARON: It's nothing to get angry about.

THE MARQUISE: Indeed it is. You must imagine a woman to be completely brainless, if you hope to succeed with that kind of recipe. Do you think she finds it amusing to pass her life listening to a perpetual flow of balderdash and to have her ears filled with nonsense from morning to night? Really, I think if I were a man and saw a pretty woman, I'd say to myself, 'Now there's a poor creature who must be overwhelmed with compliments'. I would spare her, pity her, and if I wanted to try to please her, I'd do her the honour of speaking of something other than her wretched face. But no. Always 'You're beautiful'; and then 'You're beautiful'; and again 'Beautiful'. Heavens, we know that. Do you need me to tell you that all you men of fashion are nothing but confectioners in disguise?

THE BARON: Well, Marquise, you are charming, take it how

you will. (*The bell is heard.*) There's the bell again. Goodbye. I'm going. (*He gets up and opens the door.*)

THE MARQUISE: Wait a moment, I was going to say… I forget what exactly… Oh yes. will you by any chance be going near Fossin's, the jeweller's, this afternoon?

THE BARON: It won't be by chance, Marquise, if I can be of service to you.

THE MARQUISE: Yet another compliment! Heavens, you're so tiresome. It's a ring I've broken. I could quite easily send it, but it's simpler to explain… (*She takes the ring off her finger.*) Look, it's the setting. There's a little leaf there, do you see? It opens at the side, like that. I must have knocked it this morning and the spring is broken.

THE BARON: Tell me, if it's not indiscreet to ask, but isn't there a lock of hair inside?

THE MARQUISE: Perhaps. What is there to smile at?

THE BARON: I'm not smiling in the least.

THE MARQUISE: You're being impertinent. It's my husband's hair. I don't hear anyone coming. Who can have rung the bell?

THE BARON: (*Looking out of the window.*) Another girl with another box. One more hat, I suppose. That reminds me, you have something to tell me.

THE MARQUISE: Shut the door then, you're freezing me.

THE BARON: I'm just going. You promise to tell me what's being said about me, don't you, Marquise?

THE MARQUISE: Come to the ball tonight, we'll have a little talk.

THE BARON: A little talk at a ball! A fine place for conversation, with an accompaniment of trombones and a tinkling of lemonade glasses! Someone steps on your foot, someone else jogs your elbow, while a footman drops ice cream down your neck. I ask you if it isn't too…

THE MARQUISE: Do you want to go or stay? I tell you again, you're making me catch cold. As no one's coming, what's driving you away?

THE BARON: (*Shutting the door and sitting down again.*) It's because I feel, against my will, in such a bad mood that I'm really afraid of annoying you. I must definitely stop coming here.

THE MARQUISE: How very polite! Why exactly?

THE BARON: I don't know, but I bore you. You said so yourself just now and I know it's true. It's quite natural. If only I didn't live immediately opposite. I can't go out without seeing your windows and I come in here automatically without for a moment thinking why.

THE MARQUISE: Although I said you were boring me this afternoon, you don't every time you call. No, seriously, I should be sorry; I'm very pleased to see you.

THE BARON: Are you? Most certainly not! Do you know what I'm going to do? I shall return to Italy.

THE MARQUISE: Oh. What effect will that have on Mademoiselle…?

THE BARON: What mademoiselle, may I ask?

THE MARQUISE: Mademoiselle… I don't know. Mademoiselle…your protégée. How can I know the names of your chorus girls?

THE BARON: Oh, so that's the story you've been hearing about me?

THE MARQUISE: Exactly. Do you deny it?

THE BARON: A very likely tale!

THE MARQUISE: It's annoying that you've been seen quite plainly at the theatre with a certain pink hat with flowers on it; the sort of flowers that only bloom backstage at the ballet. You've been dallying with the chorus, my friend. Everyone knows about it.

THE BARON: Like your marriage to Monsieur Camus.

THE MARQUISE: Back to that again! Very well then, why not? Monsieur Camus is a very worthy man; he's a millionaire several times over; he may no longer be young, but he's just the right age for a husband. I'm a widow; he's a bachelor. And he looks very fine when he's wearing gloves.

THE BARON: And a nightcap. That must suit him.

THE MARQUISE: Will you please be quiet! People don't say such things.

THE BARON: Indeed they do, to someone who'll see them.

THE MARQUISE: It must be those young ladies of yours who've been teaching you such manners.

THE BARON: (*Rising and taking his hat.*) Well, Marquise, I'll say goodbye before you make me say something foolish.

THE MARQUISE: What excessive delicacy!

THE BARON: No, but really you're too cruel! It's quite enough to forbid me to love you, without accusing me of loving someone else.

THE MARQUISE: Better and better! What a tragic voice! Have I forbidden you to love me?

THE BARON: Certainly. At least to speak to you about it.

THE MARQUISE: Very well, I give you permission. Let's hear your eloquence.

THE BARON: If you said it seriously...

THE MARQUISE: What does that matter? Provided that I do say it.

THE BARON: Only that although it might be a joke, there could be someone here who would be running a certain risk.

THE MARQUISE: Oh, oh! Would it be a great peril?

THE BARON: Perhaps. Unfortunately the danger would only be for me.

THE MARQUISE: When one's frightened, one doesn't usually appear to be brave. Very well, let's see. You say nothing? You threaten me; I'm defenceless; and you don't move? I expected to see you at least throw yourself at my feet like a romantic hero or even Monsieur Camus. He'd have been down there ages ago in this situation.

THE BARON: Does it amuse you a great deal to make fun of unfortunate people?

THE MARQUISE: And you? Does it surprise you that I'm brave enough to face you?

THE BARON: Take care. You may be brave, but I've been a soldier, let me tell you, and not so long ago either.

THE MARQUISE: Really! How splendid! You're going to declare your love like a soldier, that will be strange. I've never heard that in my life. Would you like me to send for

my maid? I think she might know how to reply. Let's see
your performance. (*The bell is heard.*)

THE BARON: That bell again! Goodbye then, Marquise. But
I won't let you off. We'll continue this conversation.
(*He opens the door.*)

THE MARQUISE: I shall see you this evening, shan't I?
What can that noise be?

THE BARON: (*Looking out of the window.*) The weather
has suddenly changed. It's raining hard and there are
hailstones as big as pebbles. Someone's bringing you a
third hat and I'm very much afraid it only means another
cold for you.

THE MARQUISE: That noise! Can it be thunder? In the
middle of January? In spite of the almanacs?

THE BARON: No, only a hurricane. A sort of whirlwind.

THE MARQUISE: It's terrifying. Do shut the door. You can't
go out in this weather. What can have caused such a thing?

THE BARON: (*Shutting the door.*) It's celestial rage which
is chastising roofs, windowpanes, umbrellas and ladies'
ankles.

THE MARQUISE: And my horses which are out in it.

THE BARON: They're not in any danger, unless something
falls on their heads.

THE MARQUISE: It's your turn to joke! But I'm a very
spick-and-span sort of person and I don't like my horses to
get covered in mud. It's unbelievable. Only a moment ago
it was a lovely day.

THE BARON: With this hail you can be quite certain no one
will visit you today. That's one reception less in your life.

THE MARQUISE: Not at all, as you're here. Do put your hat
down, it's making me restless.

THE BARON: A compliment, Marquise. Take care. As you
profess to hate compliments, you might be taken at your
word.

THE MARQUISE: I do say so and it's true. Your coming to
see me gives me a great deal of pleasure.

THE BARON: (*Sitting down next to her.*) Then allow me to be
in love with you.

THE MARQUISE: I've told you, I'm delighted. It doesn't annoy me in the least.

THE BARON: Then let me speak to you about it.

THE MARQUISE: As a soldier, do you mean?

THE BARON: No, Marquise. Do believe that in spite of my love I've enough sense to treat you with respect. But I think that without offending a woman one respects, one has the right to...

THE MARQUISE: To stay until the rain stops, you mean? You came in here just now without knowing why; you said so yourself. You were bored, you didn't know what to do, you could even be said to have been grumbling. If you'd found two or three other people here sitting round the fire, you'd now be talking about literature or railways and then you'd go out to dinner. Because I happen to be here alone, you immediately find yourself obliged, yes obliged, for the sake of your honour, to pay court to me – this eternal, unbearable, paying court, that's so useless, so ridiculous, so hackneyed. What have I done to you? If someone else came in, you'd show some wit; but, because I'm alone, here you are, as trite as a music-hall joke. Soon you'll finally get to the point and, if I'm prepared to listen, you'll recite your love for me. Do you know what men look like, when they do that? Like poor, unsuccessful dramatists whose pockets always contain some unpublished, unactable tragedy which they produce to overwhelm you with as soon as they're alone with you for five minutes.

THE BARON: So you tell me you don't dislike me, I reply I love you and, as far as you're concerned, that's that.

THE MARQUISE: You don't love me any more than the Sultan of Turkey.

THE BARON: Oh really, this is too much! If you don't think I'm in earnest, just listen to me for one minute.

THE MARQUISE: No, no, definitely no! Heavens, do you think I don't know what you could say to me. I've a very high opinion of your learning, but because you're well-educated, do you think I'm quite unread? Listen. I once knew an intelligent man who'd bought somewhere or other a collection of fifty letters, quite well-phrased, excellently worded; love letters of course. These fifty letters were composed progressively to form a little story and introduce every possible situation. They provided for proposals, rejections, hopes, moments of hypocrisy where one limits oneself to friendship, misunderstandings, despair, attacks of jealousy, fits of bad temper, and even for rainy days like we have at present. I've read these letters. The author professed in a foreword to have used them himself and never to have found a woman who could resist later than number 33. Did he indeed? I resisted the entire collection. I ask you if I'm not well-read. Do you think you can flatter yourself you could teach me something new?

THE BARON: You're very blasé, Marquise.

THE MARQUISE: Insults now? I prefer them. They're less insipid than your sugary compliments.

THE BARON: Yes, it's true. You're very blasé.

THE MARQUISE: Do you think so? Not in the slightest degree.

THE BARON: As blasé as an old dowager who's given birth to fourteen children.

THE MARQUISE: As blasé as the feathers in my new hat. Do you think that it's some profound science to be able to see into men's hearts? There's no need to study to learn that. All you have to do is relax and think. It's quite a simple process. There are very few men brave enough to respect our poor ears by avoiding sugary compliments. Besides, in those sad moments when men try to lie to attempt to please, you can't deny you all behave like ventriloquists' dummies. Happily for us women, heavenly justice hasn't endowed you with a very extensive vocabulary. You all have a single refrain, so that the mere fact of hearing the same phrases, the mere repetition of the same words, the same thought-up gestures, the same tender glances, the mere sight of all those different faces, which may be more or less handsome individually, but which all in these funereal moments adopt the same humbly conquering look, all this saves us either by making us want to laugh or just by boring us. If I had a daughter and I wanted to save her from these so-called dangerous situations, I should take good care to forbid her to listen to the romanticising of the men she waltzes with. I should simply say, 'Don't listen to one of them. Listen to the lot. Don't shut the book and mark the page; leave it open, let these gentlemen tell you their little absurdities. If unfortunately one of them pleases you, don't do anything, just wait. Another will soon appear, exactly the same, and he'll make you hate them both. You must be fifteen, I think. Well, my child, this will continue till you're thirty and it will always be the same.' There, that's my experience and my science. Do you call that being blasé?

THE BARON: Horribly so, if what you say is true. And that seems so unlikely that I must be allowed to be a little sceptical.

THE MARQUISE: What do I care whether you believe me or not?

THE BARON: Better still. Is it really possible for you at your age to despise love? The words of a man who loves you have the same effect on you as a badly written novel. His looks and acts and feelings seem to you a joke. You pride yourself on telling the truth and only see lies in other people. Who can have taught you these theories? Where have you learned them?

THE MARQUISE: Over a long period of years, my friend.

THE BARON: From your nurse's gossip when you were a child. Women think they know everything in the world. They know absolutely nothing. I ask you what experience you can possibly have had. You're like a traveller who sees a single red-haired woman his first day abroad and notes in his diary, 'The people in this country have red hair'.

THE MARQUISE: I asked you to put a log on the fire.

THE BARON: (*Putting a log on the fire.*) I can understand a woman being a prude, saying no, stopping up her ears, hating love. But to deny its existence is laughable. You discourage a poor wretch by telling him, 'I know what you're going to say to me'. But hasn't he the right to answer, 'Yes, you may know, and indeed I know, what people usually say when they're in love, but when I speak to you I forget it all'? There may be no new thing under the sun. But it's my turn to ask 'What does that prove?'

THE MARQUISE: Well done! You speak admirably. Almost like a book.

THE BARON: Yes, I can speak well enough. And I assure you, if you're really the sort of person you like to pretend to be, I'm sincerely sorry for you.

THE MARQUISE: Don't stand on ceremony. Make yourself at home.

THE BARON: I've said nothing to hurt you. If you've the right to attack us, aren't we justified in defending ourselves? When you compare us to unsuccessful dramatists, what do you think you're reproaching us with? Heavens, if love's a play...

THE MARQUISE: The fire's going out. That log has fallen off.

THE BARON: (*Attending to the fire.*) If love's a play, it is after all as old as the world, and unsuccessful or not it's the one that's been found to be the least bad. The parts are hackneyed, I admit. But if the play were worthless, the whole world wouldn't know it by heart. Besides I'm wrong to say it's old. Can it be old if it's immortal?

THE MARQUISE: Sir, that's poetry.

THE BARON: No, Marquise. But all this nonsense which bores you, these compliments and protestations, all this rubbish, are very fine old things, conventional if you like, tiresome, sometimes ridiculous, but they accompany something else, which is always young.

THE MARQUISE: You're getting confused. What is always old and always young?

THE BARON: Love.

THE MARQUISE: Sir, that's eloquence.

THE BARON: No, Marquise, I mean this: love is immortally young, but the ways of expressing it are and always will be eternally old. All the worn-out phrases, repetitions, scraps of novels, which for some unknown reason spring up from one's heart, all this verbiage is like a crowd of old chamberlains, ministers, and diplomats gossiping in the anteroom of a king. That all dies away, but the king never dies. Love is dead, long live love.

THE MARQUISE: Love?

THE BARON: Love. And in any event just to think that…

THE MARQUISE: Give me that screen over there.

THE BARON: This one?

THE MARQUISE: No, the silk one. Your fire is blinding me.

THE BARON: (*Giving her the screen.*) In any event just to think that one's in love is surely rather pleasant?

THE MARQUISE: I tell you, it's always the same.

THE BARON: And always different, so they say. What do you want us to think up? Must we make love to you in Greek? That Venus over there on your clock is always the same, but does that make her any less lovely? If you resemble your grandmother, are you any less beautiful?

THE MARQUISE: There's the refrain again, 'Beautiful'. Give me that cushion next to you.

THE BARON: (*Taking the cushion and holding it in his hand.*) That Venus was made to be beautiful, to be loved and admired, and it doesn't bore her in the least. If there was ever a model for the Venus de Milo, that glorious creature must have had more men in love with her than she knew what to do with. And of course she let herself be loved, like any other woman. Like Astarte and Aspasia and Manon Lescaut.

THE MARQUISE: Sir, that's mythology.

THE BARON: (*Still holding the cushion.*) No, Marquise; but I cannot say how troubled I am, to see in a young woman this fashionable indifference, this jesting and disdainful coldness, this air of experience that reduces everything to nothing. You're not the first woman I've met who's like this. It's a sickness one finds in every drawing room. They all turn aside, and yawn, as you're doing now, and say they don't want to listen to any talk of love. Then why do you wear that lace? What is that ornament doing in your hair?

THE MARQUISE: What is that cushion doing in your hand? I asked you for it to put under my feet.

THE BARON: Very well. Here it is; and here am I too. And I'll make you a declaration, as old as the hills and as silly as a goose, whether you like it or not. Because I'm furious with you. (*He puts the cushion on the floor in front of THE MARQUISE and kneels on it.*)

THE MARQUISE: Will you please do me the favour of removing yourself from there.

THE BARON: No. You must listen to me first.

THE MARQUISE: You refuse to rise?

THE BARON: No, no, definitely no; as you said just now. Not unless you agree to listen to me.

THE MARQUISE: I have the honour to bid you good day. (*She rises.*)

THE BARON: (*Still on his knees.*) Marquise, for heaven's sake! This is too cruel. You're driving me insane.

THE MARQUISE: It will pass off at the club.

THE BARON: No, I swear, I'm speaking from the depths of my heart. I'll agree as much as you like that I didn't come here for this reason. I only expected to see you for a minute; witness this door that I've opened three times to try to leave. The conversation we've just had, your jesting, your coldness even, have made me go further than was perhaps necessary. But it's not only today. From the first time I saw you, I've loved you, adored you. I'm not exaggerating when I say this. For more than a year I've adored you. I only dream…

THE MARQUISE: Goodbye. (*She goes out, leaving the door open.*)

THE BARON: (*Left alone, remains kneeling for a moment, then rises.*) Yes, this door does make the room icy. (*He goes to the door and sees THE MARQUISE.*) Ah, Marquise, you're making fun of me.

THE MARQUISE: (*Leaning against the half-open door.*) So you're on your feet.

THE BARON: Yes. I'm leaving and I'll never see you again.

THE MARQUISE: Come to the ball tonight. I'll keep a waltz for you.

THE BARON: I shall never, never see you again. I'm in despair. My life is ruined.

THE MARQUISE: What's the matter?

THE BARON: My life is ruined. I love you like a child. I swear by all I hold most sacred in the world...

THE MARQUISE: Goodbye. (*She wishes to leave.*)

THE BARON: No, I am going. Don't move, I beg you. I'm the most miserable man in Paris.

THE MARQUISE: (*Seriously.*) What is it you want?

THE BARON: Why, I want, I should like...

THE MARQUISE: What! Now you're making me lose my patience. Do you imagine I'm going to be your mistress and succeed to those little pink hats? I warn you the very thought does more than displease me. It revolts me.

THE BARON: You, Marquise? Great heavens, I want to devote my whole life to your service. I'm offering you my name, my wealth, even my honour. How could I confuse you for one second, not merely with one of those creatures, but with any other woman in the world? Did you really think that? Do you believe I've lost my reason? A moment ago you said it gave you some pleasure to see me, you had some feelings of friendship for me. Isn't that so, Marquise? Do you think a man you've found worthy of your friendship could be incapable of appreciating you? Could I be so insane? I'm not asking you to be my mistress but my wife.

THE MARQUISE: Oh well, if you'd said that when you arrived, we wouldn't have had this argument. So you want to marry me?

THE BARON: I'm dying to do so. I've never dared to tell you, but I've thought of nothing else for over a year. I'd give my right hand to have the slightest hope...

THE MARQUISE: Wait a moment. You're richer than I am.

THE BARON: Oh, heavens, I don't think so, and what difference does it make? I beg you, don't let's talk of such things. Your smile at this moment makes me tremble with hope and fear. One word, for pity's sake. My life is in your hands.

THE MARQUISE: I'm going to give you two maxims. The first – 'There's nothing like making oneself understood.' So we'll have a little talk.

THE BARON: Then what I've told you doesn't displease you?

THE MARQUISE: Why, no. Here is my second maxim. It's that a door must be kept open or shut. Now this one, for three quarters of an hour, thanks to you, has been neither one thing nor the other, so the room is completely frozen. As a further result you are going to escort me to my mother's, where I shall dine. And after that you will go to Fossin's.

THE BARON: Fossin's? Why should I go there?

THE MARQUISE: My ring.

THE BARON: Of course. I'd forgotten. Well then, your ring, Marquise?

THE MARQUISE: 'Marquise', did you say? Well then, you see it's a signet ring engraved with a Marquise's coronet. Tell me, Baron, what do you think? Should the coronet perhaps be changed to that of a Baroness? Let's go. I'll get my hat.

THE BARON: You make me so happy. How can I ever…

THE MARQUISE: Do shut that wretched door before the room's uninhabitable.

YOU CAN'T THINK OF EVERYTHING
(On ne saurait penser à tout)

Characters

THE BARON, Valberg's uncle

GERMAIN, Valberg's valet

THE MARQUIS DE VALBERG

VICTOIRE, the Countess' maid

THE COUNTESS DE VERNON

Scene: The Countess de Vernon's country house.

You Can't Think of Everything

THE BARON and GERMAIN enter.

THE BARON: You say my nephew's not here?

GERMAIN: No, sir. I've looked everywhere.

THE BARON: Impossible. It's five o'clock precisely. Isn't this where the Countess lives?

GERMAIN: Yes, sir. There's her piano.

THE BARON: Perhaps my nephew's no longer in love with her?

GERMAIN: Oh yes, sir. As much as ever.

THE BARON: Perhaps he doesn't come to see her every day?

GERMAIN: He does nothing else.

THE BARON: Perhaps he didn't get my letter.

GERMAIN: He did. This moming.

THE BARON: Then he must be here, as he's not in his own house. I wrote that I should leave Paris at one fifteen and so be at Montgeron at three. Montgeron is two and a half leagues from here, say five quarters of an hour, that is supposing the roads were bad which, all in all, they're not.

GERMAIN: No indeed, sir, they're very good.

THE BARON: Therefore I should definitely be at the village by four fifteen. I had to call on Monsieur Duplessis and then, allowing for the time to come on here, I couldn't be later than five o'clock. I set all this out in my letter in the greatest detail. Now, it's five o'clock precisely, even a few minutes after. You see how correctly I worked it out.

GERMAIN: Perfectly, sir. But my master's not here.

THE BARON: Even so, everything is ready?

GERMAIN: Ready for what, sir?

THE BARON: His trunks are packed?

GERMAIN: Not as far as I know, sir. Not one.

THE BARON: But I said in my letter that the Grand Duchess had given birth to an heir. The Duchess of Gotha, Germain. That is no trifle.

GERMAIN: So I imagine.

THE BARON: I'm telling you all this, so you can note how exact I am in everything.

GERMAIN: Yes, I do see that.

THE BARON: In this world precision is the first of virtues. One might even say it's the foundation, the prime element, of all others. Just as the loveliest theme of a symphony or the finest peroration mean nothing out of their context, so the rarest of virtues, the most exquisite of manners, will only produce their full effect at a precise and carefully chosen moment. Remember that, Germain. Nothing is more pitiful than to arrive at an ill-chosen time. Why, I've seen men, who have attained the highest distinction in the army or the government even, lose their fortune for want of a good, well-regulated watch. By the way, does yours go well?

GERMAIN: I adjust it whenever necessary, sir.

THE BARON: Excellent. Now, I'll have you know that His Excellency received me yesterday at half past two and was gracious enough to inform me himself that the Duchess of Gotha had given birth to an heir, as I told you, and that the King had selected me and my nephew to go and congratulate her.

GERMAIN: To Gotha, sir?

THE BARON: To Gotha. It's a great honour for your master.

GERMAIN: Yes, sir. But he's not here.

THE BARON: That's what I can't understand. Do you mean he's still as absent-minded as ever? Always forgetting everything?

GERMAIN: You can't imagine, sir. But it's not that he forgets, he thinks of something else.

THE BARON: But tomorrow morning without fail he must be on the road to Germany. Has he given no instructions at all?

GERMAIN: No, sir. But only today, before going out, he opened a big travelling trunk and walked round and round it for a very long time.

THE BARON: Well, what did he put in it?

GERMAIN: A sheet of music.

THE BARON: A sheet of music?

GERMAIN: Yes, sir. Then he closed the trunk with the greatest of care and put the key in his pocket.

THE BARON: A sheet of music! As mad as ever! If the King knew of this weakness of his, they'd never dare to entrust him with a mission of such importance. Luckily he's in my care. Well then, what did he say? What did he do?

GERMAIN: He sang, sir, all day long.

THE BARON: Sang?

GERMAIN: Beautifully, sir. It was a pleasure to listen to him.

THE BARON: A fine beginning to an embassy. You're an intelligent fellow, Germain; tell me, do you really think he's capable of conducting himself correctly on a mission of such delicacy?

GERMAIN: What, go to Gotha and pay his congratulations? I could do it myself.

THE BARON: You don't know what you're talking about.

GERMAIN: Why, sir, the Grand Duchess. You told me yourself she'd produced an heir.

THE BARON: It is true she has given birth to a new scion of an august line. What else has my nephew done?

GERMAIN: He's come here, I don't know how many times, to call on the Countess.

THE BARON: Well, where is the Countess?

GERMAIN: She's not up yet, sir.

THE BARON: At this time of day! I've never heard of such a thing. Doesn't the woman take lunch?

GERMAIN: No, sir, dinner.

THE BARON: Another half-wit! A fine neighbour for a lunatic!

GERMAIN: My master would be very angry, sir, if he heard you speak of him in that manner. If anyone dares to notice the slightest forgetfulness on his part, he flies into a frightful rage. Only the other day he practically killed me, because he sprinkled snuff instead of sugar on his strawberries. And yesterday…

THE BARON: Great heavens! Would anyone believe that a man of talent, of the greatest talent, Germain, for my nephew is most distinguished, could behave with such deplorable, infantile absent-mindedness?

GERMAIN: It's very sad, sir.

THE BARON: Haven't I seen him with my own eyes, at a royal ball, put his hands in his pockets and stride through the middle of a quadrille, as if he were taking a country walk?

GERMAIN: Good lord, sir, he did much the same here the other evening. The Countess had a reception and Monsieur Vertigo, a poet who lives nearby, was reading a dramatic tragedy. At the most touching moment, sir, when the heroine has just been poisoned and recognises her father among the murderers, every woman in the room was in tears, and my master gets up and drinks the glass of water on the speaker's table. The whole effect of the scene was ruined.

THE BARON: It doesn't surprise me. He once put thirty sous in a cup of tea that was offered him by a charming lady, because he thought she was collecting for charity.

GERMAIN: Last winter, you were abroad at the time, sir, he was the host at his brother's wedding reception and I went to his room in the evening to help him dress. He sends me away, undresses on his own, and walks up and down for a whole hour in, with all respect, sir, his underclothes. Then he suddenly stops and looks at himself in the mirror with amazement. 'What the devil am I doing?' he says. 'Good lord, it's dark, it's time for bed.' And he goes to bed, forgetting all about the wedding and the reception if we hadn't come to fetch him.

THE BARON: You think a man like that is capable of going to Gotha?

GERMAIN: He's improving, sir, slowly. But he doesn't like anyone to contradict him. If you'll believe me… Here he is.

(*THE MARQUIS enters.*)

THE MARQUIS: Well, is this a joke of some sort? Someone's always stealing my papers.

GERMAIN: Sir, here's the Baron.

THE MARQUIS: You rascal, what have you done with a sheet of music I had this morning? Where have you put it? Where's it got to?

THE BARON: Good afternoon, Valberg. What's the matter?

THE MARQUIS: I'll make a clean sweep of you all, one of these days. I'll dismiss every one of you. (*To THE BARON, who is laughing.*) You, you scoundrel, will be the first.

GERMAIN: Sir, it's the Baron.

THE MARQUIS: Oh, my dear uncle, I am sorry. Have you come from Paris? The fact is I've lost a sheet of music.

GERMAIN: It must be the one he locked up in the trunk.

THE BARON: You see, my dear nephew, how punctual I am. I've arrived exactly on time. What about you, are you ready to go?

THE MARQUIS: To go?

THE BARON: Yes, tomorrow morning.

THE MARQUIS: Yes, I promise you, if I'm refused, I'll go at once and you'll never see me again for the rest of your life.

THE BARON: Refused? What do you mean?

THE MARQUIS: Yes, I swear it, if I'm received coldly, if my action's unwelcome, my mind is made up, definitely.

THE BARON: What are you afraid of, as you're acting on behalf of the King?

THE MARQUIS: Is the King concerned with this?

THE BARON: He would seem to be, as you'll have a letter in his own handwriting.

THE MARQUIS: For the Countess?

THE BARON: For the Grand Duchess. Have you forgotten you're…

THE MARQUIS: I was getting confused. You see, I have a letter to write to the Countess. Have you seen her?

THE BARON: No, she's asleep.

THE MARQUIS: Well, what do you think of all this? Isn't it a good idea?

THE BARON: All what?

THE MARQUIS: Oh yes, I know what you're going to say. You've never liked her, you've quarrelled with her and now you've sued her: well, I ask you, what good will that do?

THE BARON: It's about our embassy. Have you read my letter?

THE MARQUIS: Our embassy? Yes, of course. I'm always at the King's command.

THE BARON: Good.

THE MARQUIS: His Majesty knows my devotion.

THE BARON: Excellent. Then you'll be ready...

THE MARQUIS: Of course. My orders are given. Germain, is everything ready?

GERMAIN: I haven't received any orders, sir.

THE MARQUIS: What, you rascal! What about the trunk I made you get out this morning?

GERMAIN: Well, sir, if you want to sing on your journey...

THE MARQUIS: Sing, you impertinent wretch!

GERMAIN: Sir, your music's in the trunk and the key's in your pocket.

THE MARQUIS: In my...good heavens, so it is. He must have given it me this morning with my handkerchief. These fellows never pay attention to anything.

GERMAIN: Sir, I can assure you...

THE BARON: Don't say any more. Go and get everything ready. (*GERMAIN goes out.*) Now, Valberg, I must go to Monsieur Duplessis to get these letters from the court. I have only this to say to you. Remember, my dear fellow, that ours is no ordinary mission and your whole future may depend on the skill which you display in it.

THE MARQUIS: Unfortunately I know only too well.

THE BARON: So you must promise to make a strong effort to conquer these little lapses of memory, these weaknesses which are sometimes so embarrassing, so that you can conduct matters sensibly.

THE MARQUIS: Oh, that I promise.

THE BARON: Seriously?

THE MARQUIS: Very seriously.

THE BARON: Then go and give all the necessary instructions. It's now twenty minutes to six. I'm going to

Monsieur Duplessis, it's not far, I'll be back for dinner. Well then, you promise to follow my advice in everything? You know what it is with these gentlemen of the court.

THE MARQUIS: Oh, don't worry, I know how to handle them. I'll write letters to everybody. I must simply know the name of your lawyer and I'll go myself...

THE BARON: I haven't got a lawyer. What do you mean?

THE MARQUIS: If you haven't got a lawyer, it isn't time to ask for the hearing.

THE BARON: Hearing? Of what?

THE MARQUIS: Your law case.

THE BARON: I haven't a law case.

THE MARQUIS: What? Didn't you tell me to see these gentlemen of the court?

THE BARON: I am speaking of the Court of Gotha.

THE MARQUIS: Ah, yes. It's about our embassy. I have a great deal on my mind. It's the Countess who has a law case and I am conducting it for her. What a charming woman!

THE BARON: Yes, yes, we know you're infatuated with her, and the reason you bury yourself in your country house is because she's your next-door neighbour. But this attachment of yours must not interfere with our plans. if you please.

THE MARQUIS: There's nothing to be afraid of, you can put your mind at rest. When I don't think, you see, I may appear a little careless, but when I have to deal with matters of importance, no one could be more prudent.

THE BARON: I'm delighted to hear it.

THE MARQUIS: Go to Monsieur Duplessis; don't worry; I shall look after everything.

THE BARON: We shall see how careful you are.

THE MARQUIS: I shall keep an eye on Germain, in case he forgets something.

THE BARON: Very good.

THE MARQUIS: I shall finish putting my papers in order. I have so many.

THE BARON: Don't stop my going, please.

THE MARQUIS: Heaven forbid! Go, sir, get the King's letters. For my part, I shall write to my mother. And it's only proper I should thank the minister; I'll send my dogs to Madame de Belleroche; I'll inform all our relations; and by the time you return, I hope the marriage will be settled.

THE BARON: (*Stopping at the door.*) What? The marriage? Whose marriage?

THE MARQUIS: Mine. Didn't you know?

THE BARON: What kind of a joke is this? Your marriage, do you say?

THE MARQUIS: Yes, to the Countess. Didn't I tell you I was going to marry her?

THE BARON: No, really! This is another of them.

THE MARQUIS: It gives me so much to do, as you see.

THE BARON: No one gets married the day before a long journey. You must be speaking of your return.

THE MARQUIS: No, I'm not. My fate will be decided today.

THE BARON: My dear fellow, you're not thinking.

THE MARQUIS: I'm thinking very hard. I shall only go after, and according to, her answer.

THE BARON: What has it got to do with our embassy what her answer is? You're not thinking of taking her with us, I presume?

THE MARQUIS: Why not, if she's willing?

THE BARON: The Lord preserve us! A woman on a journey! Hats and gowns and ladies' maids! A torrent of trunks and cushions and cries for *sal volatile*!

THE MARQUIS: You are speaking of trifles.

THE BARON: I am speaking of what is decent and that certainly is not. These letters don't say you're bringing a wife. I don't know if it will be acceptable.

THE MARQUIS: I care very little about that.

THE BARON: I, sir, care a great deal. And if you insist, I tell you… (*THE MARQUIS sits at the piano and begins to play.*) Really, the boy's mad. He can't possibly go to Gotha. What can I do? I can't go alone, his name appears in the King's letter. If I explain, there'll be a scandal. Even if I arranged for my name to be substituted for his, which would be only right, there'd be a considerable delay and the point would be lost. (*A bell is heard.*) Great heavens, there's the Countess. I shall miss Monsieur Duplessis. My dear nephew, do please listen to me.

THE MARQUIS: Sir? I thought you'd gone.

THE BARON: You are in love with the Countess.

THE MARQUIS: That is my secret.

THE BARON: You've just told me.

THE MARQUIS: If it escaped me, I shall not conceal it.

THE BARON: Stop joking, please. I can't speak to the Countess on your behalf. She hates me and I'm in a hurry. This is what I suggest. There are two matters to be arranged, your marriage and your embassy. Don't sacrifice one to the other.

THE MARQUIS: I entirely agree.

THE BARON: Then see the Countess and obtain her answer. If she accepts you, I shall not oppose her coming to Germany, but that can't be arranged at a moment's notice. You understand, of course?

THE MARQUIS: Of course.

THE BARON: She could join us later.

THE MARQUIS: That's an excellent idea.

THE BARON: Isn't it? If she refuses you…

THE MARQUIS: If she refuses me, I'll leave her forever.

THE BARON: Yes, indeed. You'll be leaving an ungrateful…

THE MARQUIS: Ah, but I'll adore her always.

THE BARON: Of course. (*Aside.*) He's not wicked and even his absent-mindedness could be turned to his advantage with a little skill. Until now, no one has thought of guiding him. Yes, he can come to Gotha. (*Aloud.*) Then this is what we've agreed. I'm going now. When I return, you will have spoken to the Countess and received, I hope, a favourable reply. I take it she's expecting your proposal.

THE MARQUIS: I don't really know. I've come here several times to speak to her, but, I don't know how, I always forget. However this time I've put a note in my snuffbox, to remind me.

THE BARON: I can see the whole thing's practically settled.

THE MARQUIS: I don't know whether she'll accept because it's difficult to keep her on one subject for very long. When you speak to her, she seems to be listening, but she's a hundred miles away.

THE BARON: Is she perhaps absent-minded?

THE MARQUIS: Yes, she is absent-minded. It's a deplorable failing.

THE BARON: I agree with you. I'm going to Monsieur Duplessis.

THE MARQUIS: Yes, please do. This marriage and our embassy and the lawsuit take up so much of my time. I've a thousand letters to answer. There's a new novel she wants me to read. I can't do everything, you understand.

THE BARON: Yes, yes. Think of your marriage.

THE MARQUIS: Quite right. The wretched business is driving me mad. I can never remember it. I won't show you to the door.

THE BARON: Oh, no, no, of course not. (*Aside, as he goes out.*) He says he'll keep an eye on Germain, but I'm going to see that Germain keeps an eye on him. (*Goes out.*)

THE MARQUIS: Hey. Is anyone there?

(*VICTOIRE enters.*)

VICTOIRE: Do you want something, sir?

THE MARQUIS: Give me my dressing gown.

VICTOIRE: You're joking, sir.

THE MARQUIS: Eh, ah… Yes, yes.

VICTOIRE: The Countess has been told you're here, and she's just coming.

THE MARQUIS: Why? I'll order the carriage and go to her house.

VICTOIRE: Sir, you're there, this is her house.

THE MARQUIS: You're right… I was thinking…

VICTOIRE: Here she is, sir.

(*THE COUNTESS enters.*)

THE COUNTESS: (*As she enters.*) François, tell Victoire to come here.

VICTOIRE: I am here, madam.

THE COUNTESS: Good. Monsieur de Valberg, I'm

delighted to see you. Yesterday you were absent-minded in the most amusing manner. I adore you when you're like that.

THE MARQUIS: That's not the way to correct me, madam, quite the opposite. But they do say that opposites sometimes coalesce.

THE COUNTESS: Victoire, I simply must have my dress.

VICTOIRE: Yes, madam.

THE COUNTESS: Give me another collar. (*Sits at her dressing table.*) This one doesn't fit at all. (*To THE MARQUIS.*) Do sit down.

VICTOIRE: Madam, if you don't like it, you've only got to send it back. It's quite all right really. You see, there's a fold… Wait a moment… (*She adjusts it.*)

THE COUNTESS: Yes, a fold… there! (*Looks in the mirror.*) Well, that's what I mean. It fits beautifully like that. Now take care that Mademoiselle Dufour makes me another exactly the same, but exactly the same, do you hear?

VICTOIRE: Yes, madam. When would you like it?

THE COUNTESS: When? Tomorrow morning. All you have to do is to send François at once. I'm in a great hurry.

VICTOIRE: There might not be enough time.

THE COUNTESS: Oh, of course, whatever I want, you always think impossible, and then you say you're devoted to me.

VICTOIRE: I am, really I am. You're angry with me, madam.

THE COUNTESS: All right, all right, give me my rouge. Well, Monsieur de Valberg, you don't say a word?

THE MARQUIS: You don't listen to me.

THE COUNTESS: (*Dressing.*) I'm sorry, I'm sorry. Weren't you speaking of opposites?

THE MARQUIS: Opposites? Wasn't it perhaps opportunities?

THE COUNTESS: It might well have been. Victoire.

VICTOIRE: Yes, madam.

THE COUNTESS: Now I can't remember what I was going to say, what with those opportunities of yours.

THE MARQUIS: I shall have something to say, when you're good enough to listen to me.

THE COUNTESS: I'm always delighted to listen to you.

THE MARQUIS: Will you be having any guests today?

THE COUNTESS: No, if you'd rather I didn't. That's what I was going to say. Somehow all the most boring people in town use my grounds for their afternoon drive. Victoire, I'm not at home to anyone.

VICTOIRE: I'll see to it at once, madam.

THE MARQUIS: I'm greatly obliged to you, because I have to speak to you very seriously.

THE COUNTESS: (*To VICTOIRE.*) Except my sister-in-law.

VICTOIRE: Yes, madam.

THE COUNTESS: She's infatuated with you, Monsieur de Valberg.

THE MARQUIS: And I find her charming. There are some women who captivate you the first moment you see them.

THE COUNTESS: Victoire, say I'll be at home to Monsieur de Clervaut.

VICTOIRE: Is that all?

THE MARQUIS: Don't forget Monsieur de Latour, please.

THE COUNTESS: Monsieur de Latour? Why, yes, Monsieur de Latour; with pleasure.

VICTOIRE: I'll see to it at once.

THE COUNTESS: Wait. The same list as yesterday.

VICTOIRE: But, madam, yesterday you were at home to everybody.

THE COUNTESS: Was I?

VICTOIRE: I'm sure you were.

THE COUNTESS: Well, in that case, everybody.

VICTOIRE: Do you need me any more, madam?

THE COUNTESS: No, no. Don't go far away. Tell me when my dressmaker arrives with the new materials.

(*VICTOIRE goes out.*)

THE MARQUIS: You're buying some new dresses?

THE COUNTESS: Yes. For this winter.

THE MARQUIS: You're very fond of society?

THE COUNTESS: Of course. I don't know anything else. You know how miserable my husband made me when he kept me locked up with him in the country for three years.

THE MARQUIS: Three years?

THE COUNTESS: Yes, really. Except for that journey we made in the Rhine Valley.

THE MARQUIS: The Rhine Valley?

THE COUNTESS: Yes.

THE MARQUIS: Is it beautiful?

THE COUNTESS: I can't really tell you, I don't know it at all. You tire yourself out visiting all sorts of places and they all seem the same to me. It's a failing of mine. I'm shown castles and forests, rivers and churches – oh heavens, the churches, the chill of those Gothic churches! They gave me a perpetual cold. I can still recall waking in the morning in a nice warm bed, broken by posting all the previous day, and then my husband would come in with a plan in perspective of a cathedral.

THE MARQUIS: Yes, that must be very annoying.

THE COUNTESS: Worth going into a harem to stay at home. And remember, it wasn't enough to catch pneumonia in a crypt or break one's neck to look at a gargoyle. My husband's triumph was to mount to the top of every steeple and hoist me up after him. Do you know what that means? You climb round a pillar in a suffocating turret, up and up and round and round, like a corkscrew piercing your brain, until you're overcome by seasickness and close your eyes to avoid falling. It's then that your guide gives you a pair of field glasses and forces you to admire the countryside. That's how I saw Germany.

THE MARQUIS: That must be the road we're taking with the Baron.

THE COUNTESS: Is the Baron here?

THE MARQUIS: Yes, he's just arrived. He came from Paris this morning in all this rain. That must be what's upset the weather.

THE COUNTESS: (*Laughing.*) The Baron's arrival! Oh, you're enchanting!

THE MARQUIS: Why? Weren't you talking about him?

THE COUNTESS: Yes, yes, indeed. It's wonderful!

THE MARQUIS: I thought you were. Sometimes I make a mistake and it's unbearable.

THE COUNTESS: No, no. I think you're charming, just as you are. (*She looks for something.*)

THE MARQUIS: What do you want? Some snuff? Mine is excellent. (*He opens his snuffbox.*) Oh, I was forgetting.

THE COUNTESS: What?

THE MARQUIS: You see this piece of paper. Guess.

THE COUNTESS: I can never guess, tell me at once.

THE MARQUIS: Well, if you want to marry again…

THE COUNTESS: (*Searching on her piano.*) Yes.

THE MARQUIS: What are you looking for now?

THE COUNTESS: (*Still looking.*) Go on, go on.

THE MARQUIS: You'd be the happiest woman in the world, with me.

THE COUNTESS: (*Still looking.*) With you?

THE MARQUIS: Definitely.

THE COUNTESS: I can't find it. It's unbelievable.

THE MARQUIS: What are you looking for?

THE COUNTESS: A piece of paper I had just now.

THE MARQUIS: Is it anything important?

THE COUNTESS: Yes and no. It's a song.

THE MARQUIS: I have an anthology. I'll lend it to you, if you like. It contains everything published since 1650.

THE COUNTESS: This was a new song.

THE MARQUIS: My book is full of them.

THE COUNTESS: New songs?

THE MARQUIS: Yes, for the period.

THE COUNTESS: (*Laughing.*) For 1650! You're always the same.

THE MARQUIS: Yes, I never change. And that, you know, is not always popular with wives.

THE COUNTESS: You complain about wives?

THE MARQUIS: Oh, if you would only be mine! Here's one of your guests.

THE COUNTESS: No, it's your servant.

(*GERMAIN enters.*)

GERMAIN: Excuse me, madam, the Baron asked me to give this paper to the Marquis.

THE MARQUIS: It must be about… How peculiar, it's a song. Is this the one you were looking for?

THE COUNTESS: Let me see. I think it is. You must have stolen it from me. (*She sits at the piano and plays.*)

GERMAIN: (*Aside.*) He did, it's the one from the trunk. (*Aloud.*) Sir, the Baron told me to ask you.

THE MARQUIS: Yes? What is it?

GERMAIN: If you'd remembered what you had to do.

THE MARQUIS: Yes, yes. You've interrupted us.

GERMAIN: You see, the Baron's just received an urgent message from the palace and it's upset him. He's gone back again to Monsieur Duplessis. He seemed quite overcome.

THE MARQUIS: Really?

GERMAIN: Yes, and I brought you this song, to have a reason for coming in and to remind you at the same time that you must get an answer at once.

THE MARQUIS: Well done. But I think… (*To THE COUNTESS.*) No, no, no, that's wrong. It doesn't go like that. (*He goes to the piano.*)

THE COUNTESS: I can see quite plainly. Look. (*She plays.*)

GERMAIN: It doesn't seem to me they're talking very much about what matters. The Baron told me to try to catch a little of what they were saying. (*He withdraws slowly.*)

THE COUNTESS: You can see it's written like this.

THE MARQUIS: Yes, for the melody. But the words…

THE COUNTESS: I don't know the words.

THE MARQUIS: What? They're by… (*He sings.*) 'Oh, Madeleine, the happy man who hears your every word…'

GERMAIN: (*At the door.*) That won't get them to Gotha. (*Goes out.*)

THE MARQUIS: I've forgotten the rest. How strange!

THE COUNTESS: Very strange, with your memory!

THE MARQUIS: Yes, as a rule I remember everything I want to.

(*GERMAIN and VICTOIRE enter.*)

VICTOIRE: Here are the materials, madam.

THE COUNTESS: Good.

THE MARQUIS: Are you wanted? I won't keep you any longer.

THE COUNTESS: Won't you come with me? You can give me your advice.

THE MARQUIS: No, I shan't go out today. I'm waiting for someone I have to speak to.

THE COUNTESS: Here? In my house?

THE MARQUIS: Yes. And by the way…it's you.

THE COUNTESS: Me?

THE MARQUIS: Yes. Didn't I tell you?

THE COUNTESS: What?

THE MARQUIS: That I wanted very much to marry you.

THE COUNTESS: Now when can that have been?

THE MARQUIS: Just now. It's the only reason I came here.

THE COUNTESS: I don't remember.

THE MARQUIS: What are you thinking about? Really, your absent-mindedness is unbelievable. Still I do think…

THE COUNTESS: Go on.

THE MARQUIS: That I spoke to you about my journey.

THE COUNTESS: What journey?

THE MARQUIS: To Germany.

THE COUNTESS: No, no. I spoke to you about mine.

THE MARQUIS: What do you mean, yours?

THE COUNTESS: Yes, the journey in the Rhine Valley I made with my husband.

THE MARQUIS: Excuse me, I assure you…

THE COUNTESS: You're talking nonsense; come and see my materials. I'll give you my book by I can't remember who, and you'll find the rest of our song.

THE MARQUIS: (*As he goes out.*) It's I…

THE COUNTESS: (*Also going.*) I tell you it's I…

(*THE COUNTESS and THE MARQUIS go out.*)

GERMAIN: Well, Victoire, what do you say about that? You know he loves her.

VICTOIRE: And I know she loves him.

GERMAIN: And he wants to marry her.

VICTOIRE: And she'd like nothing better.

GERMAIN: Are you sure?

VICTOIRE: Certain.

GERMAIN: Perhaps you don't know we're going on an embassy.

VICTOIRE: Where?

GERMAIN: To Gotha. It seems, as far as I can gather, that the Duchess has had a child and we're going to congratulate her on behalf of the King.

VICTOIRE: What does that mean?

GERMAIN: It means that my master wants the Countess to say yes or no, before he leaves, so he can set his mind at rest. That we're going tomorrow morning with the Baron, that it only needs one word to settle everything, and instead of saying it, they're singing.

VICTOIRE: Still he did mention marriage and a journey.

GERMAIN: And she answered with a song.

VICTOIRE: Why doesn't your Baron come and help?

GERMAIN: He's afraid of spoiling everything, because he's quarrelled, so he thinks, with your mistress.

VICTOIRE: Monsieur Germain.

GERMAIN: Mademoiselle Victoire.

VICTOIRE: Our employers are just children; we must settle the matter. You brought in a sheet of paper. Isn't that what they were singing?

GERMAIN: Yes. Here it is.

VICTOIRE: Give it to me; and now… (*Writes on the song.*)

GERMAIN: What are you writing?

VICTOIRE: Don't worry. Let's put it on the piano.

GERMAIN: (*Reading.*) But if they get angry?

VICTOIRE: Do you think they can? She dreams about him all day long. Besides…

GERMAIN: Here they come. Let's go.

VICTOIRE: And listen.

(*GERMAIN and VICTOIRE go out.*
THE COUNTESS and THE MARQUIS enter.)

THE COUNTESS: You don't like this carnation-pink silk?

THE MARQUIS: (*A book in his hand.*) No, it's not what I'd

choose. (*Reading.*) 'Oh, Madeleine, the happy man who hears your every word...'

THE COUNTESS: How happy you are now. With your book in your hand, you can be quite sure of your memory.

THE MARQUIS: Good heavens, I didn't need the book, it would have come back to me in a moment. (*Reading.*)

'Oh, Madeleine, the happy man who hears your
every word
Must know the abundant blessings heaven has on
him conferred.
He sees you blush, he sees you smile...'

THE COUNTESS: You say it with such expression.

THE MARQUIS: It isn't difficult to express what you feel deeply. Doesn't it seem that these lines were written simply to be said to you? 'Oh, Madeleine, the happy man...'

THE COUNTESS: I take it you're joking.

THE MARQUIS: No, I swear by my soul, by everything I hold most sacred in the world, I... I find those lines charming.

THE COUNTESS: Well, come and sing them. I'll accompany you. (*Sits at the piano.*)

THE MARQUIS: (*Next to her.*) You'll see that I can do without the book. What are you thinking about?

THE COUNTESS: That carnation-pink silk. You don't like it?

THE MARQUIS: No, I prefer the autumn russet taffeta.

THE COUNTESS: It's too old.

THE MARQUIS: It seemed quite new to me.

THE COUNTESS: Come now. It's at least a year out of date.

THE MARQUIS: What a very feminine remark that is!

THE COUNTESS: Feminine remark? What do you mean?

THE MARQUIS: Good lord, yes. Always in search of novelty. That's all you want, you women.

THE COUNTESS: 'You women'! You are polite!

THE MARQUIS: All you care about is the present. You don't worry about what happened yesterday and you don't think about what might happen tomorrow. I promise you, if I were married, my wife wouldn't have such silly ideas.

THE COUNTESS: You'd make her wear autumn russet taffeta?

THE MARQUIS: Autumn russet, yes, if I liked it.

THE COUNTESS: She'd laugh at it and never wear it.

THE MARQUIS: She'd wear it all her life, if she really loved me.

THE COUNTESS: Well, in that case you'll remain a bachelor.

THE MARQUIS: Do you really mean that?

THE COUNTESS: Yes, I advise you to give up all hopes of finding a willing victim.

THE MARQUIS: Oh heavens, you've just pronounced my death sentence.

THE COUNTESS: What? Your death sentence?

THE MARQUIS: Certainly. I'm not like you, I don't have to be told things twice. Oh, I was afraid you'd receive me like this, but though I foresaw it, I wasn't expecting it. For heaven's sake, don't say it again.

THE COUNTESS: What on earth's come over you?

THE MARQUIS: Do you really think I can be anywhere in the world away from you, away from everything I hold most dear? Life would be unbearable. Oh yes, laugh: laugh as much as you please. I know you'll say a hasty journey is bound to be upsetting, though I have my plans, you have yours. You'll think of hundreds of reasons, hundreds of obstacles. But do any of them matter when you're in love? Is it your law case which worries you? I've told you it's already won. I've been to see your lawyer a dozen times. He doesn't live very near, but what does that matter? No, that's not the trouble, oh no! You don't love me.

THE COUNTESS: Would you mind telling me what this rigmarole is all about?

THE MARQUIS: I'm only speaking the exact truth. But as you don't wish to hear it, I shall go. Goodbye.

THE COUNTESS: My dear Marquis, there is something you should know. It's that your absent-mindedness only pleases me as long as it is pleasant. When you put on my uncle's hat or call my lawyer 'mademoiselle', no one thinks of getting angry. But that mustn't encourage you to lose your reason and start talking about an autumn russet dress as if you're going to commit suicide. You must understand that then our role is no longer one of gaiety but of patience, and that is never very wise; it's the mortal enemy of women.

THE MARQUIS: That means I'm boring you. Yet another reason for me to say goodbye.

THE COUNTESS: Really, you're going out of your mind.

THE MARQUIS: Better and better. How miserable I am!

THE COUNTESS: You're not dining with me?

THE MARQUIS: No. I'm going away. Goodbye. (*He sits in the corner.*)

THE COUNTESS: Heavens above, do whatever you like. You're intolerable and incomprehensible. Now leave me alone with my music. (*She returns to the piano.*) What is the meaning of this? (*She reads in a whisper what is written on the song.*)

THE MARQUIS: (*Seated.*) I loved her so tenderly. How can I have displeased her? What have I done to annoy her? I come here deeply in love with her, to place my whole life at her feet. I declare my love with the utmost sincerity. I ask for her hand as politely and plain-spokenly as you could wish for. And she repels me with such cruelty. It's unbelievable. The more I think about it, the less I understand it. (*He rises and strides up and down without seeing THE COUNTESS.*) Yes, there's no doubt I must unknowingly have committed some unforgivable mistake.

THE COUNTESS: (*Presenting the music to him, as he passes her.*) Look, Valberg. Just read that.

THE MARQUIS: (*Continuing.*) Unforgivable? That's impossible. When I see her again, she'll forgive me. Hey, Germain, I'm going home. Yes, of course, I must see her again. She's so good, so kind. And so gracious, so beautiful. There's no other woman like her.

THE COUNTESS: (*Aside.*) This is absent-mindedness I can forgive.

THE MARQUIS: (*Continuing.*) It's true that she's outrageously flirtatious, and pitifully lazy. Her continual forgetfulness…

THE COUNTESS: The portrait's being spoiled. (*Presenting the music.*) Monsieur de Valberg.

THE MARQUIS: Her continual forgetfulness couldn't really suit a reasonable man. Would she have the calm and common sense and evenness of temper which one needs in a wife? I should have a great deal of trouble with that woman.

THE COUNTESS: This is worth listening to.

THE MARQUIS: But she's such a good musician. Germain! Ah, how happy we'd be alone in some peaceful retreat with a few friends, and everything she loves. Yes, then I know I'd love her.

THE COUNTESS: Excellent!

THE MARQUIS: No, she likes society, parties. Germain! Well, I shouldn't be jealous. Who could be, with such a woman? Germain! I'd let her do what she wanted. For her sake I'd like these pleasures, that bore me now. I'd take pride in seeing her admired. I'd trust her as I do myself and if ever she betrayed me... Germain!... I'd plunge a dagger into her heart.

THE COUNTESS: (*Taking his hand.*) Oh no, not that.

THE MARQUIS: You, Countess! Good heavens, I didn't think...

THE COUNTESS: Before you kill me, just read this.

THE MARQUIS: Well, what is it? (*Reads.*) 'The Marquis is respectfully requested to remember to marry the Countess before leaving for Germany.' There, you see, it was I, not you, who mentioned that journey.

THE COUNTESS: So you're really going, are you?

THE MARQUIS: You ask me that! And for two hours I've exhausted myself repeating it.

THE COUNTESS: You must have mistaken my maid for me, this is her writing.

THE MARQUIS: Really? She doesn't write badly.

THE COUNTESS: No. But most impertinently.

THE MARQUIS: Not at all. It's what was in my mind.

THE COUNTESS: What are you going to do in Germany?

THE MARQUIS: Present the King's compliments to the Grand Duchess.

THE COUNTESS: When are you going?

THE MARQUIS: Tomorrow morning.

THE COUNTESS: So you want to marry me on the road?

THE MARQUIS: Exactly. I want to take you with me. It would be the most delightful journey.

THE COUNTESS: An abduction?

THE MARQUIS: Yes, a proper abduction.

THE COUNTESS: It sounds most improper to me.

THE MARQUIS: No, we'll publish our banns…

THE COUNTESS: At each posting stage, you mean. And the witnesses?

THE MARQUIS: We've my uncle.

THE COUNTESS: And our relations?

THE MARQUIS: There's nothing they'd like more.

THE COUNTESS: And society?

THE MARQUIS: What could they say? We're honourable people, surely. Because we go off in a post chaise, they're not suddenly going to think we're absconding criminals.

THE COUNTESS: Your plan is so absurd, so extravagant, that it rather amuses me.

THE MARQUIS: Do come. It will be so simple.

THE COUNTESS: I'm almost tempted to.

THE MARQUIS: I'm delighted. Hey, there! Germain!
(*GERMAIN enters.*)

GERMAIN: You called, sir? (*Aside.*) I think the danger's passed.

THE MARQUIS: Go and get that big trunk from downstairs and bring it here at once.

GERMAIN: Here, sir?

THE MARQUIS: Yes. And hurry.
(*GERMAIN goes out.*)

THE COUNTESS: (*Laughing.*) This is madness. You're sending for your trunk?

THE MARQUIS: Yes. We must pack immediately. When you have a good idea, you know, you mustn't let it pass. That's one of my principles.

THE COUNTESS: One moment, Marquis. Before starting at
full speed for the Golden East, one needs a passport. Are
you quite sure I have all the necessary qualities to make
a suitable companion for you in one of those enormous
castles you have in Spain?

THE MARQUIS: Spain? I don't understand.

THE COUNTESS: Have I the calm and common sense and
evenness of temper which one needs in a wife? Especially
when the husband sets an example.

THE MARQUIS: You're joking. Do I have to repeat to you
what everybody knows, that in you are to be found every
attribute, every talent, every grace?

THE COUNTESS: You forget that I'm flirtatious, pitifully
lazy and forgetful, above all, forgetful…

THE MARQUIS: Whoever said that?

THE COUNTESS: One of my friends.

THE MARQUIS: A most impertinent man.

THE COUNTESS: Not always. He's an original who paints
portraits in front of his mirror and in his own image. Guess
who it is. He's a diplomat who is quite a good musician. A
poet with a knowledge of ladies' dresses. A good shot who
always hits a keeper. A whist player greatly to be feared by
his partner. An intelligent man who says stupid things and
a very courteous man who sometimes does them. In short
he's a lover, of the utmost delicacy, who, in order to gain
a woman's heart, pays her compliments out of habit and
insults her out of absent-mindedness.

THE MARQUIS: If I've done that, it will be the last time in
my life and you'll see on this journey whether…

THE COUNTESS: This journey now… Do I agree to it?

THE MARQUIS: You said 'Yes'.

THE COUNTESS: I almost said 'Yes'. And between those
two sentences lies a whole world of meaning.

THE MARQUIS: Agree to it, and this portrait you've drawn
won't be mine any longer. Yes, I protest that if it resembles
me today, it's thanks to you. It's the doubts, fears, hopes,
worries, which were my constant companions and
prevented me from seeing or hearing or understanding

anything which was not you. Don't insult me by thinking that if I'd loved you less, I'd have lost my reason. It remains there in your eyes and it only needs one word from you to restore it to me.

THE COUNTESS: What you're saying gives me a rather charming idea. You see it could be that quite unknowingly we have each stolen the other's reason. You're absent-minded, you say, through love for me; perhaps I'm forgetful through friendship for you. What do you say then if we try to repair the damage we've done to each other? As I've taken your good sense and you've taken mine, why don't we each act according to the other's advice? It might be an excellent way of attaining great wisdom.

THE MARQUIS: I'd like nothing better than to obey you.

THE COUNTESS: It's not a question of obedience but of a simple exchange. For example, I'm lazy, so you told me…

THE MARQUIS: But…

THE COUNTESS: So you told me, and I agree. You, on the other hand, are always active. You return from shooting when I'm getting up. Your fingers are always stained with ink and for me it's painful to write a word. It's the same with reading; you devour even tragedies with a ferocious appetite, while the first alexandrine sends me to sleep. In society, you don't know what to do; you say nothing or speak to yourself without caring who you're with. I, yes I admit it, I like conversation; I'd willingly go so far as to gossip, if so many other people didn't do so; and while you're in a corner, sulking so savagely, the noise amuses me, transports me; and a ball fascinates me. Don't you think that with all these differences we could make a picture? Let's find a frame to take you with your autumn russet and me with my carnation pink, our virtues and our defects, where we could play in turn the blind man and his dog. Wouldn't this be a fine example to set? A man sufficiently in love to renounce the right to say 'I want', and a woman sacrificing even more, the pleasure of saying 'Suppose I wanted…'

THE MARQUIS: You enchant me, delight me. Oh, if you

were willing to take charge of my whole life, I'd die of joy at your feet.

THE COUNTESS: Please don't. What good would that do me?

(*GERMAIN enters with the trunk.*)

GERMAIN: Here is your trunk, sir.

THE MARQUIS: And my uncle?

GERMAIN: He hasn't returned yet.

THE MARQUIS: (*To THE COUNTESS.*) Well then… What do you say?

THE COUNTESS: Well then… Let's try.

THE MARQUIS: Quickly, Germain, François, Victoire, fetch everything you can find.

THE COUNTESS: Is that the way you thank me?

THE MARQUIS: Oh, I'll have plenty of time for that.

THE COUNTESS: What! Plenty of time? How polite!

THE MARQUIS: Certainly. Because from now on I want to do nothing else for the rest of my life.

(*VICTOIRE enters.*)

VICTOIRE: Do you want me, madam?

THE COUNTESS: It seems to be you, Victoire, who have taken the liberty.

THE MARQUIS: Don't scold her. If I had the crown jewels, I'd give them to her. (*Gives her a purse.*)

THE COUNTESS: Is this what you call being reasonable?

THE MARQUIS: Oh, please, let that be enough for today. Now, first of all let's pack all your music.

THE COUNTESS: That's a good beginning.

THE MARQUIS: (*Arranging the music.*) Music's so popular in Germany. We'll find that everybody loves it. I do so look forward to seeing you sing for them. (*Sings.*) 'Oh, Madeleine, the happy man…' They'll all adore you. Germain!

GERMAIN: Sir?

THE MARQUIS: Go and get my violin.

(*GERMAIN goes out.*)

THE COUNTESS: Don't forget this song, whatever happens.

277

THE MARQUIS: It will remind me of the most wonderful day of my life.

THE COUNTESS: And my autumn russet dress. Victoire.

VICTOIRE: Yes, madam.

(*She brings the dress.*
A little later GERMAIN enters with the violin.)

THE MARQUIS: You want to take it?

THE COUNTESS: As it's one of your conditions.

THE MARQUIS: Good heavens, that's why I annoyed you. Bring some other dresses, Victoire. (*He throws it on a chair.*)

THE COUNTESS: Do you know what we ought to do? Take very little with us, only absolute necessities; we'll buy everything else when we get there.

THE MARQUIS: You're absolutely right. Germain.

GERMAIN: Sir?

THE MARQUIS: My gun and my hunting horn. Yes, we'll buy the rest at Gotha.

THE COUNTESS: What? Gotha?

THE MARQUIS: Yes, that's where we're going.

THE COUNTESS: Ah! Here, take this little box.

THE MARQUIS: What's in it, family papers? (*Looking.*) No, it's tea. We can get that everywhere.

THE COUNTESS: Oh! It's the only kind I can drink.

THE MARQUIS: How happy we're going to be.

THE COUNTESS: We'll buy peasant costumes. They'll be charming for a fancy dress ball.

THE MARQUIS: Suppose we take my sundial? It works very well.

THE COUNTESS: Are you mad? What about your fine promises?

THE MARQUIS: Quite right. My watch will do. (*He puts it in the trunk.*)

THE COUNTESS: Remember, you must watch your behaviour, now you're a diplomat.

THE MARQUIS: There's nothing to worry about, I'm fully trained. (*He takes various objects at random in the room and puts them in the trunk. Still talking, he also puts in his notecase, gloves, handkerchief, and hat.*) I once went to Denmark and

was a great success. My uncle thinks he's a genius and
wanted to tell me what to do, but he's not quite right in
the head. Between ourselves he wanders a little. (*Shuts the
trunk.*)

THE COUNTESS: Here he is.

(*THE BARON enters.*)

THE BARON: I apologise for coming in unannounced and
uninvited, but an unforeseen circumstance…

THE COUNTESS: It gives me great pleasure to see you, sir.

THE MARQUIS: My dear uncle, congratulate me; and
you must congratulate her too. Everything's finished,
everything's forgotten… I mean everything's settled. You
can understand how happy I am.

THE BARON: Alas, my dear nephew, everything's ruined.
The Grand Duchess of Gotha is dead.

THE MARQUIS: What a pity. Our trunks were packed.

THE BARON: It was at Monsieur Duplessis' I just learned the
dreadful news.

THE COUNTESS: What, Valberg, aren't we going? It's the
one thing I wanted to do.

THE MARQUIS: Great heavens, are you leaving me?

THE COUNTESS: No, but take me away somewhere.

THE MARQUIS: Italy, Turkey, Norway if you like.

THE BARON: Who could ever have expected this appalling
catastrophe? All arrangements had been made, I had the
King's letter, gifts for the court; I'd prepared everything,
foreseen everything. And it must happen that the one
event which no one could have dreamt of…

THE MARQUIS: Why yes, that's what people always say.
You can't think of everything.

www.ingramcontent.com/pod-product-compliance
Ingram Content Group UK Ltd.
Pitfield, Milton Keynes, MK11 3LW, UK
UKHW031253020325
455690UK00007B/60